EXPERIENCING POVERTY

Studies in Cash and Care

Editors: Sally Baldwin and Jonathan Bradshaw

Cash benefits and care services together make a fundamental contribution to human welfare. After income derived from work, they are arguably the most important determinants of living standards. Indeed, many households are almost entirely dependent on benefits and services which are socially provided. Moreover, welfare benefits and services consume the lion's share of public expenditure. The operation, impact and interaction of benefits and services is thus an important focus of research on social policy.

Policy related work in this field tends to be disseminated to small specialist audiences in the form of mimeographed research reports or working papers and perhaps later published, more briefly, in journal articles. In consequence public debate about vital social issues is sadly ill-informed. This series is designed to fill this gap by making the details of important empirically-based research more widely available.

Experiencing Poverty

Edited by
JONATHAN BRADSHAW and ROY SAINSBURY
Soical Policy Research Unit
University of York

Ashgate

Aldershot • Burlington USA • Singapore • Sydney

Published by
Ashgate Publishing Ltd
Gower House
Croft Road
Aldershot
Hants GU11 3HR
England

Ashgate Publishing Company
131 Main Street
Burlington
Vermont 05401
USA

Ashgate website: http://www.ashgate.com

British Library Cataloguing in Publication Data
Experiencing poverty. - (Studies in cash and care)
   1. Poverty - Great Britain - Congresses 2. Poverty -
   Government policy - Great Britain - Congresses 3. Poverty -
   Research - Great Britain - Congresses
   I. Bradshaw, Jonathan, 1944 - II. Sainsbury, Roy
   362.5'0941

Library of Congress Catalog Card Number: 00-132577

ISBN 0 7546 1288 0

Printed and bound by Athenaeum Press, Ltd.,
Gateshead, Tyne & Wear.

Contents

List of Figures

List of Tables

List of Contributors

Peter Alcock
Sheffield Hallam University

Michaela Benzeval
King's Fund Policy Institute

Margaret Boneham
The Institute of Human Ageing

Jonathan Bradshaw
University of York

Julian Buchanan
University of Central Lancashire

Roy Carr-Hill
University of York

Marc Chrysanthou
University of Salford

John Coleman
Trust for the Study of Adolescence

Gary Craig
University of Humberside

Elizabeth Dowler
London School of Hygiene and Tropical Medicine

Gillian Elam
Social and Community Planning Research

Linda Grant
Sheffield Hallam University

John Hills
London School of Economics

Alper Hulusi
Social and Community Planning Research

Paul Johnson
Institute for Fiscal Studies

Ken Judge
King's Fund Policy Institute

Bob Lavers
University of York

Suzi Leather
London School of Hygiene and Tropical Medicine

Janet Lewis
Joseph Rowntree Foundation

Ruth Lister
Loughborough University

Robert Moore
Liverpool John Moores University

John M. Pitts
University of Luton

Martin Rein
Massachusetts Institute of Technology

Jane Ritchie
Social and Community Planning Research

Debi Roker
Trust for the Study of Adolescence

Roy Sainsbury
University of York

Peter Saunders
University of New South Wales

Jayne Taylor
Institute for Fiscal Studies

Christopher Winship
Massachusetts Institute of Technology

Lee Young
University of Liverpool

Preface

SIR PETER BARCLAY, CHAIRMAN
JOSEPH ROWNTREE FOUNDATION

As chairman of Joseph Rowntree Foundation, I welcome the publication of these volumes containing the proceedings of the conference sponsored by the Foundation.

The Foundation was delighted to support this event for a number of reasons:

- First and foremost, it marks the Centenary of Seebohm Rowntree's first study of poverty in York. It is indisputable that that survey constituted a large milestone in social research in this country.

  It was Beatrice Webb who called it a *'sort of Modern Doomsday Book'*. Seebohm says in his report that *'it was a contribution to the knowledge of facts in relation to poverty that any enquiry was undertaken'* and it was its factual, evidential base which gave it such impact and authority - with material gathered through unemotional objective, detailed and conscientious research. In doing so, he was making a major reference in establishing the British empirical social research tradition.

- Secondly, the Foundation, being always primarily concerned with translating research into social change, recognises and celebrates the extraordinary social policy influence which was exerted by the survey on the thinking of Liberal party policy makers in the early years of this century, which led to reform, from which, eventually, emerged the Welfare State as we knew it in the years following the last War.

His work and his ideas also had a great influence on his father Joseph and in 1904 were partly responsible for Joseph's decision to establish his three trusts.

If you read about the debates which followed the publication of the survey, in Asa Briggs' fascinating and comprehensive study of Seebohm's life, they have an uncomfortably modern ring. The Charity Organisation Society had, throughout the previous century, maintained that poverty was caused by the moral turpitude of the poor (shades of *'benefit dependency?'*) - in answer to which Seebohm was able to show that poverty was a real phenomenon with clear structural causes. He called for a minimum wage and warned his opponents, as Asa Briggs recounts, *'not to pit their uninformed feelings about poverty against his facts'*. If they saw people who by his standards were in primary poverty appearing to live well (as we see sometimes in TV documentaries today), let them not, said Seebohm confuse *'things that are seen with consequences of poverty which are not seen'* - (in our time, isolation, bad health, bad living and social exclusion in general).

Finally, the Foundation welcomes this publication because it provides a unique opportunity to review the theory method and policy relevance of poverty research. As a consequence, I hope that after 20 years in which such research has been largely ignored - in fact, in recent years only the brave even dared to mention the word *'poverty'* at all - I hope we can bring high quality research in this area back into the centre of both social research effort and informed policy debate and that we shall look back on these conference proceedings as a significant turning point.

Acknowledgements

The editors would like to acknowledge the generous financial support provided by the Joseph Rowntree Foundation to the conference to mark the centenary of Seebohm Rowntree's *Poverty: A Study of Town Life* held at the University of York in March 1998.

We would like to offer heartfelt thanks to all the contributors to this volume, not only for their excellent papers but also for their patience during the seemingly inevitable delays that accompany the preparation of an edited book.

The help and guidance of our colleagues at Ashgate Publishing has been invaluable. Our thanks to them.

And, finally, our support team at the University of York have carried out their contributions to the production of the book with their usual enthusiasm and efficiency without which we would be lost. Thank you Sally Pulleyn, Lucy Bradshaw and Nico Bradshaw.

Jonathan Bradshaw
Roy Sainsbury

University of York, March 2000

Acknowledgements

1 Editors' Introduction

JONATHAN BRADSHAW and ROY SAINSBURY

The conference to mark the centenary of Seebohm Rowntree's first study of poverty in York has resulted in three volumes of proceedings. The first volume *Getting the Measure of Poverty: The early legacy of Seebohm Rowntree* (Bradshaw and Sainsbury, 1999a) is largely devoted to papers covering the pre-Second World War era. The second volume *Researching Poverty* (Bradshaw and Sainsbury, 1999b) and this volume represent a picture of the state of poverty research in the late 1990s, after a period of 20 years when Britain had a government not particularly concerned with poverty and not much interested in funding research into it.

In 1997 after 17 years of Conservative rule a Labour Government came to power. Before the election Tony Blair had declared 'If the next Labour government has not raised the living standards of the poorest by the end of its time in office it will have failed' (reported in *The Independent* on Sunday 26 July 1996). The Government started badly. During the election they had promised not to increase public expenditure for two years and not to increase taxation in the lifetime of the parliament. Almost their first social policy act was to abolish One Parent Benefit and the lone parent premium in Income Support - thus further impoverishing more than two million of the poorest children in Britain. But the state of child poverty and the UK's comparative position has begun to seep into the political consciousness. On 18 March 1999 Tony Blair announced 'Our historic aim will be for ours to be the first generation to end child poverty, and it will take a generation. It is a 20 year mission but I believe it can be done'. In the context of both government rhetoric and action in their first two years this was a most unexpected declaration - and a brave and welcome one. The Government has claimed that policies already announced will lift 8000,000 children out of poverty and the Chancellor has promised that measures to be announced in his 2000 budget will lift another 200,000 out of poverty. We have not yet been told what poverty standard is being employed in these estimates but an indication of the challenge facing the Government is that the latest Department of Social Security statistics indicate that in 1996/7 there were 4.5 million children living in households with equivalent income below half the average. The Government is pursuing four strategies:

- redistribution (a minimum wage from April 1998, Family Tax Credit, Childcare Tax Credit, Child Tax Credit, increases in Child Benefit and the child scale rates of Income Support for children under 11, a starting rate of income tax of ten per cent)
- employment (the New Deals)
- prevention (Sure Start, Social Exclusion Unit, reducing teenage mothers)
- investment in human capital (schools, training, the NHS and the Childcare Strategy).

Poverty, particularly child poverty, is back on the political agenda in rather a big way and the poverty research community in Britain has a responsibility to respond positively to this new experience of being at the heart of a Government's domestic preoccupations.

The Rowntree Conference was deliberately aimed at a domestic audience. However, we decided to invite three papers from distinguished overseas poverty researchers. One of these by Bjorn Hallerod from Sweden was to be published elsewhere. The other two are the first two chapters in this collection. **Peter Saunders** and the Social Policy Research Centre at the University of New South Wales have made an international contribution to the study of poverty. Saunders' chapter provides an overview of the development of poverty research in Australia, focusing on the impact of Seebohm Rowntree's first study of poverty in York. It also reviews some of the recent Australian evidence on the extent of poverty, summarises the debates generated by that research and outlines recent work on poverty and living standards including the Adequacy Project launched there by the Department of Social Security.

Martin Rein is one of the leading poverty researchers in the United States but his chapter (with **Christopher Winship**) is very different. It takes Rowntree's study as an example of how in trying to answer *how* and *why* questions we are lead back to definitional issues and also how we make the leap from empirical analysis to *ought* questions. Thus it is a discussion based on poverty research and policy in the United States of the ways in which causal arguments are used to support more general moral arguments as to why certain actions ought to be undertaken.

The rest of the chapters return to the British context. **Peter Alcock and Gary Craig** have been leading figures in the movement to raise the profile of poverty at local government level. Their chapter analyses the growth of these local poverty profiles and the differing uses made of a variety of deprivation indicators and other measures, and explores how these have been used to inform local anti-poverty strategies. The conference also saw the launch of the results of a special study of poverty in York undertaken to mark to centenary of Rowntree's first study (Huby, Bradshaw and Corden, 1999).

Michaela Benzeval, Ken Judge, Paul Johnson and Jayne Taylor employ the British Household Panel Survey and the National Child Development Survey to explore the impact of poverty dynamics on various indicators of health status.

Marc Chysanthou argues that we need to recognise the interconnectedness of poverty and affluence and in particular asks whether the affluent derive health benefits through recognition of their social advantage or does the spatial separation of the affluent enable them to cope better by avoiding exposure to the realities of poverty.

Julian Buchanan and Lee Young draw on a number of studies in Merseyside to examine the relationship between poverty, problematic drug misuse and social exclusion. They also assess strategies for policy and practice initiatives aimed at reintegration and social participation.

Robert Moore draws on the 1991 census to compare the material deprivation of white and ethnic minority populations of children. He finds that children classified as Indian show the lowest deprivation and are the exception to the rule that children born overseas are more likely to experience deprivation than the UK-born. **Margaret Boneham's** is another chapter on ethnicity but in this case of older people. She reviews evidence that older people from black and ethnic minority groups are at greater risk of poverty. She argues that there is a need to raise the basic pension, to monitor community care and to provide better access to services and encourage group strategies to enhance self determination.

The next two chapters are about food. **Roy Carr-Hill and Bob Lavers** attempt to assess the adequacy of present day social security benefits by seeing how Rowntree's dietaries would costs today. Their analysis shows that families dependant on social security benefits have a standard of living today virtually the same as that enjoyed in 1950 and 1936 and only 25 per cent more than his 'poor workhouse' diet of 1899. **Elizabeth Dowler and Suzi Leather** who are nutritionists examine the history of food in poverty measurement, review the role of food and nutrition in poverty analysis and review some contemporary research on food poverty.

Gillian Elam, Jane Ritchie and Alper Hulusi explore the variety of resources that low income households employ to support their living standards.

These include help from family and friends; sale of goods; self provision; stolen goods; use of capital and credit. They also discuss how the use of these resources has changed over time and the implications of this. **Linda Grant's** chapter is based on interviews with disabled people and their carers. She analyses the impact of poverty and debt on disabled people's sense of themselves, and discusses how debt becomes an all consuming life experience and what strategies are employed in response to debt.

The next two chapters are about youth. **John Pitts** draws upon an Anglo-French comparative study of political and professional responses to youth crime and victimisation in two high crime/low income neighbourhoods and explores the implications of its findings for the corporate multi agency, crime prevention plans which local authorities are now required by government to develop. **Debi Roker and John Coleman** describe the results of research on young people growing up in family poverty and covering their physical health, education and future prospects, experience of crime, family relationships and social lives.

The Conference ended with an open session on the future of poverty research and the final chapter summarises the brief introductions that members of a panel made in order to open the discussion.

References

Bradshaw, J. and Sainsbury, R. (1999a), *Getting the Measure of Poverty: The Early Legacy of Seebohm Rowntree*, Ashgate, Aldershot.

Bradshaw, J. and Sainsbury, R. (1999b), *Researching Poverty*, Ashgate, Aldershot.

Huby, M., Bradshaw, J. and Corden, A. (1999), *A Study of Town Life: Living Standards in the City of York 100 years after Rowntree*, Joseph Rowntree Foundation, York.

2 Defining Poverty and Identifying the Poor: Reflections on the Australian Experience

PETER SAUNDERS

This paper provides an overview of the historical development of poverty research in Australia, focusing on the impact of Seebohm Rowntree's first study of poverty in York, conducted one hundred years ago. It also reviews some of the recent Australian evidence on the extent of poverty and summarises the debates generated by that research. Finally, the paper discusses several developments currently in progress in the area of poverty and living standards research. These include the Adequacy Project being run within the Department of Social Security, the recent SPRC budget standards study, the Project on *Poverty in Australia* being organised by the Academy of the Social Sciences in Australia, and the proposed National Living Standards Survey being planned by the Australian Bureau of Statistics.

Introduction

Although Seebohm Rowntree visited Australia only briefly, he has had a profound impact on Australian poverty research. The methods developed in his first York poverty study formed the basis for the Harvester Judgement of 1907 in which Justice Higgins, President of the Arbitration Court, established a basic wage by identifying the needs of working families and costing them. Rowntree met Higgins in Australia in the mid-1920s and quoted him at the beginning of *The Human Needs of Labour* on the benefits of providing working men with 'relief from their material anxiety' (quoted in Briggs, 1961, p.152).

Ronald Henderson, the founding father of Australian poverty studies, later described by Peter Kaim-Caudle as 'well on the way to becoming the Australian Beveridge' (Kaim-Caudle, 1975, p.406), was allegedly prompted to

5

establish his study of poverty in Melbourne on hearing from a colleague that there was no Australian equivalent to Rowntree on poverty (J. and D. McCaughey, 1997, p.10).

In the six decades between the Harvester Judgement and Henderson's poverty study, there were several attempts to develop and cost household budgets. In 1919, a Royal Commission on the Basic Wage estimated the cost of living of 'a man with a wife and three children under 14 years of age' to be around 50 per cent higher than Higgins' Harvester standard - an amount which, if paid to workers, would have more than absorbed the nation's entire national income at the time (Hancock, 1997).

In 1941, the Ministry of Post-War Reconstruction funded a Melbourne University Economics Professor to undertake a project on household budgets which was completed in 1945 but not published until 1952 (Prest, 1952). That study adopted the Rowntree methodology to cost budgets for a sample of Melbourne households and estimated poverty by comparing 'available income' (income after rent) with a budget that excluded housing costs (Prest, 1952).

Two aspects of these developments are worth emphasising: first, they illustrate that research on poverty and its measurement in Australia has a long history, involving both academic researchers and official agencies of government. Secondly, they highlight the close relationship between the analysis of poverty and wage determination which has been the central feature of Australian incomes policy for most of the last century.

The following discussion provides a flavour of the Australian poverty debate without straying too far into the esoteric technicalities that, like the columns of local newspapers, contain very little of interest (and generally even less of relevance) to anyone other than the locals. Although the discussion focuses mainly on current Australian debates and developments, many of these are common to other nations also and I hope that some of what I have to say will be of general interest.

Wages and Poverty

Frank Castles has captured a crucial aspect of the Australian approach to welfare and redistribution by describing its social programs as comprising a 'wage earners' welfare state' (Castles, 1985). In essence, Castles categorises welfare development in Australia as focusing on establishing adequacy of incomes primarily through a highly centralised wage determination system, supported by tariffs and labour supply controls acting through immigration policies. With wages acting as the platform for income equality, the role of social security was to provide support on a contingent and means-tested basis to those unable to provide for themselves. Residualist social security thus developed in place of extensive (and expensive) contributory social insurance programs.

From very early this century, the idea that 'need' should play a major role in Australian income determination became widely accepted as legitimate, with the result that income was redistributed on a selective basis. The idea of contributory finance was rejected in favour of general revenue financing, while the notion that benefits should be provided universally and related to earnings was regarded as both wasteful of resources and inequitable (in that previous market-generated inequalities would thereby be maintained by the state). Far better for the state to play an active role in moderating the worst extremes of market inequality through minimum wages, income-tested social benefits and progressive taxation.

The study of Australian poverty research and policy development must therefore begin by examining the wage determination system and its interaction with the benefit system. The 1907 Harvester Judgement set the basic wage at a level of seven shillings per working day or 42 shillings per week, this amount being assessed by Justice Higgins as 'appropriate to the normal needs of the average employee regarded as a human being living in a civilised community' (Macarthy, 1969, p.17).

Higgins arrived at this figure by studying the actual budgets and living costs of nine families containing between one and seven children (Macarthy, 1969, Table 2). Since the nine families contained just over three children on average, the rounded figure of 42 shillings per week was seen as applying to a family of *'about five'* - an intriguing but rather imprecise notion which was interpreted for practical purposes to refer to a family of *exactly five,* (two adults and three children).

The basic wage recommendations of the 1920 Royal Commission Report were not implemented (possibly wisely, in light of their cost!), although a proposal to automatically index the basic wage to quarterly price movements was. Subsequent work by Commission Chairman A. B. Piddington led him to propose the introduction of child endowment as a necessary complement to the basic wage, a suggestion which prompted the introduction of a modest scheme of child endowment for the federal public service (Hancock, 1997, p.4), some 20 years before universal child endowment was introduced in 1941.

The basic wage continued to underpin the entire wage system until its abolition in favour of a new minimum wage (set at a higher level - Hancock, 1997, p.7). This occurred in 1967, ironically the year after its adoption by Henderson and his colleagues as the basis on which their poverty line was established.

There is still an element of centralised determination of wages in the Australian system, although its role is diminishing. Its main purpose is to provide protection to those with the lowest wages in circumstances where enterprise bargaining is becoming the norm in an increasingly fragmented labour market characterised by declining real wages for the low-paid and greater dispersion of earnings generally (Borland, 1997).

In 1997, the Australian Council of Trade Unions (ACTU) submitted a 'living wage' claim to the Australian Industrial Relations Commission which argued that the 'needs of workers' should be reflected in the determination of wages. The ACTU Submission did not specifically argue that the Henderson poverty line should form the basis for a living wage, although they did accept that some form of external needs-based adequacy standard was required.

One possibility utilised in the ACTU Submission relied on the analysis of data from the Household Expenditure Survey. This approach was rejected by the Commission on the grounds that attempting to infer needs from actual expenditure patterns is inherently circular in its reasoning.

The Commission (or at least its Deputy President at the time) also rejected the possibility of translating needs into wage outcomes by developing benchmarks for income adequacy. Such a proposal was seen as being both 'at odds with logic and ignores historical experience' (Hancock, 1997, p.15), it being argued instead that the needs of the low paid would best be met by granting them larger wage increases than other workers.

In its decision in the 1997 living wage case, the Commission awarded a new federal minimum wage of A$359.40: a level considerably above the 1967 basic wage adjusted for movements in consumer prices, but well below what would have resulted from indexing it to movements in average earnings (Hancock, 1997).

Henderson Poverty

The above discussion of the wages debate highlights the on-going role of the current poverty line in Australia. Although never officially endorsed by government, the poverty line developed by Henderson and his Melbourne colleagues in the 1960s and reaffirmed by the Poverty Commission a decade later, has proved to be of enduring value and impact.

The original Melbourne research itself was primarily privately funded, with contributions from charitable foundations and industry, supplemented by grants from the Australian Research Council and the Social Science Research Council. Henderson himself also contributed a small amount.

The research results received very wide publicity throughout the Australian media when they were first released and this was followed by a carefully planned and coordinated release of further findings designed to generate additional publicity in academic, policy and media circles. This aspect of the study illustrates how a piece of well-conceived and timely but independent social research can, through carefully explained dissemination of its findings and implications, have a major impact on the public's awareness of the issues and thus mobilise the support necessary for political action.

The emphasis of the Melbourne survey was on identifying the extent of poverty due to inadequate income: inadequate in the sense of income being low relative to need. This was (and often still is) criticised for being too narrow a conception of poverty, although it made sense as part of a broader strategy to generate pressures for wages and social benefit levels to be increased. Poverty was measured using an austere poverty line and the study was crucial in raising public awareness about the nature and extent of poverty in Australia (Roe, 1976).

In adopting virtually the same approach, the Poverty Commission justified its emphasis on primary poverty on the grounds of both practicality and significance. In the words of the Commission:

> ... an adequate income is fundamental to a person's security, well-being and independence. It enables him to provide housing, education, food, transport and other essentials for himself and his family. An adequate income allows him freedom of choice and freedom to participate in activities of his choice. It contributes greatly to personal freedom and the extent of opportunities available.
> (Commission of Inquiry into Poverty, 1975, p.2)

Although many aspects of the Poverty Commission's 1975 Report *Poverty in Australia* have been subject to criticism, its impact has been considerable. More than two decades after its publication, the methods it developed to measure poverty still influence the collection of data on household incomes and are still used to estimate poverty. The problems identified in the Report as causing primary poverty in the 1970s - too few job opportunities and inadequate levels of income support - continue to be significant causes of poverty in Australia in the 1990s, and the Henderson poverty line continues to be used to pressure those responsible for determining basic income levels.

One criticism of the Henderson approach is that by focusing on the detailed operation of income support and related policies, broader questions surrounding the meaning and causes of poverty have become submerged in the debates over the statistics. This is despite the fact that the Poverty Commissioners themselves argued that:

> If poverty is seen as a result of structural inequality within society, any serious attempt to eliminate poverty must seek to change those conditions which produce it. Although individual members of society are reluctant to accept responsibility for the existence of poverty, its continuance is a judgment on the society which condones the conditions causing poverty.
> (Commission of Inquiry into Poverty, 1975, p.viii)

In adopting a narrow approach to the measurement of primary poverty, Henderson was in good company. Beveridge also focused on the details rather than the overall structure, yet it is difficult to claim that his work has not affected the structure of British society. The fact that this cannot be said of Henderson is primarily due to the differences in the circumstances and economic prospects of Britain in the mid-1940s and Australia in the mid-1970s. Although the poverty line used by the Poverty Commission continues to be updated and used as the basis for estimating poverty, its validity has been increasingly called into question. As implied earlier, Henderson originally set the poverty line in 1966 equal to the basic wage plus child endowment for a reference family of two adults and two children. However, it was emphasised that poverty was explicitly relative and that the poverty line should be updated in line with average earnings. This was endorsed by the Poverty Commission, whose reference family poverty line was set at the same fraction (56.5 per cent) of average weekly earnings.

Over time, those updating the poverty line initially maintained this relativity with earnings, although this was criticised in the late 1970s because fiscal drag arising from the interaction between high inflation and a progressive income tax structure meant that the poverty line rose relative to the after-tax income of the average worker. As a consequence, it was agreed in 1981 that the basis for indexing the poverty line would change towards adjustment in line with household disposable income per capita, a measure which allowed for the impact of income tax but also of changes in non-wage income and population growth.

More recently, the use of the new updating index has itself been criticised on the grounds that the household income measure includes several components that are not picked up in the income distribution surveys used as the basis for estimating poverty. These include imputed rental income from dwellings and imputed interest on superannuation, both of which have grown more rapidly than incomes generally (fueled by a buoyant housing market and the growth in occupational superannuation), leading to an upward bias in the poverty line adjustment. In addition, changes in labour force participation have caused the growth of the population of 'equivalent adults' under the Henderson methodology to exceed actual population growth, leading to a further upward bias in the updating procedures.

The net impact of these two effects has not been insubstantial. Between 1972-73, when the Poverty Commission's poverty line was set, and 1992-93, their combined cumulative impact has been of the order of 15 per cent, or just under one per cent a year on average (Saunders, 1996). The size of the impact will differ between different groups (particularly between those at different points in the life cycle), so that they are likely to have a marked impact on the overall poverty rate and on the composition of the poor.

Perhaps of greater significance, the fact that a possible upward bias in the poverty statistics may exist has taken the pressure off government. As some commentators have observed:

Disagreement over the measurement of trends in poverty has been most helpful to those who wish to see poverty kept off the policy agenda.
(Manning and de Jonge, 1996, p.354)

One way of removing the effects referred to above would be to expand the concept of income that is measured in household income surveys rather than revise the poverty line methodology. This would be desirable in its own right, although the practical problems are considerable.

However, the debate has raised the whole question of the changing meaning and measurement of income, how these have changed and what consequences this has had for the measurement of poverty. One of the most significant developments that has occurred in Australia since the early 1980s has been associated with the expanding role of the non-cash 'social wage', that is, government benefits in the form of free or subsidised health, education, housing and welfare services.

In the decade to 1994, the average value of social wage benefits for all households increased by almost 63 per cent - well above the increase in prices and cash incomes. For households principally reliant on government cash benefits, the average value of social wage benefits more than doubled in absolute terms and increased as a percentage of disposable income from 52 per cent to 63 per cent (King, 1997, Figure 7).

More recently, the trend has been towards further targeting of social wage benefits to low income households and increased reliance on user pays by the middle class, both of which would result in less measured poverty if they were incorporated into the poverty estimates. Against this, it is important to acknowledge that the social wage provides households with a notional 'income' that is conditional upon their use of services over which they have little or no effective choice. Free health care benefits may help to make the poor less sick, but not necessarily less poor. As Manning and de Jonge have noted:

> Social security and the social wage are inherently unsatisfactory as income sources for people who would rather earn their own living, particularly when everybody else would also prefer that they were doing so.
> (Manning and de Jonge, 1996, p.356)

Aside from this, incorporating the social wage into the Henderson poverty framework would not be easy and would raise many difficult conceptual problems in addition to those associated with the measurement of income and of need. What these problems suggest, however, is that the case for revising the Henderson poverty framework (or at least supplementing it with other measures) may be becoming more compelling as traditional forms of income receipt are supplemented by new ones.

Some interesting insight into the traditional poverty literature can be gained if, instead of using Australian Bureau of Statistics (ABS) income distribution data to estimate poverty, data from the Household Expenditure Survey (HES) are also used. The HES data have the advantage that they include information on both income and expenditure, so that it is possible to distinguish between poverty measures derived from income, which measures the *capacity to consume,* and those which are derived from expenditure, which more directly measures *actual consumption.*

Some of the contrasts between the two measures are particularly interesting. In a recent study, I applied the conventional Henderson poverty line framework using HES data for single income unit households in 1993-94 to produce an estimated poverty rate of 20.3 per cent (Saunders, 1997). However, further analysis of those below the poverty line reveals that of all households who were in income poverty, 12.1 per cent had recorded expenditure levels that were *above* the poverty line, while a further 5.4 per cent reported expenditures that were less than their income.

If these two groups are excluded from the poverty definition (the former on the grounds that their expenditure was more than sufficient to support an above-poverty level of consumption, the latter on the grounds that their apparent saving suggests that they are not in need), the poverty rate drops from 20.3 per cent to 2.8 per cent. The extent of the fall varies across different socioeconomic groups, with a very large decline (from 37.2 per cent to 2.0 per cent) in poverty among single people over pension age. For sole parents, the figures fall from 33.7 per cent to 6.1 per cent - again a very substantial decline, but one which still leaves their poverty rate more then twice the national average.

These estimates raise important questions about the sustainability of the observed situations and what this implies for whether or not those experiencing them are poor on a longer term basis. Borrowing to sustain a level of consumption in excess of income cannot be pursued indefinitely, particularly if income itself is very low. The estimates also draw attention to the role of saving and dissaving at different points in the life cycle in smoothing the fluctuations in living standards that would otherwise arise from periodic variations in income.

They also raise important questions about the validity of using the HES data for such purposes. Expenditure on infrequently-purchased consumer durables implies that the divergence between the weekly incomes and expenditures of *individual* households can give a very misleading impression of their longer term economic status. There are also formidable difficulties involved in interpreting the difference between income and expenditure, as recorded in the HES, as a measure of household saving.

These factors caution against drawing strong inferences from the above estimates. Even accepting this, there are nonetheless important issues raised concerning the relationship between the levels of income and expenditure recorded in household surveys and their relationship to the standard of living of those reporting them. This would appear to be fertile ground for further work.

Another area where the limitations of the Henderson poverty framework are apparent is in relation to its use to measure poverty among indigenous

Australians. It is widely acknowledged that the Henderson poverty line provides only a 'rudimentary baseline for the analysis of indigenous poverty' (Altman and Hunter, 1998, p.255). Even so, estimates suggest that indigenous poverty has declined relative to total poverty from being three to four times higher in the early 1970s to around twice as high in the early 1990s, partly as a consequence of the rise in poverty amongst non-indigenous Australians (Altman and Hunter, 1998, p.255).

However, it would be foolish to conclude from such analysis that the problem of indigenous poverty can be solved solely by increasing their incomes, whether through increased employment or higher benefits. Nor can the problem be solved by paying higher wages under the Community Employment Development Projects (CEDP) scheme, under which payment of unemployment benefit to indigenous Australians living in remote communities and small country towns is made conditional upon them undertaking work approved by community leaders. Addressing the problems of indigenous poverty will involve far more than providing access to higher incomes, however much that in itself is needed. Deriving estimates of Henderson poverty may help to track the extent of one aspect of the problem, but the problem itself requires a far more broadly-based structural response.

Despite its limitations, my assessment is that the Henderson poverty line benchmark has been far more influential than its critics are willing to admit. Many of the benefit changes of the last two decades have focused on areas where research has identified highest poverty rates and largest gaps between benefits and the poverty line. Even the current Government's decision to fix the age pension at 25 per cent of average earnings corresponds almost exactly to where the Poverty Commission set its poverty line for the aged.

The Australian experience with its (semi-official) poverty line illustrate the value in what Tony Atkinson has referred to as the institution of a poverty line that has some official status (Atkinson, 1993). It is easy to focus on the strengths and limitations of a particular poverty line and lose sight of the wider research and policy issues. Many of the esoteric debates over the relevance of the Henderson poverty line in fact mirror broader social trends concerning the nature of income, the meaning of poverty and the role of *money income* in its alleviation.

The Meaning of Poverty

The above discussion, like the Australian poverty debate in general, has proceeded without giving explicit consideration to the meaning of poverty. It is possible to construe the meaning of poverty in one of two ways. The first focuses on a limited *definitional* sense which focuses on what poverty means to those who study it. Alternatively, the meaning of poverty can be considered from a more *outcome-oriented* perspective which explores what poverty means to those who experience it.

What has been called the 'consensual approach to poverty measurement' spans these two perspectives in attempting to base a poverty line on the responses of the population to what they regard as the minimum income needed to 'make ends meet' (Walker, 1987). Here, the approach estimates what income would, on average, meet the subjectively assessed material needs of the population if they were able to meet their needs, but no more.

One of the most striking features to emerge from research on the consensual approach is that even when the minimum income question (MIQ) is worded very precisely, there is often no clear consensus in the replies. This emerged from research in which we asked a random sample of Australians on the electoral roll what they regarded as the minimum income they needed in order to make ends meet. Even after taking account of differences in the actual incomes and family circumstances of the respondents, we were never able to explain more than 30 per cent of the variation in the MIQ response.

One consequence of this is that the poverty line derived from the MIQ responses is very sensitive to the precise methods used to derive it: too sensitive in my opinion to make the method of much use for policy purposes (Saunders and Matheson, 1992).

The following version of the MIQ has been asked of Australians twice each year by the Roy Morgan Research Centre since the late 1940s:

> In your opinion, what's the smallest amount that a family of four - two parents and two children - need each week to keep in health and live decently - the smallest amount for all expenses including rent?

Analysis shows that the mean response varies considerably over time (Saunders and Bradbury, 1991; Gruen, 1995). Between February 1974 and February 1994, for example, the mean response varied in real (1988 dollar) terms between $360 in July 1991 and $430 in February 1982 - or by about 20 per cent. Overall, the mean real response at the end of the period ($372) was very close to that at the beginning ($376). The Henderson poverty line for a two-adult, two-child family in September 1994 was $402 a week, well below the mean response of $459.

It is possible to argue that these variations reflect different interpretations of the MIQ question and differences in the values and experience of respondents. However, we have also discovered that even if the MIQ is asked of a group with a similar standard of living and (recent) experience, the responses still vary considerably. For example, when the MIQ was asked as part of a recent study of the young unemployed, the response from a sample of 389 recipients of unemployment benefit aged between 16 and 24 varied between $110 and $210 a week, according to age and whether the respondents were living at home or not (King and Payne, 1993, Table 14.1). The MIQ response exceeded the actual incomes of those surveyed by between 30 per cent and 80 per cent, although the interviewers noted that many respondents had difficulty answering the question and around ten per cent chose not to.

More recently, the same question has been asked of over 1,000 participants in the first wave of a Social Policy Research Centre (SPRC) longitudinal study of Department of Social Security (DSS) clients which began around September 1995. In this instance, the mean overall response was just over $400 a week, with around three-quarters falling between $200 and $500 a week, again indicating that there is considerable variation in the perceptions of minimum income levels, even amongst those with very similar standards of living.

The conclusion I draw from this research is that it is unlikely that the consensual approach is likely to provide the basis for a new poverty line. Although it remains possible that the variation in responses reflects a systematic effect of as yet unidentified variables, the best that can be concluded at the moment is that any consensus in Australian perceptions of minimum income levels itself remains elusive.

Another aspect of what poverty means to those who experience it concerns how the notion of poverty itself is understood by those living at or close to the poverty line. Research currently underway at the SPRC has explored this issue by asking those who participated in the longitudinal study referred to above a series of questions designed to elicit information on their understanding of the meaning of poverty.

In the course of a face-to-face interview, survey participants were asked the following question:

There's been a lot written recently in the papers about poverty in Australia. Which of these statements BEST describes what being in poverty means to you?

Analysis of the 1,149 responses indicates that the vast majority (over 68 per cent) of those interviewed couched their perceptions of poverty in terms of being able to afford basic needs without having to struggle to make ends meet all the time (Table 2.1). Less than ten per cent saw poverty as having enough to 'live decently', while only 6.7 per cent accepted that poverty means having to forgo the 'good things in life', and very few saw poverty purely in terms of having less than others.

Table 2.1   Perceptions of the meaning of poverty among DSS clients (percentages)

Not having enough money to make ends meet	12.3
Having a lot less than everyone else	1.8
Not having enough to buy basics like food and clothing	41.9
Having to struggle to survive each and every day	26.4
Never having enough to be able to live decently	8.6
Never being able to afford any of the good things in life	6.7
Don't know	2.5

Source: SPRC Longitudinal Survey of DSS Clients, First Wave of Interviews.

Table 2.1 gives the overall impression that those who are themselves on low incomes regard poverty as a situation in which people do not have enough to meet their basic needs. The evidence suggests that those on low incomes have rather modest expectations of what they would need to escape poverty, although when the same group were asked what level of income they themselves needed to 'make ends meet' many said that they needed more (often a good deal more) than they were currently receiving.

These results are exploratory and preliminary, although they suggest that there is a need for more Australian research on what members of the community understand by the meaning of poverty in its various manifestations - along similar lines to that pioneered by Mack and Lansley (1985) and recently extended by Gordon and Pantazis (1997) and Halleröd, Bradshaw and Holmes (1997).

Such research will not provide 'the' answer to the definition of poverty, but it holds the promise of improving community awareness of poverty, of gaining legitimacy for any new poverty measure, and influencing how poverty can best be defined for policy purposes.

Current Developments

It is possible to separate views regarding where Australian poverty research should now be heading into two broad camps. The first of these accepts the need to refine the prevailing (Henderson) approach by developing a poverty line that has more relevance to, and hence increased legitimacy in, the Australia of the 1990s. Within this group, there is some division between those who favour revising the current poverty line to remove some of its main weaknesses and those in favour of its continued use until a clearly superior alternative has been developed. The differences between these two groups are as much to do with strategy as with poverty research itself, although this is not to deny that the need for more research is widely acknowledged.

The second camp favours the rejection of any poverty line because the normative judgements implicit in any line undermine its value as an objective indicator of adequacy. This group sees the value in the conduct of *poverty research* but sees this as possible without having to use a *poverty line*. Of particular relevance to the emergence of this position has been book *Living Decently* by Travers and Richardson (1993) which argues that traditional poverty lines 'carry too heavy a burden; they confuse issues of inequality with issues of the ability to live decently, and seek a degree of precision which is greater than they can bear' (Travers and Richardson, 1993, p.65).

Travers and Richardson argue that the best way forward involves using a range of descriptive indicators of actual living circumstances to compare different groups, leaving it to others to make the judgement as to whether or not these represent poverty. In effect, what is being proposed is that households are ranked against a range of different indicators and the characteristics of those at the bottom of each ranking (or at the bottom of several separate rankings) be identified as most in need. There is undoubtedly value in research of this kind, although the difficult problems associated with establishing on what basis to rank households (the equivalence scale issue) remains a formidable obstacle. My own view is that such research should complement not replace traditional poverty research.

Which of the two broad positions identified above will have most impact on Australian poverty research over the next decade or so will depend upon a number of important initiatives that are currently taking place. Several of these are now briefly described.

One of the most important and enduring lessons to emerge from the experience of the last three decades of Australian poverty research is the value and significance of *data* which can be used to estimate the dimensions of poverty, however it is defined. Although much of the discussion of the impact of the Poverty Commission surrounds the value and relevance of the poverty line, of equal significance was the entire framework for collecting and analysing data on household incomes in order to estimate poverty (Saunders, 1998). How income is measured and how the income unit is defined have as much impact on the nature and extent of poverty as the poverty line itself, as some of the foregoing discussion has indicated.

Equally important in practice is the frequency with which household income surveys are conducted and who pays for them. In this respect, Australia has been well served in the past by the Australian Bureau of Statistics (ABS) which has conducted a series of household income surveys and, since the mid-1980s, made the (confidentialised) unit record data available (at a price) to researchers. Until recently, however, the fact that such data were only available every five years or so has limited the ability to conduct research on the causes of poverty and to influence the current policy debate.

Since July 1994, the ABS has changed its method of conducting its household income surveys from an infrequent one-off approach to a continuous survey piggy-backed onto the Monthly Population Survey (MPS). A major advantage of this change is that household income distribution data will henceforth be available on an annual basis, allowing for trends in income poverty to be better tracked and their causes more readily identified.

Under the new methodology, about one-sixth of households who are participating in the MPS are asked to participate in the income survey when they reach their final (eighth) month of participation in the MPS. This methodology implies that the new income data will not be directly comparable with those collected in earlier income surveys, although strict consistency is often a casualty of change. The important point is that the new ABS data should provide the basis for a more informed and timely discussion of trends in poverty, although it is still too early to judge what the real impact will be.

The second development with the potential for far-reaching consequences is the study of the adequacy of social security payments within the Department of Social Security (DSS, 1995; Holbert, 1995). The long-term objective of the study is the development of benchmarks for assessing the adequacy of social security payments which; 'address both issues of opportunity and outcomes ... and to place this material in a contemporary and relevant context' (Holbert, 1995, p.45).

The project was initiated by the previous Government, although it appears to have withstood the change of government in 1996 and the restrictive budgetary stance of the new Government - so far! The initial report of the project identified two approaches to adequacy, a *prescriptive approach* designed 'to nominate a specific and independent measure against which the adequacy of payments could be assessed' (DSS, 1995, p.23) and a *descriptive approach* which 'would identify some payments as being more or less adequate than other payments' (DSS, 1995, p.23) on the basis of observing the living conditions and experience of low-income DSS households.

As an initial step, DSS commissioned outside experts to conduct research in each area. Peter Travers was commissioned to conduct a pilot study of the circumstances of low-income DSS households as a way of assessing the potential of the descriptive approach (Travers, 1996). I and a group of colleagues at the SPRC were commissioned to undertake the development of a set of indicative budget standards for Australia, along the lines of those developed for the UK by the Family Budget Unit in York.

Our budget standards study has been more ambitious (and better funded) than the York study - possibly too ambitious. We have developed a series of modest but adequate and low cost budgets for no less than 46 different household types, a huge task which has just been completed and published (Saunders *et al.*, 1998). The fact that we in Australia have now joined the increasing number of countries that have developed their own budget standards using the techniques pioneered almost a century ago by Rowntree in his first York poverty study (Rowntree, 1901) points to the strength and enduring value of his contribution to poverty research.

Although any detailed discussion of these findings is not appropriate here, I am doubtful whether the low cost budget standard will replace the Henderson poverty line. Our low cost standard, like the lower living standard proposed two decades ago for the US by Harold Watts (1980) is intended to allow 'economic and social participation consistent with community standards' even though it also requires 'frugal and careful management of resources'. These descriptions imply a higher standard of living than that achievable at a poverty line described by its originators as 'so austere as to make it unchallengeable that those described as poor are not so' (Henderson, Harcourt and Harper, 1970, p.1).

This does not mean that the low cost budget standard will not be useful as the basis for a new understanding of what income adequacy means in the 1990s. It will provide a systematic framework for defining adequacy and assessing its achievement in various dimensions - both of which are of central importance to determining the level of social security payments.

At the same time as these developments have been taking place, additional work is being conducted within the somewhat narrower confines of the traditional Henderson approach. Two specific initiatives are worth mentioning briefly. The first has involved the preparation of a volume of essays designed to provide a perspective on Australian poverty in the 1990s using the Henderson framework. The book, *Australian Poverty: Then and Now* has just been published and contains a thorough evaluation of the contribution of Henderson and the Poverty Commission and an assessment of what is known about the magnitude and various dimensions of Australian poverty in the 1990s (Fincher and Nieuwenhuysen, 1998).

In what should eventually be an important companion volume, the Academy of the Social Sciences in Australia (ASSA) has been funded to undertake a project on Poverty in Australia which will draw on expertise from a range of social science disciplines, to define key areas and issues in poverty research, develop strategies for improving its quality and to recommend broad objectives for such research in the context of current and future trends. Particular attention is being given to the scope for improved international cooperation in poverty research and how this can complement other activity being undertaken by ASSA and other bodies such as ABS.

Among the topics that will be addressed in the project itself are situating the Australian poverty debate in the context of international trends in poverty and poverty research, the changing nature of the links between the labour market and poverty, the geography of poverty and disadvantage, the various dimensions of poverty and deprivation among indigenous Australians and the nature of family poverty from the perspective of children.

In addition, specific attention will be directed to the much neglected but very important issue of the representation of poverty in the media and advertising and the role of discourses that emerge from this in the evolution of community understanding of, and attitudes to, poverty and the poor. The final section of the project will draw out the implications for how Australia can best adapt to the future pressures impacting on poverty, including identifying the scope for further international collaboration.

The final development has evolved directly from those already described. As a consequence of the DSS Adequacy Project, the ABS has established a Living Standards Reference Group to advise it on the content of a major survey of household living standards which is being planned for implementation in around the year 2000, supported by special funding provided by DSS and other agencies. The initial fieldwork for the study began in February 1998, with the evaluation of the test data currently underway.

Amongst the topics covered by questions in the pilot survey are the degree of satisfaction with the current standard of living, comparison with the standard achieved twelve months ago, the degree of difficulty experienced meeting mortgage repayments, satisfaction with dwelling (with reasons for any dissatisfaction), satisfaction with schools, difficulty paying school expenses, satisfaction with hours of work, employment prospects, unemployment experience over the previous five years, lowest acceptable weekly take-home pay, self assessment of health status, degree of involvement in community activities, imputed rent of owner-occupied dwellings, estimated values of assets, liabilities and net worth, ability to raise $2000 in an emergency and details of cash flow problems experienced over the last twelve months. (The SPRC argued unsuccessfully for inclusion of the MIQ described earlier.)

In addition to the collection of standard demographic, income and labour force characteristics data, the survey has the potential to provide many new insights into the kinds of deprivation being experienced by different households and how these relate to the objective circumstances and subjective experiences of each household. In conjunction with the detailed results from the budget standards project, the basis is being laid for a quantum leap in Australian research on living standards, though not necessarily in research on poverty.

Summary

The main aim of this paper has been to provide an overview of the issues that are currently shaping the very vibrant area of Australian poverty research in its various manifestations. That vibrancy is mirrored to some extent by the policy concerns surrounding the re-emergence of poverty and other forms of social disadvantage in a more competitive and dynamic international economy that is generating 'winners and losers' at an increasing rate.

One of the themes running through the paper is that much of the

Australian poverty literature has been rather narrow in its focus on measurement issues, to the relative neglect of developments in the international literature in the way that poverty is conceptualised and identified. Yet at the same time, the imperative for action is being fueled by the emergence of new forms of poverty associated with the persistence of unemployment and growing labour market inequalities.

Several current initiatives have the potential to provide an optimistic basis for future Australian poverty research. These include the development of improved national statistics on income and other dimensions of living standards, the SPRC research on budget standards, work on descriptive indicators of relative deprivation, the proposed ABS survey of living standards and several strands of the Academy's poverty project.

These developments suggest that the prospects for a new and improved understanding of the nature, extent and meaning of poverty in modern Australia have not been better since the Poverty Commission was undertaking its work over two decades ago.

An important feature of many of the developments described in the final section of this paper is the degree to which they involve the active participation and/or encouragement by key agencies of government, particularly DSS and ABS. The close interaction between the academic and bureaucratic spheres has long been one of the features of Australian policy research generally. There are obvious dangers in this, particularly in sensitive areas like poverty where research often becomes a source of pressure for government.

On balance, however, these dangers have not in my view materialised to date, although this is not to deny that government has been all too willing to challenge poverty research findings when it has been in their interest to do so. As a researcher who has worked actively in the field for the last two decades, I would far rather work in a cooperative (if guarded) way with the bureaucracy than in an environment where the word poverty is no longer recognised by some people as either a helpful research construct or as a practical reality.

References

Academy of Social Sciences in Australia (1985), *Women, Social Science and Public Policy*, Allen and Unwin.

Altman, J. and Hunter, B. (1998), 'Indigenous Poverty', in R. Fincher and J. Niewenhuysen (eds), *Australian Poverty: Then and Now*, Melbourne University Press, Melbourne, pp. 238-57.

Atkinson, A.B. (1993), *The Institution of an Official Poverty Line and Economic Policy*, Discussion Paper WSP/98, Welfare State Programme, London School of Economics, London.

Borland, J. (1997), 'Earnings Inequality in Australia: Changes and Causes', Paper presented to the 1997 National Social Policy Conference, University of New South Wales, July.

Bradshaw, J. and Lynes, T. (1995), *Benefit Uprating Policy and Living Standards*, Social Policy Research Unit, University of York, York.

Briggs, A. (1961), *Social Thought and Social Action. A Study of the Work of Seebohm Rowntree 1871-1954*, Longmans, London.

Castles, F.G. (1985), *The Working Class and Welfare. Reflections on the Political Development of the Welfare State in Australia and New Zealand, 1890-1980*, Allen and Unwin, Sydney.

Commission of Inquiry into Poverty (1975), *First Main Report. Poverty in Australia*, AGPS, Canberra.

Department of Social Security (DSS) (1995), *Developing a Framework for Benchmarks of Adequacy for Social Security Payments*, Policy Discussion Paper No. 6, AGPS, Canberra.

Fincher, R. and Niewenhuysen, J. (eds) (1998), *Australian Poverty: Then and Now*, Melbourne University Press, Melbourne.

Gordon, D. and Pantazis, C. (1997), 'The Public's Perception of Necessities and Poverty', in D. Gordon and C. Pantazis (eds), *Breadline Britain in the 1990s*, Ashgate, Aldershot, pp. 71-96.

Gruen, F.H. (1995), 'The Australian Welfare State: Neither Egalitarian Saviour Nor Economic Millstone?', *Economic and Industrial Relations Review*, vol. 6, no. 1, pp. 125-38.

Halleröd, B., Bradshaw, J. and Holmes, H. (1997), 'Adapting the Consensual Definition of Poverty', in D. Gordon and C. Pantazis (eds), *Breadline Britain in the 1990s*, Ashgate, Aldershot, pp. 213-34.

Hancock, K. (1997), 'The Needs of the Low Paid', 1997 Cunningham Lecture to the Annual Symposium of the Academy of the Social Sciences in Australia.

Henderson, R.F., Harcourt, A. and Harper, R.J.A. (1970), *People in Poverty. A Melbourne Survey*, Cheshire for the Institute of Applied Economic and Social Research, Melbourne.

Hills, J. (1995), *Enquiry into Income and Wealth*, Joseph Rowntree Foundation, York.

Kaim-Caudle, P.R. (1975), Review article. 'Poverty in Australia', *Journal of Social Policy*, vol. 5, no. 4, pp. 401-6.

King, A. (1997), *The Changing Face of Australian Poverty. A Comparison of 1996 Estimates and the 1972-73 Findings From the Commission of Inquiry*, Discussion Paper No. 23, NATSEM, University of Canberra.

King, A. and Payne, T. (1993), *Living Conditions and Costs of the Young Unemployed*, Reports and Proceedings No. 110, Social Policy Research Centre, University of New South Wales, Sydney.

Macarthy, P.G. (1969), 'Justice Higgins and the Harvester Judgement', *Australian Economic History Review*, vol. 11, pp. 16-38.

Mack, J. and S. Lansley (1985), *Poor Britain*, George Allen and Unwin, London.

Manning, I. and de Jonge, A. (1996), 'The New Poverty: Causes and Responses', in P. Sheehan, B. Grewal and M. Kumnick (eds), *Dialogues on Australia's Future. In Honour of the Late Professor Ronald Henderson*, Centre for Strategic Economic Studies, Victoria

University of Technology, pp. 351-62.

McCaughey, J. and D. (1997), *Ronald Frank Henderson 1917-1994. A Tribute*, Melbourne Institute of Applied Economic and Social Research, University of Melbourne, Melbourne.

Poverty Commission Data (1980), *Interim Evaluation Report on the Programme to Combat Poverty: Report from the Commission to the Council.*

Prest, W. (1952), *Housing, Income and Saving in War-Time*, Department of Economics, University of Melbourne.

Holbert, R. (1995), 'Issues in Assessing the Adequacy of Social Security Payments', *Social Security Journal*, June, pp. 31-48.

Roe, J. (1976), *Social Policy in Australia. Some Perspectives 1901-1975*, Cassell, Sydney.

Rowntree, B.S. (1901), *Poverty. A Study of Town Life*, Macmillan, London.

Saunders, P. (1996), 'Poverty in the 1990s: A Challenge to Work and Welfare', in P. Sheehan, B. Grewal and M. Kumnick (eds), *Dialogues on Australia's Future. In Honour of the late Professor Ronald Henderson*, Centre for Strategic Economic Studies, Victoria University of Technology, pp. 325-50.

Saunders, P. (1997), 'Living Standards, Choice and Poverty', *Australian Journal of Labour Economics*, vol. 1, no. 1, pp. 49-70.

Saunders, P. (1998), 'The Role of Indicators of Income Poverty in the Measurement of National Progress', in R. Eckersley (ed), *Measuring Progress: Is Life Getting Better?*, CSIRO Publishing, Collingwood, pp. 223-37.

Saunders, P. and Bradbury, B. (1991), 'Some Australian Evidence on the Consensual Approach to Poverty Measurement', *Economic Analysis and Policy*, vol. 21, no. 1, pp. 47-78.

Saunders, P. and Matheson, G. (1992), *Perceptions of Poverty, Income Adequacy and Living Standards in Australia*, Reports and Proceedings No. 99, Social Policy Research Centre, University of New South Wales, Sydney.

Saunders, P. (1996) *Unequal but Fair?: A Study of Class Barriers in Britain*, Institute of Economic Affairs, Health and Welfare Unit.

Saunders, P., Chalmers, J., McHugh, M., Murray, C., Bittman, M. and Bradbury, B. (1998), *Development of Indicative Budget Standards for Australia*, Policy Research Paper No. 74, Department of Social Security, Canberra.

Travers, P. (1996), 'Deprivation Among Low Income DSS Australian Families: Results from a Pilot Study', in R. Thanki and C. Thomson (eds), *Mortgaging Our Future? Families and Young People in Australia*, Reports and Proceedings No. 129, Social Policy Research Centre, University of New South Wales, pp. 27-45.

Travers, P. and Richardson, S. (1993), *Living Decently. Material Well-Being in Australia*, Oxford University Press, Melbourne.

Walker, R. (1987), 'Consensual Approaches to the Definition of Poverty: Towards an Alternative Methodology', *Journal of Social Policy*, vol. 17, no. 2, pp. 213-26.

Watts, H.W. (1980), *New American Budget Standards: Report of the Expert Committee on Family Budget Revisions*, Special Report Series, Institute for Research on Poverty, University of Wisconsin, Madison.

3   The Dangers of Strong Causal Reasoning: Root Causes, Social Science, and Poverty Policy

MARTIN REIN and CHRISTOPHER WINSHIP

Introduction

Rowntree's classic study of poverty in York in 1898 made an important contribution to policy debate about poverty in England at that time. A testament to the importance of his study is that it is being celebrated 100 years later at this conference. He tried to answer the question: 'Is it the case that' the proportion of the population in poverty is large enough to require a collective response to try to alleviate it? His conclusion that 'nearly 30 per cent of the population is forced to live in poverty' was a fact of the gravest concern (Rowntree, 1901). This conclusion, however, rested on the assumption that he had defined poverty appropriately and in a way that was agreed upon by others.

Rowntree was also interested in the nature of poverty. He explored this question by examining different types of poverty (primary and secondary), as well as poverty over the life course of the family. He asked two different kinds of questions: 'How' can families with sufficient resources end up being poor?, and 'Why' do people enter and leave poverty at different points in their lives? Someone who asks why something is the case typically knows, or thinks he knows, what constitutes an exemplar of the case. To answer a how and why question presumes the definitional problem of 'what is the case' has been answered in a way that is adequate.

Rowntree's research raises interesting and important questions about how to study the size and nature of the problem of poverty. In particular, his study raises two issues: (1) the way in which why and how questions lead back into definitional issues; and (2) how the normative leap is made by the empirical analyst to the 'ought' question - what ought to be done to deal with poverty and its consequences. The main contribution of this essay is to consider these issues in the current context, principally within the United States. In part we are interested in the way in which claims about causality are used to answer the definitional question of 'what is poverty?'. More importantly, we want to examine the ways in which causal arguments are used to support more general moral arguments as to why certain actions ought to be undertaken.

Our interest in not in the use of causal arguments to justify specific policy programs. Rather we are concerned with the ways in which claims about causality are used to argue for broad collective action or policy. One example is the argument that the American government should aggressively alleviate childhood poverty, which is based on the assertion that children clearly are not responsible for their poverty and the strong belief that childhood poverty has substantial long-term negative consequences. More generally, one might argue for generous support for the poor if one thought that individuals were poor because of employment dislocation due to technological change or, more simply, the forces of a competitive capitalist market (Blank, 1997). Conversely, one might contend that the government should provide only the most limited forms of support for the poor because one believed that such support led individuals to rely on the dole instead of seeking to support themselves (Murray, 1984).

These broad prescriptions for societal action all rely on what we term 'strong causal' reasoning, the belief that specific factors lead to particular outcomes. Social science, however, has had little success in demonstrating strong causal relations among factors. Rather the research literature is littered with small, or at best modest-size, estimates for the effects of different variables on each other. In the vast majority of cases most of the variance in the dependent variable is unexplained. As a result, the use of strong causal arguments to justify claims about what we ought to do often is highly problematic.

Before turning our discussion to the present, we review in more detail the issues that Rowntree's study presents for poverty researchers. We start by providing a brief analysis and then a critique. We want to argue that in examining poverty types and the life course Rowntree developed a typology of poverty types that subverted his moral claim for action. His focus on the 'why' of poverty led him to define to two different types - primary and secondary. This in turn undermined the normative basis from which he could conclude that poverty was a severe problem.

Next we examine Rowntree's analysis of poverty in some detail, and then we consider the current policy context with respect to poverty in the United

States. The following section explores the failures of causal thinking. Social science potentially fails policy making in two ways: first, the causal theories it offers often are empirically weak, having little predictive power, and can be quite sensitive to different model specifications. Thus the definitional and moral conclusions based on such analysis are tenuous at best. Second, social science fails even when causal analysis is successful in that it is incomplete because there are normative and moral questions that extend beyond even the most successful research.

The subsequent section examines the dangers in the unthinking use of causal thinking in the policy process. We discuss six issues: overselling, fragile rationales, weak causal chains, over-generalisation, elimination of personal responsibility, and the confounding of issues. We end by discussing what we see as the implications of making policies with 'weak' as opposed to 'strong' causal theories. We conclude that policy should involve direct interventions and be as much concerned with the amelioration of poverty as with its abolition, and that public discourse needs to focus on creating consensus around a set of values to deal with poverty.

Rowntree's Analysis of Poverty and a Critique

Rowntree's objective was to understand 'not only the proportion of the population living in poverty, but the nature of that poverty'. (All references about Rowntree are based on Peter Kaim-Caudle, 1998.) At the time, the definition of poverty was based on the very unrealistic assumption that 'every penny earned by each member of the family went into the family purse and was judiciously expended on necessaries'. He defined primary poverty as a condition in which the family's total earnings were not sufficient to maintain mere physical efficiency. Secondary poverty existed when the level of resources was sufficient but the expenditure pattern was wasteful, resulting in the lack of resources to maintain physical efficiency. Rowntree skilfully avoided all of the conceptual problems of measuring 'wasteful expenditure' or 'squandering'. As Kaim-Caudle explains, secondary poverty is defined as 'the difference between those assessed by visible evidence to be in poverty ... and those estimated to have been in primary poverty' (Kaim-Caudle, 1998, p.2). So the methodological problem was in measuring primary poverty and in judging 'obvious want and squalor'. The issues surrounding 'visible evidence' appear not to have been addressed at all, although these are all the well-known issues that every study of poverty must confront.

There were two problems with Rowntree's analysis dividing poverty into 'primary' and 'secondary'. First, the two types were very unevenly distributed. Primary poverty accounted for nine per cent of the population of York in 1899; secondary poverty accounted for 18 per cent of the population. Second, the moral and policy implications of what 'ought to be done' differed by individuals and families found in each type of poverty. Those in primary poverty deserved societal support since presumably they were already making the best possible effort to support themselves, but still found themselves lacking. The situation of those in secondary poverty was more complex. On the one hand, since they have the adequate means to support themselves, they were not deserving of welfare. On the other hand, to deny them support would jeopardise the welfare of their children, who through no fault of their own live in less than adequate circumstances.

The second dimension of the nature of poverty that Rowntree introduced was that there was a poverty cycle which varied over the life course. 'The life of the labourer is marked by five alternating periods of want and comparative plenty.' When young couples had children, especially a large number (four or more), they lacked the resources to provide for all of them. However, as the children grew up and remained at home, they began to earn and to contribute to the family resources, thus moving the family out of poverty. When the children establish independent households and no longer contribute to the family income, their parents reenter poverty during old age. Thus the poverty cycle varied with the age of the head of household.

How did Rowntree get himself in trouble? From a normative point of view these two dimensions of poverty move in opposite directions. Rowntree's distinction between primary and secondary poverty suggests that 'hard-core' poverty - that is, primary poverty - is only a problem of a relatively small portion of the population. From a life course perspective, however, the proportion of the population poor over time was much larger than the proportion poor at a specific point in time. When seen dynamically, poverty has even 'graver significance'.

The condition of being poor is presumed a priori to be problematic on normative grounds. Poverty defined as a lack of resources to maintain mere physical efficiency, or to participate in society, or to realise one's capability, and so on has a normative implication, since it implies (silently, of course, because the moral premise on which it is based is simply taken for granted) that we 'ought to' do something about this undesired state, i.e. action should follow discovery. For purposes of this discussion, let us bracket the question of who are the agents doing something to relieve poverty, and focus on the implied social obligation that we 'ought' to collectively intervene to relieve the unwanted condition. The larger the proportion of the population experiencing the problem, the greater the necessity to act.

However, the study of poverty also involves developing a methodology appropriate to the question that is being asked. There are three different research questions that the study of poverty confronts: What is the case? (What people are poor?); What is this a case of? (What does it mean to be poor?); Why did this become a case? (Why are particular individuals/families poor?).

The foundation on which why and how questions depend is the presumption that we can provide an account of the question 'what is the case' that is (to paraphrase Max Weber) 'adequate as to its meaning'. Why and how questions must, by their nature, presuppose that the phenomenon of interest has therefore already been meaningfully identified (Ragin, forthcoming). By contrast, 'what' questions provide the empirical foundation for the deeper 'why' questions, but they are sometimes trivialised and regarded as being merely descriptive. Yet in practice, separating the 'what' from the 'why' and 'how' questions can prove to be difficult, as we have illustrated with reference to Rowntree's research on poverty.

Much of the serious social science research appears to be more interested in the 'why' rather than the 'what' questions. 'Why' questions seek to provide additional information that helps to explain the phenomenon of interest by trying to understand its causes. However, before a 'why' question can be studied we must assume that the cases described in answering the 'what' questions are sufficiently alike to be treated as instances of the same thing. The main research task is to uncover what 'independent variables' can help to explain the outcome.

'How' questions are attempts to identify the social mechanisms, the concrete social processes, that are at play in producing the outcome or the event that is, in the context of variable-oriented research, referred to as the dependent variable. This exercise requires that we explore how the different parts of the phenomenon fit together and constitute a pattern or a configuration of the case in review. To answer the 'how' question it is necessary to assure that the definition of the dependent variable 'does not vary substantially across the cases selected for study' (Ragin, forthcoming). The 'how' questions seek to explain more or less the same outcome. One of the tasks then is to reduce 'the observations made over time and space to a social process that connects events', such as the rise or fall in poverty rates (Burawoy, 1998, p.15).

'What is the case' questions presume that we are considering broadly the same conditions. To generalise to a population, Rowntree should have been measuring the same thing - poverty - and providing in its operationalisation a clear definition and a clear boundary (Ragin, forthcoming). What he actually measured was two different types of poverty: those individuals who do not have enough resources to maintain physical efficiency, and those who did but squandered the money on wasteful expenditure and therefore ended up without enough to make ends meet.

When the same outcome of a lack of resources is produced by quite different processes, then the question shifts to 'what is this a case of?' and the normative implication suggests a quite different set of issues. Instead of showing poverty as a clear social wrong, the research calls attention to a value conflict between the norm which affirms an unconditional obligation to help poor children who are victims of the environment into which they were born, and the norm of not helping the family who violates the norm that people should live within their own means. This is particularly troubling since most of the cases appear to fall into this category of secondary poverty. The issue of personal responsibility does not appear to be a factor for those in the much smaller category of primary poverty - but still, one could ask why the family had more children than they could support. Thus the distinction between primary and secondary poverty points to the tension between social and personal obligations.

It has always been difficult to define the 'truly needy', even in provincial towns in the late 19th century. The judgement is always relative to some value position about what low-income people 'should' do. Studies of living wages in the early 1900s often concluded that working people could get along 'just fine' if only they knew more about nutrition, how to conserve their resources, and so on, and therefore even primary poverty could be judged as wasteful; as always, the poor were to blame for their own poverty. Still, it is a continuum, and at the lower end there could be consensus about the truly needy. Of course, the relative size of the primary versus secondary categories is a key question for policy, but it takes values as well as analysis to answer it. The normative issue and the methodological issue are intertwined. To say you are interested in 'all people who can't make ends meet and thus are in poverty' is the only way to avoid the normative issue, but this decision involves a cost since it requires embracing a diverse population that may defy meaningful generalisations.

Most of the papers in this conference appear to have neglected Rowntree's interest in poverty types and the life course. We think this is a mistake. We also believe that it is a mistake to study these questions in the same way that one studies the question of poverty rates in a population. Rowntree identified two forms of diversity: diversity over time (relative to the life cycle), and cross-sectional diversity (the diverse ways of not being able to make ends meet). To answer the 'what is this a case of' question requires using evidence and making something of it, and then generating a back and forth process among definition, causes and normative conclusions. By contrast, a 'what is the case' question is based on the assumption that you have data on all possible relevant cases, and the problem is one of coming up with a definition of the subset of the possible relevant meanings of poverty that works, makes sense, and is acceptable to the audience that the study is trying to influence. As we discuss below, this distinction does not resolve the normative leap between understanding processes and outcomes, but it permits a more direct confrontation of the connection between 'is' and 'ought' by clarifying what question is being asked and how it might best be answered.

Our argument is not about the limits of 'what is the case' questions, nor are we arguing to support one or another method or normative position. Above all, it is not an argument to switch to the more mainstream questions concerning the causes of poverty and the mechanisms that maintain it. Indeed, the primary purpose of this paper is to explore the problems that do arise from the focus on 'why' and 'how' questions in the search for normative justifications for broad policy actions.

The Current U.S. Context

The federal welfare reforms enacted in 1996 constitute a new chapter in the long history of American poverty policy. As has occurred so frequently in the past, there was sharp disagreement about the causes and consequences of poverty and, as a result, what types of reforms were needed and what their likely consequences would be. When a reform package was finally enacted, two of President Clinton's key poverty advisors (Bane and Primus) were so appalled by the legislation that they resigned in protest.

Reaching a policy consensus on an issue as divisive as poverty in a society as ideologically, economically, and ethnically diverse as the United States is an enormous challenge. Public support for different solutions has historically swung between interest in outdoor relief or its modern equivalent welfare, and formal institutions such as the poorhouse and orphanages (Katz, 1986; Rothman, 1971). The question of the poor's relation to work has always been highly contested in the United States, with the right arguing for 'workfare' and the left declaring all such requirements as 'slavefare'. In the past decade the political process has been in near-gridlock over what to do. The discourse, which was dominated by ideological elites with their argument for extreme solutions (Teles, 1996), has now surrendered to a broad-based political consensus with wide public support. The original ADC programme introduced in 1935 provided cash grants and did not require work. The new consensus is based on the view that work is a central objective of policy, but the debate over how to motivate recipients to find jobs has continued unabated.

In the U.S., it was primarily during the depression years that poverty viewed simply as a problem of economic deprivation. Recently it has been more broadly conceived as a whole set of related behaviours, with the focus shifting from moral hazard to employment opportunities, norm-violating behaviour like single-female- headed households, and law-violating behaviour like delinquency and crime. While much empirical work has remained at a descriptive level, the goal of the more ambitious poverty research has been to identify the causal links between different dimensions of poverty - economic impoverishment, crime, family breakdown, unemployment, and so on - with the aim of developing broad policies consistent with the analysis. James Q. Wilson, attacking liberals for their failure to pay attention to policies that deal with deterrence and incarceration, has argued that the social science view is one that believes that 'the only morally defensible and substantively efficacious strategy for reducing crime is to attack its "root" causes' (J.Q. Wilson, 1985, p.47). The same point could just as easily be made about poverty. Of course, this does not mean that the objective of all or even most social science research is to discover the causes of specific phenomena. Rather, the argument is that the liberal search for policy solutions solely in the causes of phenomena is misplaced.

The recent discussion in the *Economic Report of the President* (February 1998) about the economic well-being of children illustrates what social scientists typically do in the field of poverty research and how they link these efforts to policy recommendations. The starting point of the analysis is a simple description that two things appear to be associated with each other - economic status and child well-being. This association is assumed to be valid, robust and especially relevant to understanding the consequences of poverty on later development. The Report asserts that:

> children who grow up in low income families score lower on standardised academic achievement tests, are less likely to complete high school, complete fewer years of school, and are likely to have lower earnings when they enter the labor market than children who grow up in higher income families.
> (*Economic Report of the President*, February 1998, p. 90)

Of course, low-income needs to be defined and the report does so using three measures of poverty: the conventional approach, half the poverty line, and twice the poverty line. Let us assume that the results are robust and supported by most similar studies, so that we have confidence that we are dealing with a real and important relation.

The next task, then, is to offer an explanation of the event. One common way to explain something, though not the only way, is in terms of its causes. The cause of an event is 'anything that contributes, or makes a difference, to the realisation of the event in one or more of its aspects. Causes of economic events, typically, are ensembles of things and relations - agents, intentions, beliefs and actions, endowments, social positions, rules, institutions, the constituents of the physical world, and so forth' (Runde, 1998, p.154). The *Economic Report of the President* asks a modest causal question: How is it that income has this constellation of impacts? It offers three plausible explanations: Parents can't afford to invest as much in the things that improve children's well being; the neighbourhoods the children reside in have more limited access to mainstream activities, like good schools; or perhaps, the report suggests with detachment, the finding is not really an effect of income, but something else which is related to income (like the value that parents place on education) so that raising the income level will not affect academic achievement.

The causal explanation in terms of social mechanisms is not pursued further. Instead the report shifts ground, and while assuming that income is important, proceeds to ask a 'why' question, namely, why have poverty rates changed between 1979 and 1996? Again, three causal explanations are offered: changes in family structure; changes in macro-economic and labour market conditions; and changes in transfer policy. The next step in analysing these multiple causes is to determine 'the full impact of each of these factors on poverty', noting cautiously that 'these estimates may also be sensitive to the order in which each income source is accounted for in the analysis'. The analysis that follows involves how a specific per cent change in the official poverty rate is attributable to a per cent change in each of the three independent variables.

The last step is to relate the 'scientific' analysis to conclusions about policy initiatives that the Administration is pursuing in order to create positive incentives to promote work and personal responsibility, assuming of course that income and children's well-being are linked.

From this concrete example of an official policy analysis we learn the following lessons: 1) the sources for developing casual hypotheses are a mixture of data, theory, belief, and political preferences; 2) the set of possible causes is always much larger than the specific analytic exercise; 3) the explanation tends to be inconclusive; 4) whatever evidence is brought to bear does not undermine the starting generalisation; and 5) inadequate income must somehow be a important cause of the failure of children to develop later in life. We will examine this case in more detail later in this paper. The example illustrates the subtle ways in which a soft analysis fails to displace the casual analysis when evidence must be brought to bear on the current policy debate.

This approach to poverty is based on a type of reasoning we term 'strong' causal reasoning, even though the actual study may only provide evidence of a weak causal relation. The analysis assumes that the particular symptoms of concern - economic deprivation, female-headed households, joblessness, crime-- can be dealt with by determining their particular causes and then developing policies that are directed at these factors. We term this type of reasoning 'strong' causal reasoning because any approach of this type will work only if the causal factors strongly affect the symptoms. In addition, typically it is necessary for the number of causal factors to be limited. Just as we want to attack the bacteria or virus that cause a disease, so with poverty we want to attack its 'root' causes.

Poverty policy in the U.S., even in the most recent decades, certainly has been driven by factors other than science. In fact, the newest round of welfare reform was passed over the objections of most of the social scientific community doing research on poverty (Weaver and Dickens, 1997). Science, however, has greatly influenced the process and the public understanding of what would constitute a policy solution to the problems of poverty. For example, the current welfare reform was critically influenced by the finding that poverty for many individuals was not a permanent state, but rather represented a spell of bad luck (Rein and Rainwater, 1977; Bane and Ellwood, 1994), often due to divorce, loss of job, sickness, and so on. The conclusion was that the

State should provide temporary short term relief to poor families as opposed to indefinite support.

The Failure of Causal Analysis

Causal analysis can fail in one of two ways. First, social science has been able to provide only what we would call 'weak' causal theories. In the vast majority of cases, the effects that are found are of modest size and only a small amount of the variation in the dependent variable is explained. As Jon Elster (1991) argues, it is doubtful that complete explanations will ever be forthcoming in most social science. Furthermore, empirical results can be quite sensitive to the particular model specification employed. The use of 'weak' theories as the basis for social policy implies that the policy's effectiveness is far from assured. Second, causal analysis in the social sciences fails because it is incomplete in that there are essentially normative questions that it can not answer. This can happen in two ways. First, there is the question of what problem is to be addressed, for example, is the concern the material standard of living of some individuals or is it that there are so many children being raised by single parents? Second, in cases where there are multiple factors involved in a problem, there is the question of on which factor societal or government policy should focus. For example, assume that youth violence is a function of both family breakdown and the absence of formal institutions in inner city neighbourhoods. The question is then, where should policy intervene?

Weak Theories

It is a common observation that quantitative empirical models in the social sciences have extremely weak predictive power. R-square, which measures the total variation in the dependent variable explained by a model, is almost never greater than 50 per cent. Most of the time it is less than 30 per cent, and often it is below 20 per cent. This holds true in all cross-sectional analyses. (This is not the case in time series analysis, which we discuss below.) In most cases, social science is able to explain only a small portion of the outcome of interest. Although the empirical weakness of social science models is well recognised, the implications of this weakness for public policy are often not fully appreciated. Perhaps the strongest and best known analysis is Christopher Jencks's (1972) book *Inequality*. Jencks addresses the assumption popular on the left in the 1960s and early 1970s (and still fashionable in some circles today) that by equalising educational opportunity and attainment, the problems of economic inequality in the U.S. can be largely resolved. Jencks shows that most of the variance in economic outcomes is unexplained by education as well as other observed variables. Jencks finds, as have many others, that education affects earnings and income only at a general level. For example, Ashenfelter and Rouse (1996), in reviewing the decades of research that have been carried out on this topic, state that estimates of the returns to schooling in the literature typically range between four per cent and ten per cent per year of schooling. Despite this substantial effect of education on earnings, Jencks shows that most of the variance in economic outcomes is unexplained by education as well as other observed variables. As a result, equalising educational attainment will have only modest effects in reducing economic inequality.

The problems of social science, however, go beyond weak predictions. Not only are models typically not very powerful predictors, but the results they do produce can be quite sensitive to how the models are specified. This is often the case with time series in which R-squares may be high, but they are also high on the same set of data for a wide variety of different models. This makes it difficult, if not impossible, to determine the importance of different causal factors.

As an example of the problem of model sensitivity, consider the fact that according to standard indicators, child poverty has risen considerably over the past several decades. Jencks and Mayer (1996) provide basic trends and important counter-arguments. In a recent and massive edited volume, Duncan *et al.* (1998) carry out a set of parallel cross-sectional analyses that examine the effect of poverty on a wide variety of outcomes for children. They brought together 12 studies, each of which tried to replicate the same causal model. Each of the studies used similar variables on family income, mother's education, and family structure in order to predict children's performance as adults in two broad areas: school performance and latter work behaviour on the one hand, and health and behavioural problems on the other. Behavioural problems were based on an index that measured whether children had problems in school with emotional well-being, and whether they had children out of wedlock. In brief, the findings show that family income during the early childhood experience has a strong positive impact on school performance. 'In contrast, virtually none of the behaviour, mental health, or physical health measures ... were predicted strongly by family income' (Duncan and Brooks-Gunn, 1997, p.4). This positive effect is non-linear. The probability is that a child will spend on average one-sixth of the year more in school for the population as a whole, but when the bottom end of the income distribution is considered, it increases school attendance by eight-tenths of a year. The critical question is whether these results are spurious and obscure an understanding of the true causal factors. There is the question of possible simultaneity and the direction of causality and omitted variables. An example of simultaneity is that if a young child is developing in a mature way the mother feels that she can enter the labour market; this then has an income effect on the child's well-being. Separating the simultaneity requires variables that affect one outcome but not the other: for example, the volume of crime and the number of police are simultaneous events; in order to study the relationship it is necessary to find a variable that affects one outcome but not the other. The number of policemen often increases during electoral years, but this is independent of the amount of crime that is committed. Thus, electoral voting is a way to resolve the problem of simultaneity. Duncan *et al.* (1998) did not find simultaneity to be a major problem in understanding the consequences of growing up poor.

The second technical problem in arriving at a causal analysis is that of the omitted variable: the true cause of a child's later performance in school or in the labour market is not the family's income but some omitted variable that was not taken into account in the regression analysis. It is hard to get agreement on the importance of the final result since a critic can always challenge the estimate by arguing that a variable has been omitted from the analysis. As a result, causal analysis is always in doubt. In a multi-causal world where family income is one cause rather than **the** cause of later performance of children, omitted variables are particularly troublesome.

In the conclusion of his book Duncan is forced (despite his political inclinations) to acknowledge that even the relatively small effects he and his colleagues have identified may overstate the effect of poverty on children's well-being. He also discusses Susan Mayer's book *What Money Can't Buy* (then forthcoming, published 1997) that argues that income has almost no effect on child well-being. Specifically, Mayer carefully analyses the problem of omitted variable bias in work of the type done by Duncan and others. She finds that when one controls for future income, the effect of current income is reduced substantially. She argues that since it is difficult for future income to affect the current well-being of children, future income is really a proxy for unmeasured characteristics of a child's family that have not been controlled for. She also examines the effects of income other than earnings (for example, government benefits), and finds the effect on a variety of outcomes to be quite small. She suggests this is evidence that the estimated effect of current earnings in part reflects the effect of unmeasured variables. If this is correct, then the effect of poverty on child well-being may well be quite minimal.

Since the publication of the book, Mayer (1997) developed a path diagram (see Appendix A to this chapter) which graphically shows the relative strengths of the mechanisms through which parental income influences children's outcomes. The final outcome is the product of the two coefficients. In none of the causal mechanisms are there two strong effects associated with parental income and family. For example, parental income has a strong effect on family living conditions but this has a weak effect on children's outcomes, so the resulting effect of income through family living conditions on the child's outcome is small. A strong effect multiplied by a weak effect is small. Similarly, parental income has a moderate effect on a parent's psychological well-being which has a moderate effect on children's outcomes; a moderate effect multiplied by a moderate effect is also small. This illustrates the problem of indirect intervention when causal effects are anything but large. Because of the multiplicative nature of effects, the resulting effect of an indirect intervention on the final outcome is almost always small.

Mayer's results are not unusual. In fact, social science models almost always have weak explanatory power and that results are often sensitive to the model specification used. What is problematic is that in arguing for particular policies we often argue as if social science's findings imply that there are strong determinative relations between particular causes and outcomes. Certainly, education affects earnings, but this does not mean that equalising education will have much effect on earnings inequality. Similarly, economic poverty certainly affects child development, but this does not mean that reducing economic poverty will substantially improve child development. Weak causal links do not lead to strong policy effects.

Incompleteness

Poverty is not one problem, but many. To some people it is an issue of economic inequality; to others it is a question of the lack of a minimally adequate standard of living for those at the bottom of the social ladder. Some consider poverty a problem of crime and deviance, and for still others it is a question of who will take care of those who cannot care for themselves. When we have strong explanatory theories of behaviour, then the findings of research may provide a reliable guide as to which policy question to focus on. Take, for example, the link between economic poverty and crime.

The claim that economic poverty 'causes' crime is ambiguous. Leaving aside the obvious ambiguity that there are many types of crime, the causal proposition linking poverty to all crime is too general. It can mean that economic poverty is one of several causes of crime, or it can be interpreted as meaning that poverty is **the** cause of crime. If economic poverty is the cause of crime then even if our primary concern is with crime, it is economic poverty that policy should address since it is the causal factor. There are two reasons for this: first, since economic poverty is the cause of crime, attacking poverty should effectively reduce crime. Second, if economic poverty is the cause of crime and an individual is poor through no fault of their own, then we are compelled to address poverty on moral grounds. It makes no sense to hold an individual responsible for their behaviour, if they behave that way due to factors outside of their control.

Of course, social science is almost never able to show that one factor in isolation from all other factors is the cause of a phenomenon. In fact, even claims about a factor being one of several possible causes typically need to be tentative. There are at least two issues here: first, the relationships between different dimensions of poverty are often quite weak. For example, Tittle, Villemez and Smith (1978) summarise the results of a host of studies on the relationship between social class and crime/delinquency, and suggest that the best estimate of the association between social class and crime/delinquency (as measured by the ordinal measure of association gamma) is .09. (Also see Tittle and Meier, 1990.) Second, there is always the persistent question of whether association represents causation. Are poverty and crime possibly associated because they are mutually dependent on some third factor? Even if this is not the case, there is the question of the direction of causality. Is it poverty that produces crime, or is it crime and deviance more generally that leads to poverty? These questions are difficult to answer with any degree of certainty.

There are at least two normative issues here. If there are multiple symptoms of poverty that are only weakly inter-linked, then there is the question of where policy should focus. First, if we are unable to argue that one factor is causally prior to others and it has substantial effects, then causal analysis provides little or no guidance as to where intervention should occur. We must decide on normative grounds (generally conceived and including cost-benefit analysis) where intervention should occur.

Second, even if there is agreement about which symptom should be of concern, if a symptom has multiple causes (which it almost always does), there is always the question of which cause on which to focus policy intervention. Consider the problem of youth violence. Youth violence might be thought of as a function of: (1) the breakdown of family structures; (2) the accessibility of guns; (3) the lack of aggressive policing; (4) the drug trade; or (5) the absence of formal institutions in the inner city. There is the potential for policy intervention in each of these domains. Such intervention might ameliorate the problem of youth violence, though it would be highly unlikely that intervention in any single area would be totally effective.

Analogous to the multi-symptom situation, in the multi-causal situation we must decide where to intervene. Two sets of criteria come into play. First, there is the question of where policy can possibly make a change. James Q. Wilson's, elaborated the argument about policy analysis versus causal analysis:

> Policy analysis, as opposed to causal analysis ... asks not what is the 'cause' of a problem, but what is the condition one wants to bring into being, what measure do we have that will tell us when that condition exists, and what policy tools does a government (in our case, a democratic and liberal government) possess that might, when applied, produce at reasonable cost a desired alteration in the present condition or progress towards the desired condition. ... A policy analyst would ask what feasible changes in which of these instruments would, at what cost (monetary and non monetary), produce how much of a change in the rate of a given crime. ... A commitment to causal analysis, especially one that regards social processes as crucial, will rarely lead to discovering the grounds for policy choices, and such grounds as are discovered (for example, taking children away from their parents) will raise grave ethical and political issues.
> (Wilson, 1985, pp. 49-50)

Wilson makes the obvious, but often neglected, point that factors that are causally critical are not necessarily factors that can be easily changed. The effects of gender and age on crime are examples. In the end these are questions of cost effectiveness. It may be difficult to nearly impossible to affect family structures, but relatively inexpensive to substantially reduce the accessibility of guns. Second, however, there are normative questions. Although reducing the accessibility of guns may be cost effective, some actors, like the National Rifle Association, may take the position that as a society we have a legal and normative commitment to having guns easily accessible. Conversely, although changing family structures may be difficult, there are groups such as the religious right that strongly believe children should be brought up in two-parent households. Feminist groups or others on the left may well take the opposing position that the choices individuals make about family structure are none of the government's business.

What we see here is that in situations where there are multiple symptoms and multiple causes, the type of causal analysis that social science has been able to achieve is unlikely to provide definitive answers as to where policy intervention would have a substantial effect on reducing poverty. The weak and fragile links that social science typically finds imply that efforts to build policies on the identification of specific causes are likely to fail. Second, decisions about where policy should intervene involve choices with cost-benefit and normative considerations. These are outside the purview of causal analysis.

The Dangers of 'Strong' Causal Reasoning

Social science theories are weak and incomplete. So what? These are hardly new observations. Many would argue that although social scientific knowledge is imperfect, it is the best basis we have for developing policy. Despite its weaknesses, social science should be the principal tool for the development of sound policy.

Although we concur with this position, we think that there are many dangers in its unthinking and unconditional acceptance. Consider the following analogy: it is quite a different matter to start on a cross-country trip in a new car that has been thoroughly road tested and inspected by a mechanic than it is to start off in a twenty-year-old 'clunker' that has a history of breaking down with several hundred thousand miles on the odometer. Although the 'clunker' (social science) may be the best alternative available, we need to prepare for its failure and we certainly want to take bus money. To assume that our 'clunker' is in great shape is only to court disaster. Our argument is that social science is a 'clunker' - flawed, but still hopefully useful transportation.

There is an additional issue. A car, by itself, is also not sufficient for a cross-country trip. One will need gasoline, food, maps, and money. Similarly, in even the best of circumstances it is unlikely that social science by itself is sufficient for policy making. Thus our argument is first that social science is a critical, but not fully dependable vehicle for policy making, and second, that normative and moral factors that fall beyond science also need to be considered. What are the dangers to the policy process of an overly confident adoption of a scientific approach based on 'strong' causal analysis? We identify six.

Overselling

If we believe deeply in our causal models, then we are likely to construct social policy based on them and make strong assertions about their future effectiveness. There can be perhaps no better examples of 'overselling' than those which occurred during the War on Poverty in the 1960s when social science was at its zenith in its claims about what problems it could understand and solve. As we saw above, President Johnson argued that eliminating economic poverty would go a long way to ameliorating a host of other problems, and there is no reason not to assume that he believed what he said. Strategically, he tried to convince Congress that the programme was important to support, hence the overselling. He also wanted to find not so much what would work, which required a long time horizon, but what was viable in the local political scene, and these were the programmes that he promoted in the next round of national legislation. Charles Murray (1995) has argued in a recent Op-Ed in the *New York Times* that the War on Poverty was a total failure, as evidenced by the fact that since the 1960s, welfare, out-of-wedlock births, and crime rates have all risen dramatically.

There are also more current examples of overselling. Recently, Donna Shalelah, Secretary of the U.S. Department of Health and Human Services, offered the following account of the purpose of new welfare reform legislation to set time limits on eligibility for benefits: 'The whole purpose of this is to eliminate poverty in the United States, not just to get people off of welfare' (*New York Times*, 1997, p.A-16).

Of course, the new welfare reform effort to mandate work cannot eliminate poverty or the problematic behaviours associated with it, but overselling led the Secretary to promise more than the programme is able to deliver. Oddly, her statement seems to echo Charles Murray's (1984) claim that welfare was its own cause, and that eliminating welfare by forcing people to work would actually reduce poverty rather than cause hardship.

Fragile Rationales

'Strong' causal analysis holds the promise of providing an objective rationale for a policy. If the causal analysis is believed, then we can avoid confronting other arguments for a specific policy; but what happens to our rationale when we discover the analysis is wrong and/or that the causal relations are quite weak?

This is precisely the situation we are in today with respect to school desegregation. The lower courts paid special attention to such arguments, but it was the modest reference to social science and desegregation in the famous *Brown v. Board of Education*, that made it a landmark decision for social science. Based on scientific evidence, the Regents in Yonkers concluded in 1960 'that segregated schools "damage the personality of minority group children" and "decrease their motivation and thus impair their ability to learn". Such schools should therefore be eliminated in the name of good education practice' (Danielson and Hochschild, 1996, p.7). Social scientists had argued strongly that black children were being given an inferior education by being kept in segregated schools, and that they would learn considerably more in integrated schools. This argument had two implications. First, it became the principal rationale for school desegregation; the more general question as to whether integration was as an important value in and of itself was not pursued. Second, because it was blacks who were going to benefit from integration, many cities adopted policies that resulted in black children bearing most of the direct costs of desegregation - in most cases it was blacks, not whites, who were bused in order to integrate schools.

We are facing a situation today in which the effects of integration promised by social science have not materialised. Both research and the experience of black parents suggest that the benefits have been minor and the community opposition strong. As a result, support for desegregation is now disappearing even among black parents. In Evanston, Illinois, one of America's most liberal communities and the first city in the country to voluntarily desegregate, there is a now a coalition of black and conservative white parents arguing for the return of neighbourhood schools.

In part, the problem is similar to the War on Poverty and the new Welfare Reform - a problem of overselling. The benefits of desegregation have not been as substantial as social scientists argued. Furthermore, because of the perceived objectivity of the causal reasoning, the strong predictions made by social scientists, and the consequences of this for policy design, other arguments for integration were crowded out. Most importantly, after we change the rationale and terms of the justifications for the intervention we propose, it is difficult, if not impossible, to successfully advocate a position which justifies integration as an important societal value in and of itself and not merely a means to promote the education of children.

Weakness of Indirect Intervention

We saw above that if effects are anything but strong, then indirect interventions are likely to have only small effects. For example, if we believe that growing up in a single-parent household adversely affects child development, then we may want to argue for policies that increase the attractiveness of marriage. This argument, however, only makes sense if the effects are large enough to justify the cost. With indirect interventions the effects need to be especially large since the policy must first substantially effect marriage rates, which in turn must substantially effect child development, if the policy can hope to have any effect on child development. It may well prove more efficient to develop policies that intervene directly to promote child development.

Over-generalisation

The last two decades have seen considerable discussion of poverty as a problem of the urban underclass. The seminal book in this debate has certainly been William Julius Wilson's *The Truly Disadvantaged* (1996). There has been much argument about the usefulness of the underclass concept (Jencks, 1992; Katz, 1986) and its potential for stigmatising the poor. A further criticism is that the use of the term underclass leads us to think about the poor as a single homogenous group. This is a problem more generally with 'strong' causal thinking. If individuals are in some particular situation or behave in some way because of some specific factor, then if the causal effect is strong, it should hold true for most individuals where this factor is present. Let us return to the question of economic poverty and crime. If economic poverty is the cause of crime, or even if it has an especially strong effect on criminality, then most (if not all) poor individuals should be criminals. Of course, as we have noted above, this is not the case. Without even getting into the difficult questions of causality, we noted that the correlation between economic poverty and crime is quite weak. Notice, however, that if we accept the premise that economic poverty is the cause of crime, this has a potentially stigmatising effect on the poor (Anderson, 1994). More generally, 'strong' causal thinking inclines us to think of the poor as a homogenous group facing a common set of issues and thus exhibiting a common set of behaviours. As is well known (Blank, 1997), the poor are anything but a homogenous group. Certainly, the vast majority of poor individuals are not criminals.

Elimination of Personal Responsibility

One of the virtues of 'strong' causal reasoning is that it identifies who is responsible. This, however, is only a virtue when the reasoning is correct and convincing. A whole array of poverty researchers have argued that poverty and the behavior of the poor needs to be understood as being solely determined by their environment and structural factors. A vivid example of this strain of thinking, related to the Moynihan Report (1965), was the phrase made famous by William Ryan's (1971) book, that we must avoid 'blaming the victim'.

As Orlando Patterson has forcefully argued in his new book (1997), the theory that individual behaviour is fully determined by structural factors eliminates the possibility of individual will and responsibility. The poor are no longer fully human individuals capable of making choices for which they are held responsible. As Patterson shows, this involves us in the deep and complicated argument that philosophers have been engaged in for centuries: the question of free will versus determinism. Patterson argues, as have many others (for example, see March, 1991; J.Q. Wilson, 1985), that the assumption of complete determinism is unworkable in a society in which social order is based on holding individuals, poor or otherwise, accountable for their actions. More specifically, he explains the logical contradiction of an over-deterministic view. 'The cry of the victim, then, is doubly futile: not only does it demean the victim by attributing all agency to the victimiser, but in assuming and legitimising a wholly determinist social and moral universe, it explains away the injustice of the victimiser.' After all, his hatred is also conditioned by the racist culture in which he was raised (Patterson, 1997, p.97). Strong causal reasoning forces out discussion of individual moral responsibility, thus leading to an ethical stalemate (J.Q. Wilson, 1985).

Confounding of Issues

As we argued above, if economic deprivation is the cause of crime, then we are morally compelled to alleviate economic deprivation of the criminal. Punishing him for his behaviour is morally unacceptable. 'Strong' causal reasoning can imply narrow policy interventions both for empirical and moral reasons. In his recent book, *Whose Welfare* (1996), Steve Teles argues that in the last couple of decades American politics has become polarised around the extreme positions of ideological elites. Specifically, he sees three different positions competing with each other: an elite concerned with economic equity, a group concerned with the need for hierarchy in order to achieve social control, and libertarians who are concerned with individual freedom. Each group believes in a different form of 'strong' causal reasoning: that the poor are poor due to structural and environmental constraints; that it is necessary to constrain the poor from engaging in self-destructive behaviour; that the poor are poor because of the choices they have made as individuals. Teles argues that the 'strong' causal positions of these different ideological elites have led to a policy gridlock where each group has argued for policies that are in conflict with the principles of the others. Thus the commitment to 'strong' causal reasoning has led each group to support one set of policies and to strongly oppose others.

Consider the case of equality. Proponents of this value position need to add a referent: equality of what? And the answer implies not only an elaboration of the value, but a specification of the instruments for its realisation. Egalitarians can argue for equal status, for equal opportunity, for equal resources and outcomes, or equality in the distribution of specific goods. In practice, there is no way of calibrating, for example, the dimension of equal resources except 'by reference to the welfare effects produced by alternative portfolios of resources holdings', and this must imply a causal theory for how the value can be realised in practice (Goodin *et al.*, 1998, p.12).

What is wrong here is the commitment to 'strong' causal thinking. Social science has shown that different dimensions of poverty are, at best, weakly linked. Attempting to deal with crime and to improve child development by reducing economic deprivation makes little sense if poverty and crime are not causally connected and money does not matter for child development. Such an effort is likely to be expensive and ineffective. Given the weak linkages that social science has found, it is much more sensible to think of policies in a de-coupled fashion. If one's goal is to ameliorate the economic deprivation of the poor, then develop programmes directly aimed at this. If one's goal is to reduce crime, then develop programmes directly aimed at crime. If one's goal is to improve child development, then create programmes directly aimed at improving child development. If we accept for the moment that the different dimensions of poverty are weakly interconnected, then there is much less reason for ideological gridlock over what policy should be given priority. Poverty is not a problem, but is a set of problems that at best are loosely interrelated. As such, we need a variety of policies to deal with poverty.

Conclusions: Making Policies with Weak Theories

We started this paper by examining how Rowntree's analysis of poverty led to a typology of different poverty types based on his analysis of the different causes of poverty. In one instance, he distinguished between primary and secondary poverty. Since only a small portion of the population suffered from primary poverty - a lack of resources - his causal analysis undermined his moral claim that poverty was a problem of the gravest concern. In the other instance, however, he showed that poverty varied over the life cycle as a function of family dynamics and thus potentially affected a large portion of the population at some point during their lifetimes. Perhaps poverty was a problem of the gravest concern. In both cases causal claims underpinned different moral claims about what society ought to do about poverty.

Does it make a difference to realise that social policy needs to be based on 'weak' as opposed to 'strong' causal theories? 'We believe that it does. At the obvious level, if the theories that we base policy on are wrong or misconstrued in terms of their empirical strength, it is likely that our policies will be ineffective. We are in danger of overselling our policies, basing them on potentially fragile rationales, and over-generalising our results. Besides these general points, however, we think that there are two specific lessons to be learned that are of critical importance.

Direct Intervention and Amelioration

We discussed above Murray's 1995 op-ed piece that described the War on Poverty as a total failure. In an op-ed written just prior to Murray (1995), Mayer and Jencks (1995) declared that the War on Poverty was a considerable success in that its programmes did much to ameliorate the social and economic hardships suffered by the poor. They argue that this must have been the goal of the programme, since almost all of the money spent on fighting poverty since 1964 was of this kind. The money spent on education, training, and so on was tiny by comparison. Thus the programme's intention is inferred from it what it actually did. They further point out that these programmes were not designed to deal with the types of dysfunctional behaviors among the that poor Murray is concerned with: single-parent households, crime, joblessness, and so on. The more modest goal of relieving hardship is a manageable goal that a compassionate society can realise.

The alternative evaluations of the War on Poverty in these two op-ed articles reflect different understandings of what its goals were. Murray wants to evaluate the War on Poverty in terms of its stated goals, in the inflated language of President Johnson cited earlier (Murray, 1995, p.26). In the conservative view, the underlying problem is the dynamic of welfare dependency created because welfare benefits were simply given away to relieve hardship, without an expectation of reciprocal obligations. It was an entitlement, a right unaccompanied by an expectation of a behavioural change on the part of the welfare client. Mead (1997) has argued that we must expect clients to work because work engenders self-discipline and provides a routine which organises and structures time. It also engenders cooperation and demands consistent behaviour responses from a set of demands imposed by the authority of the supervisor. Taken together, these beneficial effects of work has an important impact on an individual's personal character. This analysis from the conservative side is strikingly similar to the argument developed by William Julius Wilson on the liberal side about the deleterious effect of jobless ghettos. Where they differ is in the prescription they recommend. Murray and Mead reject job creation as a social obligation and insist on the supervision of the poor as a way to create personal responsibility. By contrast, Mayer and Jencks want to evaluate outcomes with respect to the more modest objectives that were built into the limited aims of specific programme designs, for example, a food programme designed to reduce hunger (Mayer and Jencks, 1995).

What does this teach us? What is to be learned here, besides the perils of overselling, is that in a world of weak causal relations policy should have two objectives. First, policy should be designed to directly intervene. If you want the poor to have better medical care, provide them with better access. If you want to improve their financial status, directly transfer funds to them. Indirect interventions are unlikely to have effects. One way to understand the debate between Murray and Mayer/Jencks is that the War on Poverty's programmes had the direct effects they were designed to have, but not the indirect effects that wishfully had been promised by Johnson and others. Second, at least at this time, poverty policy can be much more effective at ameliorating the conditions of poverty than in eliminating its underlying causes. For now, we can achieve much more by dealing with the symptoms.

Societal Values

The second consequence of having 'weak' causal theories is the recognition that as a society we need to develop consensus on a set of values for dealing with the poor. This consensus must be based on moral arguments about justice and fairness combined with social science knowledge. Despite the substantial investment in research about poverty in the United States it has been difficult to reach political agreement about a coherent approach to the issues of welfare and poverty. Kenneth Burke puts the argument with clarity and force: 'We should not expect a dualism of motives to be automatically dissolved, as with those apologists of science who believe that in a scientific world ethics become unnecessary' (Burke, 1969, p.38). On the contrary, the stronger the influence of social science the greater the need for moral and ethical principles to act as a guide.

The difficult question that this issue poses is: What is the relationship between social science and morality? We can't develop the argument in detail here, but it raises an important question about the appropriate relationship between social science, and ethics and morality. Many will object that in a society as ideologically diverse as ours, connecting morality and science is impossible. However, in actuality progress has been made in the last decade. In *Poor Support* (1988), David Ellwood argued strongly that individuals and families who 'play by the rules' should not be poor. Families in which at least one adult worked full time throughout the year should have an income above the poverty line. This argument has been the basis for the earned income tax credit (EITC), which President Clinton was able to substantially expand during his first term. The EITC has received greater bipartisan support than has any other poverty programme. This example suggests that moral evaluation could be an integrated part of the test for truth and not simply a causal add-on (Burke, 1941, p.183). It is true that moral judgements are not subject to tests of their truth value, but involve giving reasons for why we should want to pay attention to the welfare of our fellow citizens; 'But it would nevertheless be wrong to draw an overly sharp distinction between the two sets of concerns. Moral norms matter, socially and politically (and hence ultimately morally as well), only insofar as people can actually be motivated to act upon them' (Goodin, 1998, p.1). And, we would add, this commitment to act must also depend on being convinced that the consequences of a particular moral view have the desired outcomes. There is little sense in affirming a moral position that has no implications for any course of action to be followed and that cannot be realised in practice. Hence a good policy must be both morally acceptable and effective.

It appears that a new consensus seems to have been forged on the issue that work should come first, being mandated with time limits for welfare mothers with young children. However, the political and moral issues have not gone away but have been reconfigured around a triad of work, services and poverty. As Larry Lynn has astutely pointed out, the pragmatists have tried to combine work and services, while the conservatives say 'we will take the time limits but skip the services' (Lynn, 1998, p.19). Turning to the issue of poverty, the rationale on which Ellwood's position is based is that work and welfare go together, since the low wages require an income package supplemented by universal tax credits and other programmes that make work a condition of eligibility. In the past, the welfare need was the basis for entitlement and work incentive programmes were added to welfare. On these questions we have to come to a value consensus separate from social science, but not wholly independent of it.

For all of its problems, the recent welfare reform has been based on principles, some of which have been accepted by many members of both parties and much of the American public, that the poor deserve to be helped but that there is a reciprocal responsibility that the poor contribute and help themselves also. Thus the core of the new legislation involves the requirement that individuals who have the capability of working work in the private sector, or if they cannot find a job there, in community service. Where the new welfare legislation failed was in not incorporating a requirement that the government provide jobs to the poor if it was going to require them to work, a position that the American public also supports (Teles, 1996). At the present, with an unemployment rate of less than five per cent, this is not much of a problem. Only time will tell whether the government, federal or state, will meet their reciprocal moral obligations to provide jobs when unemployment is much higher.

Acknowledgments

A number of people have generously commented on an early version of this paper. We particularly want to thank Christopher Jencks, whose detailed comments were especially challenging. In addition, Libby Schweber, Jeff Page, Langly Keyes, Jonathan Bradshaw, Steve Teles and Jonathan Imber made useful criticisms. Of course, we are responsible for any errors that remain.

References

Anderson, E. (1994), 'Code of the Streets', *Atlantic Monthly*, vol. 273, May, pp. 90-4.

Ashenfelter, O. and Rouse, C. (1996), 'Schooling, Intelligence, and Income in America: Crack "The Bell Curve"', unpublished, Princeton University.

Bane, M-J. and Ellwood, D. (1994), Welfare Realities, Harvard University Press, Cambridge.

Blank, R. (1997), *It Takes a Nation: A New Agenda for Fighting Poverty*, Princeton University Press, Princeton N.J.

Booth, C. (1893) *Life and Labour of the people in London*, London.

Burke, K. (1941), *The Philosophy of Literary Form*, Louisiana State University Press, Louisiana.

Burke, K. (1969), *A Grammar of Motives*, University of California Press, Berkeley.

Burawoy, M. (1998), 'The Extended Case Method', *Sociological Theory*, vol. 16, no. 1, March.

Danielson, M. and Hochschild, J. (1996), 'Can We Desegregate Public Schools and Subsidised Housing? Lessons from the Sorry History of Yonkers, N.Y.', Paper prepared for a conference on 'Changing Urban Education', University of Maryland, College Park, November 22-23.

Duncan, G. J. and Brooks-Gunn, J. (eds) (1997), *The Consequences of Growing up Poor*, Russell Sage Publications, New York.

Duncan, G.J., Wei-Jun J.Yeung and Brooks-Gunn J. (1998), 'How Much Does Childhood Poverty Affect the Life Chances of Children', *American Sociological Review*.

Economic Report of the President, Transmitted to the Congress 1998, United States Government Printing Office, Washington, D.C.

Economic Report of the President (1964), U.S. Government Printing Office, Washington, D.C.

Elster, J. (1991), 'Arguing and Bargaining in Two Constituent Assemblies', The Storrs Lectures, Yale Law School.

Ellwood, D.T. (1988), *Poor Support: Poverty in the American Family*, Basic Books, New York.

Goodin, R.E. *et al.* (1998), *The Real Worlds of Welfare Capitalism*.

Goodin *et al.* (1998), *Social Welfare and Individual Responsibility*, Cambridge University Press.

Gordon, D. and Pantazis, C. (1997), *Breadline Britain in the 1990s*, Ashgate, Aldershot, Hants.

Jencks, C. (1992), *Rethinking Social Policy: Race, Poverty, and the Underclass*, Harvard University Press, Cambridge.

Jencks, C. (1972), *Inequality: A Reassessment of the Effects of Family and Schooling in America*, Basic Books, New York.

Kaim-Caudle, P. (1998), 'Misleading Data - Comments on the First and Third Social Surveys of York', Rowntree Poverty Conference, University of York, 1998.

Katz, M. (1986), *In the Shadow of the Poorhouse*, Basic Books, New York.

Lynn, L.E. (1998), 'The View from the Cellar: Reflection on the Incrementalist House of Anti-poverty', *Poverty Research News*, Joint Center of Poverty Research, Northwestern University, University of Chicago.

March, J. (1991), 'Social Science and the Myth of Rationality', unpublished.

Mayer, S.E. (1997), *What Money Can't Buy: Family Income and Children's Life Chances*,

Harvard University Press, Cambridge.

Mayer, S. and Jencks, C. (1995), 'War on Poverty. No Apologies, Please', Op-Ed, *The New York Times*, November 14.

Mayer, S. and Jencks, C. (1996), 'Do Official Poverty Rates Provide Useful Information About Trends in Children's Economic Welfare?', Discussion Paper, Institute for Policy Research, Northwestern University, May 30.

McClements, L.D. (1978), *The Economics of Social Security*, Heinemann, London.

Mead, L. (ed) (1997), *The New Paternalism: Supervisory Approaches to Poverty*, Brookings Institution, Washington D.C.

Moynihan, D.P. (1965), 'Employment, Income and the Ordeal of the Negro Family', in T. Parsons and K.B. Clark (eds), *The Negro Family*, Beacon Press, Boston.

Murray, C. (1984), *Losing Ground*, Basic Books, New York.

Murray, C. (1995), 'Welfare Hysteria', Op-Ed. *The New York Times*, November 14, *New York Times* (1977).

Patterson, O. (1997), *The Ordeal of Integration: Progress and Resentment in America's "Racial" Crises*, Civitas Counterpoint, Washington, D.C.

Rein, M. and Rainwater, L. (1977), 'Patterns of Welfare Use', Social Service Review, December.

Rothman, D.J. (1971), *The Discovery of the Asylum: Social Order and Disorder in the New Republic*, Little Brown, Boston.

Rowntree, B.S. (1901), *A Study of Town Life*, Macmillan, London.

Runde, J. (1998), 'Assessing Causal Economic Explanations', in *Oxford Economic Papers*, vol. 50, no 2, April, pp. 151-72.

Ragin, C.C. (forthcoming), *Fuzzy-Set Social Science*, University of Chicago Press, Chicago.

Ryan, W. (1971), *Blaming the Victim*, Random House, New York.

Teles, S. (1996), *Whose Welfare? AFCD and Elite Politics*, University of Kansas Press, Lawrence, Kansas.

Tittle, C.R., Villemez, W.J. and Smith, D.A. (1978), 'The Myth of Social Class and Criminality: Empirical Assessment of the Empirical Evidence', *American Sociological Review*, vol. 43, October, pp.643-56.

Tittle, C.R. and Meier, R.F. (1990), 'Specifying the SES/Delinquency Relationship', Criminology, vol. 28, no. 2, pp. 271-99.

Weaver, K.R. and Dickens, W.T. (1997), *Looking Before We Leap: Social Science and Welfare Reform*, Brookings Occasional Paper, The Brookings Institution, Washington, D.C.

Weaver, K. R. (1997), *Caught in a Trap?: Wage Mobility in Great Britain 1975-94*, LSE Centre for Economic Performance.

Weber, M. (1994), *Political Writings*, Cambridge University Press.

Wilson, J.Q. (1985), *Thinking About Crime*, 2nd edition, Vintage Press, New York.

Wilson, W.J. (1996), *The Truly Disadvantaged: The Inner City, the Underclass and Public Policy*, University of Chicago Press, Chicago.

APPENDIX A

STRENGTH OF THE MECHANISMS THROUGH WHICH INCOME WORKS

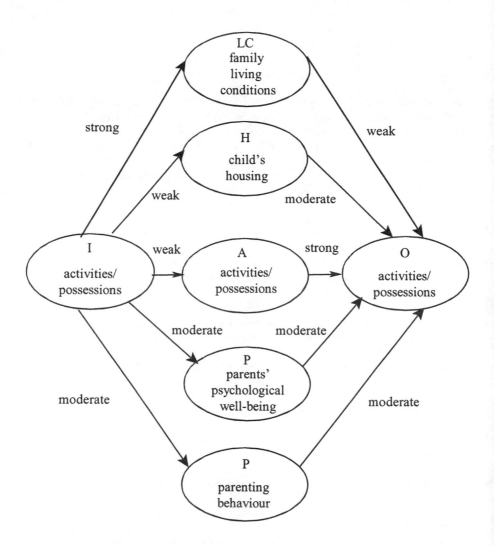

Source: Susan Mayer. Unpublished diagram presented at a lecture at Harvard University,
           7 February 1988

4 Local Poverty Profiles and Local Anti-Poverty Work

PETER ALCOCK and GARY CRAIG

Local Poverty: Research, Poverty and Action

The seminal work of Seebohm Rowntree on poverty in the City of York in the 1890s has been taken as establishing an important benchmark for research on the scale of the problem of poverty in Britain, and as providing the empirical basis on which to construct policies to combat poverty it. Rowntree expected his research to provoke a national debate and hoped that it would provide the kind of evidence that would inform national action. In both cases his expectations were largely, if not immediately, realised. Other researchers have followed Rowntree's lead, and he himself repeated his survey in York on two later occasions. Rowntree's findings were later directly taken up by Beveridge in constructing the benefit levels for his report on social insurance in 1942, a report which was to determine the development of British social security policy in the latter half of the twentieth century.

It is as a national figure contributing to a national debate that Rowntree is therefore perhaps best remembered. However, his survey of poverty and living standards in the 1890s (and later) was in fact, of course, a local study of the extent and depth of poverty in his home town of York. Rowntree chose to study York both because it was his home town and because he thought that it might provide complementary evidence to Booth's earlier study of poverty in Metropolitan London. However, he was also concerned about the particular local features of poverty in York, and this concern with the local dimensions of poverty is one which has been taken up and reworked by both researchers and policy-makers since. This is particularly the case in the last decade or so of the twentieth century - a hundred years after Rowntree first began his local research.

Although Rowntree's research on poverty was important in influencing the national policy planning of Beveridge in the 1940s, in recent times the influence of research on the development of national anti-poverty policy has been much less marked. This is particularly so since the 'rediscovery of poverty' in the 1960s and the mushrooming of surveys and other studies which have revealed the shortcomings of the post-war social security scheme(s) in removing poverty from Britain. Although there have been many changes to the social security scheme, sometimes responding to evidence of inadequate benefit support, and which have resulted in shifts in the focus and structure of social security policy, there has been no major overhaul of national social security provision in order to combat poverty in the way that Beveridge had initially intended. In the last two decades in particular, there has been growing political support for the view that, in so far as poverty is a national problem in the country (itself a matter of political contention), it is not one to which national policy changes are an appropriate response.

Accompanying this shift away from a national policy response to continuing evidence of the poverty problem in Britain has been an increasing emphasis on locally-based policy intervention. Loosely underlying this is a belief that, where national policy development may have failed, local action - focusing attention and resources onto poor people in poor neighbourhoods - may perhaps succeed. This shift towards local action on poverty can be traced back to the 'positive discrimination' strategies of the 1960s. These were intended in part as a policy response to the 'rediscovery of poverty' and drew heavily upon similar policy initiatives being developed in the US. The US 'War on Poverty' relied upon targeting (limited) Federal resources onto community action programmes in urban neighbourhoods known to have high levels of deprivation (Higgins, 1978). In Britain similar targeting was implemented, for instance, in the Education Priority Areas (EPAs) and Community Development Projects (CDPs) (see Berthoud *et al.,* 1981; Alcock *et al.,* 1995).

Much has been written about the achievements, and the failures, of these targeted anti-poverty programmes (for example Loney, 1983), and central government support for both the EPAs and CDPs was relatively short-lived. However, as we shall discuss below, the focus on local poverty which underlay them has been continued in a range of other policy developments by both central and local government; and their ideas of targeting extra support onto failing institutions in deprived local areas can still be found in the health and education 'action zones' of the late 1990s and, potentially, the work of the new government's 'Social Exclusion Unit'.

Despite the withdrawal of central government support for some of the high profile local anti-poverty programmes of the 1960s and 1970s, a large part of the practical anti-poverty action which they initiated did remain in place; and the commitment to supporting such local action - targeted on deprived local areas - was increasingly taken up by local government. In the 1970s and 1980s a number of local authorities, notably the large urban metropolitan authorities with some of the highest levels of poverty, began to provide active support for anti-poverty initiatives within their local area, in particular, welfare rights work to encourage take-up of social security and other benefits.

In the 1980s the Association of Metropolitan Authorities (AMA) set up a small unit to provide support and advice for such anti-poverty work; and, in a review of activity within metropolitan authorities carried out by the unit (Balloch and Jones, 1990), at least twelve English authorities claimed to be developing, or delivering, a local anti-poverty strategy. In the 1990s this commitment to local anti-poverty action from a local authority base in England, Wales and Scotland has expanded dramatically. For a start it is no longer confined to urban metropolitan authorities, with rural county councils and small district councils also now developing anti-poverty work. This is reflected in the support provided for this work by the Local Government Anti-Poverty Unit (LGAPU), which is now supported by all local authorities in England and Wales and located in the Local Government Management Board. In a recent survey carried out by the authors with the LGAPU as part of ongoing research on local anti-poverty strategies, 161 authorities in England and Wales reported that they were engaged in local anti-poverty work (Pearson *et al.*, 1997). In the 1990s a campaigning organisation representing elected members committed to local authority anti-poverty work has also developed - the National Local Government Forum Against Poverty. More recently central government too has begun to take an interest in this work with the Department of Environment (DoE, now Department of Environment, Transport and the Regions, DETR) commissioning research from the authors into the policy and organisational links between local anti-poverty activity and government regeneration programmes (Alcock *et al.*, 1998).

At the end of the twentieth century therefore local government anti-poverty action has become an important and growing element of the broader policy response to poverty in Britain. This trend is also replicated in other European countries, and is supported too by the European Union. Local projects to combat disadvantage and promote activation of citizens can now be found in most major EU nations. The European Commission has supported three programmes of funding for locally-based anti-poverty action, the most recent ending in 1994, and continues to support the European Anti-Poverty Network, a forum for local projects engaged in anti-poverty activity.

To some extent the growth in the scale and scope of local anti-poverty action is a product of declining UK national commitment to combat poverty through significant social reform - in Britain this has certainly produced a frustration amongst many local councillors and officers which has fuelled their commitment to local action. However, it is also a product of the growing evidence of the extent of poverty in many local areas which has been revealed in recent research. Local anti-poverty action has created a demand for research to reveal the location and distribution of poverty which can then act as a basis for the targeting of resources. Research into local poverty has also been undertaken, however, in order to stimulate a commitment to action amongst local politicians. As with Rowntree's earlier research into local poverty, the relationship between research and policy development is one of both cause and effect.

The Geography of Poverty

The demand from local authorities for evidence on the extent and distribution of local poverty has produced a major stimulus to the revival of local studies of poverty in the 1990s, and we examine these local authority studies in more detail below. However, concern with the local distribution of poverty is not just a product of demands of local politicians for robust databases for policy planning. Recent independent research on poverty and inequality has also begun to focus more directly upon the spatial dimensions of the poverty problem.

Part of the stimulus for this new direction in research has been the entry of geographers into the field of poverty research. In the 1990s some social geographers have extended their analysis of socio-economic trends to look at the spatial distribution of disadvantage and exclusion; and they have been assisted and encouraged in this by the development of new information technologies such as geographical information systems packages (GIS). In 1995 the Child Poverty Action Group (CPAG) published a booklet on the social geography of poverty, exploring the hitherto under-developed analysis of the inequitable distribution of poverty within the UK (Philo 1995). It revealed, as we might expect, that not all areas are equally poor and that poor people are not evenly spread throughout the country, both regionally and locally; but it also discussed some of the more complex issues involved in the spatial analysis of poverty, for instance, the particular problems of identifying poverty within less densely populated rural areas, the problem of hidden poverty in affluent areas, and the need to pay attention to different indicators of need in different kinds of areas.

Spatial distribution and analysis has also begun to feature in recent major research programmes into poverty and inequality in Britain. For instance, in the extensive research programme under-pinning the Joseph Rowntree Foundation *Inquiry into Income and Wealth* in the early 1990s, (Barclay, 1995; Hills, 1995) some of the projects focused directly upon the geography of poverty - most notably Green (1994) which examined regional disparities in income and wealth and Noble *et al.* (1994) which compared the local distribution of poverty in Oldham and Oxford. The regional and local dimensions of poverty are therefore now much more likely to be regarded as an integral element of the research agenda.

The process has been accentuated also by the continuing concern of central government to establish means for measuring and mapping disadvantage as a basis for determining government financial allocations at regional and local government levels. Despite the withdrawal of central government from some local anti-poverty programmes in the 1970s there has been a continuing concern with support for local regeneration and with the need to map local needs and circumstances for the purposes of budget planning within urban policy, in particular within the DoE/DETR.

In 1981 the DoE developed the DoE81 index from the decennial census (which became known as the 'z score' because of the standardisation method employed to sum the indicators) to use as a guide to urban funding and to underpin urban policy development. In 1991 a new DoE91 index was developed from the new census, called the 'Index of Local Conditions' (ILC), which is now widely used by government and other agencies for funding distribution and policy planning. In the early 1980s another index, the 'Jarman Index' was developed, with input from health professionals, as a guide to the targeting of resources for primary health care.

These, and a number of other, means of measuring and mapping the distribution of poverty and deprivation all have their strengths and weaknesses and, as we discuss in more detail below, these different strengths and weaknesses can lead to problems of standardisation and comparability, particular where the different methodologies are then picked up and used by other researchers, for instance at local authority level. Lee *et al.* (1995) provide a useful summary of the comparative advantages of many of the major composite indices, including DoE91 and Jarman, concluding that, although each composite approach has deficiencies, it is possible to identify a 'best' index for differing local circumstances. They also provide examples of the ways in which various indicators can be used to identify poor areas in Great Britain. It is approaches such as this which underpin much of the research on the mapping ('profiling') of local poverty which has developed rapidly in local authorities in the last few years, often as a precursor to the development of local anti-poverty work, and which we discuss in more detail in the next section.

Local Poverty Profiles

The minimum qualifying definition which we use here for a local poverty profile is 'the systematic collection, combination and mapping of indicators of social and economic need, drawn from a range of local, regional and national sources, on a single local authority-wide basis.' This definition leaves open many issues, (some of which are discussed below), such as the number and type of indicators chosen, the level at which they are chosen and whether and how they are combined to form composite indicators of deprivation. The documents reviewed in this chapter are all referred to as 'poverty profiles' although their actual titles vary quite widely: the full list of profiles consulted is provided at the end of this chapter. Some profiles have been updated on one or more occasions and we have only consulted the latest version here. Similarly, several authorities have produced supplementary profiles for specific population groups or issues (for instance, Rotherham for ethnic minority communities; Derbyshire for older people; or Oldham for health) - again, only the main profile is drawn upon here.

Most of the profiles discussed here are concerned exclusively with the position of the individual authority itself. A number of profiles, however, make comparisons between the position of the authority discussed and other (for example neighbouring or 'average') authorities, often to demonstrate that the authority's position is less socially or economically 'healthy' than it may more generally have been perceived to be. There are many other uses to which local poverty profiling can be put. The study of Oldham and Oxford, referred to above but not reviewed here, contrasts the 'changing patterns of income and wealth' in two contrasting authorities, to explore the extent to which national economic trends resulted in differing degrees of social and economic polarisation within and between the two areas. Other studies have drawn together indicators of poverty covering a number of local authority areas for specific policy reasons: for example, South Glamorgan County Council (1996) reviewed indicators of poverty across all 22 new Welsh unitary authority areas to inform the debates about local government responses to local government reorganisation, and specifically the distribution of government funding support; several organisations in the West Midlands (1997) contributed to a joint document on deprivation in the region, with a view, *inter alia*, to promoting its case for European Regional Assistance; and Save the Children and Glasgow Caledonian University (SPIU, 1996) have jointly reviewed the extent of child and family poverty across Scotland as part of the response to an acknowledged lack of adequate primary data sets at a national level (Craig, 1994). Some profiles for new unitary authorities, such as Denbighshire County Council, following the 1996 local government reorganisation in Wales and Scotland, have been produced by 'ancestor' authorities which disaggregated data to correspond with new authority boundaries.

The range of profiles is not comprehensive, and many are in any case updated from time to time: however, the sample collected over the past three years and discussed here (58 in all) does provide a representative range of types of local poverty profiles currently in existence. The form in which they appear, however, differs very widely. Some are lengthy and detailed documents, often with academic input, debating the technicalities of differing composite indices of deprivation; others are 'popular' versions, oriented towards the dissemination of information about local poverty to local audiences and may be as short as four pages long. The nature of the publicly-available profile is, to a large, extent, a reflection of the political and policy context in which the profile was produced. For some local authorities, a brief profile may have been produced as an aid to local consultative exercises; for others, a much more detailed and technical profile may have preceded detailed policy reviews. The following sections analyse some of the key issues which these profiles raise for local policy-oriented poverty mapping.

Type of Local Authority

Balloch and Jones's (1990) study of local government anti-poverty work was limited to urban metropolitan authorities, partly because the study was sponsored by the Association of Metropolitan Authorities but in part also because, at the end of the 1980s, this is where the greatest concentration of local authority anti-poverty strategies was to be found. Nearing the end of the 1990s, as our earlier and current studies have shown (Alcock *et al.*, 1995;

Pearson *et al.,* 1997), anti-poverty strategies can be found in every type of local authority, including unitary authorities, some of which have only been legal entities for barely a year. The sample of 58 discussed here are distributed been types of authority as follows:

- London Boroughs   10
- Metropolitan Districts   12
- Scottish Districts/Unitaries   6
- Scottish Regions   6
- Shire Counties   11
- Shire Districts   6
- Welsh Districts/Unitaries   6
- English Unitaries   1

In Wales, Scotland and England, work is evidently in progress in the unitary sector (which emerged in 1996, 1996 and 1995 respectively) to develop poverty profiles. A few profiles were published in the mid-to-late 1980s (particularly in Scotland) but the great majority have appeared in the past five years and are therefore relatively contemporaneous with each other. Although the local government elections of the mid-1990s did move the political centre of gravity of local government somewhat to the left of centre, it is also true that a recognition of the extent of local poverty has extended into local authorities of every political persuasion. One of the most marked trends in the past three years has been the extent to which traditionally conservative (both politically and attitudinally) largely rural shire counties and districts, have begun to recognise and engage with the extent of poverty within their boundaries despite government protestations that poverty did not exist.

Numbers of Indicators

The numbers of indicators mapped within the profiles varies quite considerably. Glasgow City Council's popular pamphlet uses five indicators. Typically, at the lower end of the range, a number of more detailed profiles from varying types of authority (Devon County Council, Lothian Regional Council, Monmouthshire [unitary] County Council and Carlisle City Council, for example) use six indicators. The most common numbers used in England were 13 or 14, corresponding to the range used in the DoE Index of Local Conditions (DoE91), discussed earlier, with a lower number common in Scotland and

Wales, aligned to the differing approaches of the Welsh and Scottish Offices. A few authorities, however, go well beyond this, Fife Regional Council, Newham London Borough Council and Lancashire County Council all making use of 30 or more indices. The latter's *Green Audit*, which takes a broad view of environmental deprivation, includes many indices which are not to be found elsewhere.

Sources of Indicators

There is little doubt that the publication of the results of the 1991 Census, at a time of growing awareness of the extent of local poverty, facilitated the development of many of the local poverty profiles reviewed here. As a result, it is hardly surprising that many of the profiles are heavily (in some cases, totally) dependent on census indices. However, profiles published more recently have begun to acknowledge the limitations of over-dependency on one source of data, particularly the Census which is now seven years out of date and quite unhelpful in relation to some data - for example, the undercounting of groups such as young males (Craig, 1998a), and the inadequacies of the 'ethnic' question, introduced into the Census for the first time in 1991 - but also other data sources such as unemployment statistics which have been the subject of political manipulation for many years (Craig, 1998a; see also Atkinson and Micklewright, 1989). In technical terms, advances made in the visual presentation of data through the use of GIS, has offered local authority policy departments the opportunity to present and manipulate data in much more accessible and visual ways than hitherto, thus opening up policy debates to a wider range of audiences and, in particular, displaying aspects of rural deprivation to good effect (Higgs and White, 1997).

Our earlier studies on anti-poverty work (Alcock *et al.*, 1995) suggested that profiles tended to make use of four broad sources of data:

- nationally collected data which is either readily available or can be re-analysed to provide information appropriate to local needs (notably, of course, the Census, because of its - in principle at least -100 per cent coverage). This still provides the bulk of data used in local poverty mapping.
- data already compiled by the local authority itself for other, usually administrative, purposes (such as housing or council tax benefit records). This, in our experience (see below), has been an under-utilised resource

for local poverty profiles given that most local authorities (except perhaps the smallest and least technologically-advanced) have much of this data already stored within their administrative systems.

- data accumulated by other agencies (for example, local branches of national organisations such as the Benefits Agency or local or regional bodies, such as Regional Health Authorities, reporting statistical returns to national organisations) but which can be used at a local level. Dobson *et al.* (1996) have demonstrated, for example, the way in which Income Support data can be mapped to understand the spatial concentration of deprivation in one local authority area (Leicester).

- data which is compiled by means of *ad hoc* local exercises by the local authority or other agencies (for example research organisations or voluntary agencies). Particularly given the growing constraints on local government expenditure, the capacity of local authorities to mount large primary data-gathering exercises is increasingly limited but there have been some notable studies of this kind, particularly the *Breadline Greenwich* (Greenwich, 1994) exercise, based on the Breadline Britain methodology (Mack and Lansley, 1985), Liverpool's Quality of Life Survey, and the Social Survey of Islington, carried out on behalf of the local authority by MORI. Our analysis suggests that the value of local primary data collection exercises can be overlooked as a useful complement (particularly a qualitative one) to the secondary analysis of existing quantitative data sets.

This fourfold typology remains a useful broad classification of the varying sources of data on which poverty profiles have drawn. In terms of the range and type of data used, the position has improved immeasurably since the time when Norris reported (1979) that 'certain dimensions of the problem [of poverty] receive much more attention than others merely by virtue of the greater availability of quantifiable data concerning the former'.

Some local authorities (for example Cambridge City Council) have also attempted to present longitudinal trends in poverty by, for example, using data from both 1981 and 1991 Census although this is problematic in those instances where data output boundaries have changed significantly in the inter-censal period or where, as with the 'ethnic question', some trends are not able to be analysed. Waltham Forest's profile maps trends over varying timescales for differing indices at ward level, offering a clear profile of those areas where conditions have deteriorated significantly.

Types of Indicators

Given the range of indices used, it is not possible to analyse them in great depth here. However, apart from a classification by source, it is also possible to classify the indices in terms of the broad aspect of poverty or deprivation which they address. Spicker's work for Tayside Regional Council (1992) remains the most detailed attempt at classification of this kind, offering a fivefold classification into material resources; housing and environment; health; social problems; and (unusually) status and power, covering 28 indices in all from about twelve differing sources. There is no doubt that the classification could be refined with indices arranged under other, further headings (such as education, for example) but it remains a useful broad means of classifying indices and, of course, serves as a reminder of the multi-faceted nature of poverty. Using this classification, the most commonly occurring indices used within the sample of 58 profiles analysed were as follows, with indices drawn from Census and other indices and used in the DoE *Index of Local Conditions* (ILC) marked with an asterisk (the two ILC indices not appearing frequently within local profiles were derelict land and insurance premiums):

- material resources:
    - unemployment rates (DfEE/Census)[*]
    - long-term unemployment rates (DfEE NOMIS/Census)[*]
    - receipt of free school meals (local education authority)
    - receipt of income support (Benefits Agency/housing benefit and council tax benefit records)[*]
    - receipt of housing benefit (local housing authority)
    - council tax benefit records (local authority housing or finance department)
    - low pay (DfEE)
    - access to car ownership (Census)[*]
    - no earning households with children (Census)[*]

- housing and environmental:
    - homelessness (local housing department)
    - overcrowding (housing department/Census)[*]
    - children in flats (Census)[*]
    - housing lacking basic amenities (Census)[*]

- health:
    long-term limiting illness or disability (Census)
    standard mortality ratio (Health Authority)[*]

- social problems:
    burglary (police)
    criminal damage (police)
    personal assault (police)

Spicker's fifth category of **status and power** included indices such as voter turnout, social class of mothers and illegitimacy which were represented in few, if any, of the other profiles studied. Other indices grouped under this heading such as educational participation (for example the proportion of 17 year-olds not staying on in full-time education at 17 [*]), or educational attainment (the proportion of GCSE exams not passed at Grade C or above [*]) are, however, frequently used within local poverty profiles.

What this analysis reveals is first, the continuing emphasis on indices concerned with material poverty, with 9 out of the 18 most commonly cited indices being concerned with aspects of material deprivation - despite the fact that the Census has no income question and that therefore any income profiles have to be derived either from sample or incomplete surveys or from proxy indices such as, for example, receipt of certain benefits. But secondly, that the range of indices used (and therefore, by implication the different 'faces' of poverty described) has indeed increased substantially since local poverty mapping became a significant phenomenon. Some indices used, such as the extent of mortgage repossession, reflect the impact of important social trends: in this case, both the growth of owner-occupation as a result, particularly, of the Right to Buy legislation, but also the consequence for lower-income owner-occupiers of the slump in housing prices in the early 1990s. Yet others, notably the range of 30+ indices used by Lancashire, reflect a more holistic approach taken to the quality of life, incorporating not only many of the common indicators of poverty listed above, but indices such as air and water quality, mode of travel to work, and community cohesion. Our research suggests that, for the initial development of local anti-poverty strategies, a law of rapidly diminishing returns operates beyond about 8 or 9 indices although later detailed work might helpfully draw on more extensive and detailed analyses. For authorities covering both rural and urban areas, separate (perhaps overlapping) lists of indicators might be required.

Smith and Noble confirm our own observation that local authority administrative data (particularly relating to housing benefit and council tax benefit) is a substantially under-used resource for poverty mapping, particularly as it offers a useful income proxy and is often much more contemporary than other data sets. Also in conjunction with the Local Government Anti-Poverty Unit, they have demonstrated the capabilities (and limitations) of local administrative data to good effect (Smith and Noble, 1998), using it longitudinally and geographically to map income deprivation. And the potential of this approach may now be enhanced as the Benefits Agency has agreed to lodge with the Local Government Management Board a complete sweep of Income Support data which will be made available for analysis to individual local authorities.

The other significant way to date in which local authorities have approached the mapping of poverty has been to identify those demographic groups, membership of which implies a much greater risk of poverty (regardless of whether all those individuals mapped actually were poor). The most commonly mapped groups were:

- lone parents (see for example Bradshaw and Millar, 1991)
- minority ethnic groups (Craig, 1998b)
- lone pensioners;

although some profiles (for example Nottingham) record a much greater range of 'target groups' including carers, young unemployed and the low paid. Other 'functional' groups such as renters or those in rent arrears were also recorded in some profiles.

Overall, the approach to the use of indices reflects the twin-track emphasis of an increasing number of authorities which regard an approach to combating poverty at a local level as requiring targeting of population groups as complementary to the targeting of deprived neighbourhoods. This reflects, in part, a widespread recognition of the 'ecological fallacy', recognised from the government's experimental EPAs of the 1960s onwards, that as many poor people are likely to live outside areas defined as deprived, as live within them so that geographical targeting alone will inevitably miss many of its targets - a point to which we shall return later.

In some local authorities, a particular emphasis has been placed on the circumstances of particular population groups which are disproportionately represented locally (*vis-à-vis* the UK population as a whole). The most common example of this is the mapping of the circumstances of minority ethnic groups in, for example, Newham and Oldham; a relatively unusual exemplar is the mapping of the student population in Cambridge.

Approaches to Combining Indices

Once a range of indices is chosen and mapped by local authorities, the indices can be combined in, in principle, a virtually limitless number of ways to provide refined and developed understandings of the local distribution of poverty. For example, the Suffolk profile maps the distribution of people aged 75 and over without central heating; the Central Region profile provides a gendered analysis of all indices; and Stockport's profile maps Standardised Mortality Ratios (SMRs) for under-65s, by type of disease or illness. Nottingham's profile includes an index of dependency ratios (economically inactive residents per economically active resident).

These types of simple combination are undoubtedly useful in facilitating targeted service and policy responses to local poverty. However, the most common approach to combination of indices has been the search by local authorities (in which about half of those whose profiles are reviewed here have engaged) for an appropriate composite indicator which can provide an overall 'snapshot' of poverty and deprivation either for the authority as a whole or (or, more usually, **and**) at the level of wards or enumeration districts. Many of the profiles review the relative advantages of the range of compositing approaches available (reflecting the discussion by Lee *et al.,* 1995) and some of the more sophisticated profiles mirror national debates on this issue, particularly in relation to the robustness and complementarity of the indicators used. Some indicators (for example, crime rates) are regarded as of doubtful value since they reflect levels or concentrations of police activity as much as of criminal activity. One important and illuminating trend has been the growing prominence of community safety, a relatively insignificant feature of profiles at the time of Balloch and Jones' (1990) study, as a key element of local anti-poverty work. Robust measures of this have yet to feature strongly in local poverty profiles although some authorities are beginning to explore this field, for example the location of children's accidents by ward is used within the Derby profile.

The composite approach most commonly used is the DoE *Index of Local Conditions* (or its Welsh or Scottish counterparts) not necessarily because it was regarded as the best available but because it was both the simplest (and cheapest) to apply to the locality (much of the preliminary organisation of the data already having been undertaken for the Census) and also because it both offered a publicly endorsed means of comparison between authorities and as a guide for negotiations with central government regarding central subsidies of various kinds to local expenditure. This confirms the findings of a survey of all Welsh unitary authorities (White and Higgs, 1997) which showed that more authorities used the Welsh Office Index of Socio-Economic Conditions than any other index. This survey also showed, incidentally, that 'informing anti-poverty strategies' was the second most frequent use to which such authorities put the compilation of deprivation indicators.

However, given that the DoE91, as with any mechanism for distributing government subsidies, involves winners and losers, it is hardly surprising that some authorities embrace it less enthusiastically than others. A significant number of authorities, (such as Pembrokeshire County Council) also review the available data using a range of compositing methods to establish the extent to which the same areas might consistently be regarded as deprived on the basis of differing composite approaches. Most authorities which composite indicators do so using appropriate statistical weighting methods: some, however, simply rank wards for each indicator, arriving at a composite by arithmetical addition across all scores.

Levels of Mapping

As might be expected, the level of geographical unit at which poverty is most commonly mapped within the profiles studied is either wards or enumeration districts or both. This reflects the dominance of census data and the fact that the DoE91 includes 13 indices, of which 6 are at ED scale and 7 at ward scale. However, DoE91 also maps all indicators at local authority district scale because 'data for some indicators is either not available or not robust at the smaller scales' (DoE, 1994). Politically, the mapping (for example disaggreg-ation) of county data to district level can prove helpful where inter-authority working may be possible (as, for example it has been in Cheshire or Derbyshire).

Some commonly-used indices are problematic in this regard because they are collected for administrative areas which do not correspond necessarily with the boundaries of local authority districts, the Income Support (and other benefit) 'catchment areas' of Benefits Agency local offices being the most obvious case in point. In a number of cases, particularly for local authorities which have significant or largely rural populations, the mapping of poverty at ward or enumeration district was also not regarded as appropriate. In these cases, authorities have attempted to define what they regard as 'natural communities', based, for example, on parish boundaries - data for which is generally aggregated in the Census (Lincolnshire), catchment areas of primary schools (Strathclyde) or postcodes (Fife). Many of the rural authorities (for example, Cheshire, Cornwall, Shropshire and most of the rural Welsh and Scottish authorities) dispute the robustness or appropriateness of the range of indicators used within DoE91 or its Welsh and Scottish counterparts, arguing that, for example, car ownership and proportion of children living in flatted accommodation are inappropriate indicators for measuring rural deprivation and that other measures of rural deprivation such as access to public services, quality of life or depopulation of economically active people might be more appropriate. This is a further interesting reflection of Rowntree's pioneering work in that he extended his survey work later on to investigate rural poverty, thereby helping to challenge the myth of the 'rural idyll'. DoE91 is itself currently the subject of an updating revision process (Robson *et al.*, 1997) which seems likely to accommodate at least some of these criticisms of urban bias.

Other local authorities map poverty for areas (often aggregates of wards) corresponding to areas pre-defined in relation to existing policy interventions: examples of this approach are the community development areas in Cleveland County or the priority areas of Fife Regional Council. One authority profile (Wycombe) provides a very detailed analysis of deprivation in three wards previously identified by DoE91 as the most deprived wards within the area.

Needs and Resources

Given that many, if not most, of these poverty profiles, have been developed as tools to inform developing anti-poverty strategies within local authority areas, it might be expected that an attempt would be made to correlate needs revealed through poverty mapping with the resources available (for example, the distributions of local services and agencies) to meet those needs. In practice, this approach was undertaken in a relatively very few cases, two of the later rural profiles (Shropshire and Lincolnshire) being cases in point. That they were rural authorities may reflect the growing debate about rural poverty which has been carried forward in recent years by rural development agencies throughout the UK (Cloke *et al.*, 1994; Rural Forum, 1994). In the Lincolnshire map, for example, GIS techniques were used to good effect to allow transparent maps of resources to be overlaid onto needs maps: for example, the location of children and family service outlets in relation to the lone parent indicator; or the nature of the composite indicator used within the profile, within a 10 Km radius of social services area offices. Similarly, in the Grampian profile, distributions of basic services provision (primary school, shop, petrol outlet, GP surgery and post office) are mapped by parish. In several profiles (for example, Coventry and Birmingham), data regarding service enquiries (for example calls at advice centres regarding debt) are mapped: this provides further data combining both need and service availability.

The Policy Implications of Local Poverty Mapping

The links between the mapping of needs and resources highlights the importance of the policy context of local poverty profiling. Whatever general academic interest there might be in the local distribution of disadvantage (and hopefully this is growing now), the real value of local poverty profiling is to inform policy debate and policy development - and to deliver changes in the distribution of, and access to, local resources. Policy-makers will rightly ask, what are the implications of local profiles? And local citizens might also rightly ask, what is going to happen as a result of them?

When we begin to examine the policy implications of local poverty mapping we encounter some of the limitations of policy debate and development, which to some extent have been apparent since Rowntree's local poverty mapping one hundred years ago. Local and national anti-poverty policy planning and delivery are not well-co-ordinated. Indeed in recent times the history of the relations between central and local policy planning has been characterised by conflict rather than co-ordination, most notably in the battles between local authorities and the Conservative central government over local spending and policy priorities in the 1980s. In the 1990s some of these conflicts have been continued within the competitive bidding process established for the receipt of local regeneration funding under the City Challenge and Single Regeneration Budget (SRB) programmes.

Further, the focus of area regeneration strategy in the 1980s and early 1990s on physical and economic development in inner urban areas (Alcock *et al.*, 1998) ignored increasing evidence of the diversity of the spatial distribution of poverty and disadvantage, and the many complex problems this creates for policy planners. Recent analysis of rural disadvantage is an important example of this; and yet there are relatively few policy initiatives focusing upon the problems of poverty in rural areas. The shift towards a more holistic concern with social and economic regeneration within more recent central government planning, especially since the 1997 General Election, may presage a shift towards greater harmony between central and local anti-poverty policy planning at the end of the 1990s, evidenced in the proposed broader and needs-related focus of SRB funding regimes, and the commitment to work more closely with local government, revealed in recent DETR policy statements (for example GROYH, 1997). In this context the new Regional Development Agencies are likely to play a key role in determining the spatial dimension of social policy planning and it is to be hoped that the considerable and increasingly sophisticated work that has gone into local poverty profiling over the last few years will be seen as a vital resource for any new era of regional planning.

However, it is perhaps important to conclude by highlighting some of the significant contradictions at the heart of all policy approaches which focus policy interventions upon identified areas of local poverty or disadvantage. For it is only in recognising the shortcomings, as well as the opportunities, of local anti-poverty action that effective social change is likely to be achieved.

In large part poverty profiling is concerned with the relative advantages, or disadvantages, of people living in different areas and localities. It is therefore concerned with the drawing of boundaries between areas. Inevitably, however carefully they are drawn, there is likely to be an element of (historical) arbitrariness in the placement of boundary lines; and this is likely to be revealed most markedly where it is also most politically sensitive, at the margins - the line down the middle of the street separating the residents on one side (perhaps those in a local action zone) from those on the other (who are not) is the graphic example of this. Boundaries inevitably operate to include, but also to exclude. And, although boundaries may be carefully drawn to include those most disadvantaged areas within the targets for local action, it is worth stressing again that it is almost always the case that most poor people live outside of any designated action areas. In other words targeting of resources onto particular areas will mean that those outside the target areas are going to miss out from targeted programmes

The mapping of local poverty also involves the identification of target areas or action zones - and hence, potentially at least, the identification of these areas, and the people living in them, as failing or deprived. This is what we have previously referred to as the problem of 'negative labelling'. This has a number of contradictory consequences. For a start people may not be keen for their area, and indeed themselves, to be labelled in this way - negative self-imagery is not a sound basis for survival or prosperity. This is confirmed by much local research evidence which, when it probes local people about their images of their local area, is much more likely to find positive than negative views held by residents. The problems of negative labelling contributing to a spiral of local decline rather than reversing it was recognised by the workers in the CDP initiatives in the 1970s (CDP, 1977) and it is also a problem recognised by many local councillors and officers today. In the context of broader regeneration strategy it reveals also the dilemma of basing local development activity on needs as opposed to opportunities - those areas with the best opportunities for growth and development may not be those with the highest level of needs according to local poverty profiles.

Negative labelling of areas is problematic; but it can lead to the allocation of additional resources to such areas. Thus poverty profiling can also sharpen conflict over the competition between areas for such additional resources. This competition is of major importance at the national planning level; it was the source of much of the conflict between central and local government in the 1980s, and it was institutionalised in the bidding process for programmes such as SRB in the 1990s. It also has international dimensions, as witnessed in the competition for support for 'Objective 1' and 'Objective 2' regions within the EU and the current debates about reshaping the criteria for access to European Structural Funds (ESF). Regions designated 'Objective 1', where GDP per head is below 75 per cent of the European average, receive significant additional resources to support local regeneration activity; and those designated 'Objective 2', areas experiencing structural difficulties, also receive targeted funding. ESF funding is used to support a wide range of community and employment initiatives at local or regional levels.

However, competition between areas can also become manifest within local areas where the conflict between neighbourhoods and wards for anti-poverty resources can furthermore be overlain by the political rivalries between local politicians with bases in these areas. This a conflict which we previously have referred to as 'post-code' politics, and it is a conflict in which some can only win if others also lose.

The problem of post-code politics sums up many of the dilemmas involved in local poverty profiling and local anti-poverty work. Knowledge of the spatial dimensions and complexities of disadvantage is now recognised as a valuable aspect of poverty measurement, and it plays an increasingly important role in policy planning and development. But is also produces inevitable tensions and contradictions, in particular because the targeting of resources onto some means that other targets are missed. And yet the conflicts which this targeting produces may in practice serve to obscure some of the more general, and important, features of the poverty problem.

Poverty may be experienced locally and may be distributed inequitably between different local areas; but it is not the product purely of local forces, and ultimately will not be resolved purely by local action - a point which still remains a major legacy of Rowntree's work. Those utilising poverty profiles to inform strategic action to combat local poverty would do well to remember the limits of local action in the promotion of social change and the importance of challenging too the broader social and economic forces which shape local conditions.

References

Alcock, P., Craig, G., Dalgleish, K. and Pearson, S. (1995), *Combating Local Poverty*, *Local Government Management Board*, Luton.

Alcock, P., Craig, G., Lawless, P., Pearson, S. and Robinson, D. (1998), *Inclusive Regeneration*, Sheffield Hallam University/University of Lincolnshire and Humberside/DETR, Sheffield and Hull.

Atkinson, A.B. and Micklewright, J. (1989), 'Turning the Screw' in A. Dilnot and I. Walker, (eds), *The Economics of Social Security*, Oxford University Press, Oxford.

Balloch, S. and Jones, B. (1990), *Poverty and Anti-poverty Strategy: The Local Government Response*, Association of Metropolitan Authorities, London.

Barclay, Sir P. (1995), *Inquiry into Income and Wealth*, (Volume 1), Joseph Rowntree Foundation, York.

Berthoud, R., Brown, J. and Cooper, S. (1981), *Poverty and the Development of Anti-Poverty Policy in the UK*, Heinemann EB, London.

Bradshaw, J. and Millar, J. (1991), *Lone Parent Families in the UK*, DSS Research Report No. 6, HMSO, London.

Cloke, P., Milbourne, P. and Thomas, C. (1994), *Lifestyles in Rural England*, Rural Development Commission/ DoE, Salisbury.

Community Development Project (CDP) (1977), *Gilding the Ghetto: The State and the Poverty Experiments*, CDP Information and Intelligence Unit, London.

Craig, G. (1994), *Poverty and Anti-poverty Work in Scotland*, Scottish Anti-Poverty Alliance, Glasgow.

Craig, G. (1998a), 'The Privatisation of Human Misery', *Critical Social Policy*, vol. 18, no. 1, February, Sage, London.

Craig, G. (1998b), '"Race", poverty and social security', in J. Ditch (ed.), *Social Security in the United Kingdom: Policies and Current Issues*, Routledge, London.

DoE (1994), *Index of Local Conditions*, Department of Environment, London.

Dobson, B., Trinder, P. Ashworth, K., Stafford, B., Walker, R., and Walker, D. (1996), *Income Deprivation in the City*, Joseph Rowntree Foundation, York.

Green, A. (1994), *The Geography of Poverty and Wealth*, Institute for Employment Research, University of Warwick, Coventry.

GROYH (1997), *Single Regeneration Budget Challenge Fund: Round 4, Framework for Yorkshire and the Humber Region*, Government Regional Office for Yorkshire and the Humber Region, Leeds.

Higgins, J. (1978), *The Poverty Business: Britain and America*, Basil Blackwell and Martin Robertson, Oxford.

Higgs, G. and White, S.D. (1997), 'Changes in Service Provision in Rural Areas', *Journal of Rural Studies*, vol. 13, no. 4, pp. 441-450, Elsevier.

Hills, J. (1995), *Inquiry into Income and Wealth*, Volume 2, Joseph Rowntree Foundation, York.

Lee, P., Murie, A. and Gordon, D. (1995), *Area Measures of Deprivation*, University of Birmingham, Birmingham.

Loney, M. (1983), *Community against Government: The British Community Development Project 1968-78*, Heinemann EB, London.

Mack, J. and Lansley, S. (1985), *Poor Britain*, Allen and Unwin, London.

Noble, M., Smith, G., Avenell, D., Smith, T. and Sharland, E. (1994), *Changing Patterns of Income and Wealth in Oxford and Oldham*, University of Oxford, Oxford.

Norris, G. (1979), 'Defining Urban Deprivation', in C. Jones (ed.), *Urban Deprivation and the Inner City*, Croom Helm, Beckenham.

Pearson, S., Kirkpatrick, A. and Barnes, C. (1997), *Local Poverty, Local Responses*, Sheffield Hallam University/University of Lincolnshire and Humberside, Discussion Paper No. 2.

Philo, G. (ed.) (1995), *Off the Map*, Child Poverty Action Group, London.

Robson, B., Bradford, M. and Tomlinson, R. (1997) *Updating the Index of Deprivation: A Consultation Draft*, University of Manchester, Manchester.

Rural Forum (1994), *Disadvantage in Rural Scotland*, Perth.

Scottish Poverty Information Unit (SPIU), (1996) *Child and Family Poverty in Scotland*, Glasgow Caledonian University/Save the Children, Glasgow.

Smith, G. and Noble, M. (1998), *Developing the Use of Administrative Data to Study Poverty*, unpublished paper, University of Oxford, Oxford (mimeo).

South Glamorgan County Council/NLGFAP (1996) *Welsh Unitary Authorities*, Indicators of Poverty, Cardiff.

West Midlands Low Pay Unit (1997) *Measuring Deprivation in the West Midlands*, Birmingham.

White, S.D. and Higgs, G. (1997), 'Identifying Deprivation in Wales', *Regional Studies*, vol. 31.6, pp. 614-619, Regional Studies Association.

Poverty Profiles

- Barking and Dagenham London Borough Council (1996) *Poverty profile,* Barking and Dagenham
- Birmingham City Council (1989) *Poverty in Birmingham: A Profile*, Birmingham
- Bradford Metropolitan District Council (1995) *Bradford Economic Profile*, Bradford

- Cambridge City Council (1993) *Poverty in Cambridge,* Cambridge
- Cambridgeshire County Council (1996) *Deprivation and Disadvantage in Cambridgeshire,* Cambridge
- Carlisle City Council (1995) *Towards an Anti-Poverty Strategy for Carlisle,* Carlisle
- Central Regional Council (1995) *Social Strategy,* Stirling
- Cheshire County Council (1994) *Economic Disadvantage in Cheshire,* Five Volumes, Chester
- Chester City Council/ Chester College (1995) *The experience of urban and rural poverty in Chester,* Chester
- Cleveland County Council (1993) *A New Map of Disadvantaged Areas,* Middlesbrough
- Clwyd County Council (1996) *Poverty Profile of Denbighshire,* Ruthin
- Cornwall County Council/ University of Bristol and others (1996) *Poverty and deprivation in West Cornwall in the 1990s,* Truro/Bristol
- Coventry City Council (1997) *Coventry Poverty Profile,* Two Volumes, Coventry
- Dacorum Borough Council (1996) *Tackling poverty in Dacorum,* Hemel Hempstead
- Derby City Council (1997) *Poverty in Derby,* Derby
- Derbyshire County Council (1994) *Poverty in Derbyshire,* Five Volumes, Matlock
- Devon County Council (1995) *Tackling Poverty in Devon,* Exeter
- East Ayrshire Council (1997) *Social and Economic Profile,* Kilmarnock
- Edinburgh District Council (1988) *Poverty in Edinburgh,* Edinburgh
- Enfield London Borough Council (1995) *Tackling Poverty,* Enfield
- Fife Regional Council/Kirkcaldy District Council (1995) *Aspects of Deprivation in Fife,* Glenrothes
- Fife Regional Council/A Copus *et al.* (1996) *A Profile of rural deprivation in Fife,* Glenrothes, 1996
- Glasgow City Council (1996) *Poverty and Deprivation in Glasgow,* Glasgow
- Grampian Regional Council (1995) *Social and economic disadvantage in Grampian,* Aberdeen
- Greenwich London Borough Council (1994) *Breadline Greenwich Report,* Greenwich
- Gwynedd County Council (1995) *Poverty in Caernafonshire and Meirionethshire and Ynys Mon,* Caernafon
- Hammersmith and Fulham London Borough Council (1994) *Borough Profile,* Hammersmith and Fulham
- Hertfordshire County Council (1996) *Hertfordshire's Anti-Poverty Strategy,* Hertford
- High Wycombe District Council/Buckinghamshire College (1996) *Deprivation in High Wycombe,* High Wycombe
- Hillingdon London Borough Council (1995) *A Poverty Map,* Hillingdon
- Islington London Borough Council (1990) *Poverty in the 1980s,* Islington
- Kingston upon Hull City Council (1994) *Urban Deprivation in the city of Hull,* Kingston upon Hull
- Lancashire County Council (1997) *Lancashire's Green Audit,* Preston
- Leeds City Council/Leeds CPAG (1992) *Child poverty in Leeds,* Leeds
- Lincolnshire County Council (1997) *Social Audit,* Lincoln
- Liverpool City Council (1994) *Analysis of Problems, Issues and Needs,* Liverpool
- Lothian Regional Council (1995) *Deprivation in Lothian Region,* Edinburgh

- Monmouthshire County Council (1997) *Hidden Poverty and social exclusion in Monmouthshire*, Cwmbran
- Newcastle upon Tyne City Council (1994) *Poverty profile*, Newcastle upon Tyne
- Newham London Borough Council/Steve Griffiths (1994) *Poverty on your Doorstep*, Newham
- Newport County Borough Council (1997) *Pattern of disadvantage in Newport*, Newport
- Norwich City Council (1991) *Poverty in Norwich*, Norwich
- Nottingham City Council (1994) *Poverty in Nottingham*, Nottingham
- Oldham Metropolitan Borough Council (1994) *Areas of deprivation in Oldham*, Oldham
- Pembrokeshire County Council (1996) *Indicators of Poverty and Deprivation*, Haverfordwest
- Rotherham Metropolitan Borough Council/University of Huddersfield (1993) *Deprivation Analysis*, Rotherham
- Sheffield City Council (1993) *Poverty and the Poor in Sheffield*, Sheffield
- Shropshire County Council (1996) *Poverty and Deprivation in Shropshire*, Shrewsbury
- Southwark London Borough Council (1993) *The Poverty Profile*, Southwark
- Stockport Metropolitan Borough Council (1997) *Profiling Stockport*, Stockport
- Strathclyde Regional Council (1992) *Poverty in Strathclyde*, Glasgow
- Suffolk County Council (1996) *Poverty in Suffolk*, Ipswich
- Swansea City Council (1997) *Poverty profile of Swansea*, Swansea
- Tayside Regional Council/ University of Dundee (1992) *Poverty and deprivation in Tayside*, Dundee
- Tower Hamlets London Borough Council (1996) *Profiling Poverty*, Tower Hamlets
- Waltham Forest London Borough Council (1996) *The Way it is*, Waltham Forest
- West Dumbartonshire (1997) *Social and economic profile*, Dumbarton
- West Lothian District Council/University of Glasgow (1995) *Directory of Poverty Indicators in West Lothian*, Bathgate.

5 Relationships Between Health, Income and Poverty Over Time: An Analysis Using BHPS and NCDS Data[1]

MICHAELA BENZEVAL, KEN JUDGE, PAUL JOHNSON and
JAYNE TAYLOR

Introduction

That there is a relationship between income and health, that the poor are less healthy than the rich, is hardly in dispute. Studies too numerous to mention have shown this correlation in the cross section. What is less common, though, is information on the relationship between income (or poverty) over time or in the past, and current health status.[2] It is this longer-term relationship which is addressed here.

This paper uses two longitudinal datasets - namely the National Child Development Study (NCDS) and the British Household Panel Survey (BHPS) - to look at the relationship between some measures of poverty at various points in the past and measures of health in the present. This adds substantially to the sorts of conclusions one is able to draw when using purely cross-sectional data, although it is still difficult to disentangle all the possible directions of causality in the income/health relationship. For there are three distinct reasons why there might be a correlation between income and health:

1. low income 'causes' poor health (through restricted access to basic amenities, poor housing conditions, the persistent stress of managing daily activities with limited resources or the reduced self esteem of being at the 'bottom' of society);
2. poor health 'causes' low income (perhaps by restricting labour market opportunities);
3. income and health are jointly determined by the same prior characteristics or circumstances, so that the causal relationship runs from something else (perhaps education) to both income and health.

It is likely that all three of these relationships exist within any population, and even for the same individual at different points in time. It is clear that while cross-sectional data, without any background or historical information, can illustrate the income/health correlation it can tell us precisely *nothing* about these possible causal relationships. This paper, while not able to prove causality, does present a number of indicative results which shed new light on the nature of the poverty/health relationship; results which it is only possible to produce given longitudinal data with information on income and health at different points in time.

The NCDS is a cohort study of individuals born in 1958, with measures of income and health at distinct points during their life up to the age of 33. In the BHPS information is available on a sample of individuals of all ages in each year from 1991 to 1995. The two datasets offer different but complementary information about the income/health relationship over time.

The paper begins by briefly describing the two datasets and in particular the measures of income and health which are employed.[3] It then examines various aspects of the income health relationship in each dataset: first cross-sectionally and then over time.

Data Description

The British Household Panel Survey (BHPS) first interviewed a nationally representative sample of around 5,000 households, containing 10,000 adults, in 1991. These households were followed up and re-interviewed in each succeeding year, and this paper is based on information for the first five waves of the survey (1991-95). Note though that sample attrition and incomplete information means that by wave 5 only 5,548 initial adult respondents had complete information for themselves and their household for each year.

The NCDS also suffers from sample attrition and, perhaps more seriously, from incomplete information about the 11,406 individuals who were interviewed at age 33 in the fifth sweep of the survey (NCDS5). Of these 11,406 only 6,578 have the full range of information, particularly on childhood financial circumstances, that is required for this analysis.

Both surveys contain detailed information on health. The BHPS contains a wealth of information about family income, but the NCDS is somewhat lacking in this area. Brief details are provided below.

Health Information in the BHPS

The health questions in BHPS and NCDS are similar but not directly comparable. Both contain sets of questions covering a range of aspects of people's health, including measures of both physical and mental health problems, psychological well-being, limiting illness and subjective assessments of health. For the purpose of this analysis, each health question has been used to create a simple binary dependent variable of the type healthy or unhealthy. This does mean that some of the richness of information available in the data is not used, but it makes the analysis tractable. The health measures used from BHPS are described in Table 5.1.

The most striking feature of Table 5.1 is the higher prevalence of ill health among women for each of the health measures. However, it is important to note that this table does not take into account the different age distributions of men and women, since women, on average, live longer than men part, but by no means all, of the explanation for the higher prevalence will be their greater age.

Table 5.2 tries to give an impression of the changes in health that occur to respondents in the BHPS over the five year period of the survey. The extent of change varies with the health measure considered, and it is important to bear in mind that people move in and out of different health states during the five-year period in ways more complex than this table is able to demonstrate.

Table 5.1 Health measures in the BHPS

Variable	Explanation	Sample prevalence in wave 5 (%)	
		M	W
Limiting illness	Whether or not respondent has illness which limits their daily activities	14.0	17.7
Health problems	Respondents are asked whether they have any illnesses from list of various health problems - a binary variable is created by splitting the distribution at the average number of health problems (1.09)	23.2	33.0
Psychological well-being General Health Questionnaire (12 item)	The GHQ is scored by the caseness method and a binary variable is created by splitting the distribution at those with score of 3 or more[4]	21.5	29.8
Subjective assessment of health	Five category question about overall assessment of health as excellent, good, fair, poor or very poor. Binary variable created by comparing those with fair, poor and very poor health with excellent or good health	27.0	32.7

M = men; W = women

Table 5.2 Health changes in the BHPS

Health measure	Per cent of respondents spending time in poor health		
	0 years	1-4 years	5 years
Limiting illness	73	21	6
Health problems	54	35	11
GHQ	45	51	4
Subjective assessments of health	48	43	9

Nearly three-quarters of respondents have no limiting illness over the entire five year period, while under half of respondents report only good subjective assessments of health or GHQ scores for the entire period. Conversely, only a small proportion of respondents are in poor health in every year of the survey.

Health in the NCDS

As with the BHPS there is a range of health measures in the NCDS which for the purposes of this paper are split into binary variables. The variables as used are described in Table 5.3.

Some of the main features of the health information in NCDS5 are summarised below:

- Men and women report very similar levels of excellent or good current health, but a smaller percentage of women say their health *over the past year* has been good (70 per cent compared to 78 per cent);
- A higher percentage of women (12 per cent) than men (seven per cent) have high malaise scores. Correspondingly, almost two-thirds of women, compared to less than half of men say they had some emotional/psychosocial problems between the ages of 16 and 33;
- More than half of both men and women with high malaise scores report excellent or good current health (although a higher proportion than average do say their health is only fair or poor), suggesting that these two health variables are measuring different dimensions of health;
- Looking at specific illnesses, women are more likely than men to say that they currently have or have in the past had health problems and to have consulted their GP about particular illnesses.

Because of this differential reporting of ill-health by sex (common to most sample surveys), all of the analyses are conducted for men and women separately. The BHPS analysis is also split by age, with separate results provided for those over pension age, as one might expect the determinants of health to be very different for this age group.

Table 5.3   Health measures in NCDS5 (respondents age 33)

Variable	Explanation	Sample prevalence %	
		Men	Women
Limiting illness	A two stage question – whether or not respondent has long-standing illness/disability and, if so, does it limit their daily activities	6.3	6.1
Health problems	Respondents are asked whether they have any illnesses from list of various health problems[+] in the past 12 months - a binary variable is created by splitting the distribution at the average number of health problems (1.6)	41.6	50.0
Malaise inventory (24 item)	A 24 point malaise score of symptoms of depression/psycho-social problems based on the Cornell medical index. A score greater than 7 is counted as poor psychosocial health.[5]	6.8	12.2
Subjective assessment of health	Four category question: "how would you describe your health generally" ranked as excellent, good, fair or poor. Binary variable created comparing those with fair or poor health with good or excellent	13.1	13.8

[+]This list covers a different set of health problems than BHPS (details available from the authors).

Income/Poverty

In the BHPS, and in the NCDS when the sample members are aged 23 and 33, it is relatively straightforward to construct a measure of family income net of taxes.[6] In order to compare differences in incomes between families, this income is 'equivalised' to take account of family size (otherwise families containing more than one adult will tend to appear inappropriately rich relative to those containing just one adult).

To examine the association between people's income and their health at different points in time, this paper identifies people's location in the income distribution by splitting the sample into income quintiles, so that, for example, the experience of the people in the bottom fifth can be compared with that of other groups in the population.

Income information for the NCDS waves conducted during the sample members' childhood is limited. Instead, therefore, this paper makes use of a simple categorical variable, which asks whether the family is or has been suffering from financial hardship in the 12 months prior to the interview, which was asked when the sample members were aged 11 and 16. As such, poverty during childhood is simply defined as reported financial hardship (11 per cent reported at least one period of financial hardship at age 11 and 16).

In addition in the BHPS two extra measures of poverty over time are employed. The first uses income information to calculate how many years people spent in poverty during the period of the survey, where poverty is defined as having less than half of average income.[7] The second measure of poverty experience is more subjective and is based on a question which asks respondents whether they find it difficult to manage on their income. The number of years that people found it difficult or very difficult to manage is included in the analysis.

Cross-Section Comparisons

Given the nature of the data, the most direct comparison that can be made between the two datasets is in the correlation between contemporaneous health and income. For illustrative purposes we show this association for each dataset here, before going on to explore the longitudinal relationship in more detail. Note, though, that even here direct comparisons between the datasets are difficult to make: first, because of the different health measures being used; and, secondly, because while the NCDS contains people all of the same age the BHPS contains people distributed over the entire population age range. This latter problem is corrected for to some extent by controlling for age in the logistic regression on which the BHPS results are based. The results are presented first for the BHPS and then for NCDS.

BHPS

Using the odds ratios derived from logistic regression models, Table 5.3 shows the cross-sectional association between income and health in wave 5 of the BHPS. An odds ratio indicates how much more likely a person in each of the income categories is to report poor health than someone in the reference category - the top income quintile. For example, women under 60 in the bottom 20 per cent of the income distribution are over twice as likely to assess their health as poor as those in the top fifth of the income distribution.

For all of the health measures and population groups, people in the bottom sections of the income distribution report more ill health than those at the top. The steepest associations between current income and health are for subjective assessments of health and limiting illness. For instance, men under 65 in the poorest income quintile appear to be five times as likely to be suffering from a limiting illness as men in the richest quintile. But note that this does not mean that people on low incomes are more likely to have a limiting illness *because* they have a low income; it could be that people with a limiting illness are more likely to have a low income *because* they have a limiting illness; or it could be that there is no direct causal relationship. For the moment we cannot tell and it is only by going on to exploit the longitudinal aspects of the data that we can start to see more of what is happening.

Table 5.4   BHPS5 family income and health: odds ratio for income quintiles

| | Adjusted Odds Ratios* | | | | | | | | | | | |
| | Women under 60 | | | | Men under 65 | | | | Pensioners both sexes | | | |
Income quintile	Limiting illness	Health problems	GHQ	Subjective assessment	Limiting illness	Health problems	GHQ	Subjective assessment	Limiting illness	Health problems	GHQ	Subjective assessment
1 poor	2.91	1.84	1.57	2.22	5.19	2.19	1.38	2.82	1.86	1.3^{ns}	1.1^{ns}	2.78
2	2.33	1.88	1.36	2.15	3.36	1.69	1.1^{ns}	2.45	2.29	1.5	1.3^{ns}	2.30
3	1.4^{ns}	1.3^{ns}	1.2^{ns}	1.3^{ns}	1.4^{ns}	1.42	0.9^{ns}	1.47	1.83	1.1^{ns}	1.2^{ns}	1.88
4	1.2^{ns}	1.2^{ns}	0.9^{ns}	1.3^{ns}	1.9	0.9^{ns}	1.0^{ns}	1.21	1.1^{ns}	1.1^{ns}	0.8^{ns}	1.0^{ns}
5 rich	1	1	1	1	1	1	1	1	1	1	1	1
x^2	86	65	28	44	153	159	16	109	48	48	29	62

* The models control for age and gender as appropriate; ^{ns} Not significant at the ten per cent level

In terms of the different population groups, the strongest association between income and health - in terms of goodness of fit and the number of statistically significant coefficients - appears to be for men under 65 and the weakest for pensioners. In addition, as Table 5.4 shows, men under 65 with low incomes have a much higher risk of poor health relative to other men, than comparable women or pensioners.

The weaker association between income and health for pensioners is consistent with other studies (for example, Blaxter, 1990; Fox *et al.*, 1990). There are a number of potential explanations for this. First, given socioeconomic inequalities in mortality under retirement age and the propensity for many frail older people to move into institutional care, there is almost certainly a 'healthy survivor' effect among older people who remain living at home despite their disadvantaged circumstances. Secondly, it has been suggested that current income will have a weak association with older people's health because it does not accurately reflect the lifetime resources, which will have influenced current health status (Arber and Ginn, 1993).

NCDS

Table 5.5 shows equivalent results from NCDS wave 5. It is important to remember throughout that these results are for 33 year olds only and the health measures are not directly comparable with those from the BHPS. Again, the correlation between health and income is very clear, particularly for self-assessed health and the malaise score. For example, men in the bottom income quintile are four times as likely, and women almost three times as likely, to report fair or poor general health at this age as are those in the richest fifth. And for men, the relationship between limiting illness and income is again very strong. Whilst the pattern of results does vary across health measures and by sex, these findings hold generally true. The fact that the majority of people in the bottom income quintile (almost two-thirds[8]) are not working,[9] suggests that very low income and poor health are highly correlated, but this relationship is not as strong across the rest of the income distribution.

Table 5.5   Age 33 health and income: odds ratios for income quintiles

	Men				Women			
Income quintile	Subjective assessment	Limiting illness	Malaise	Health problems	Subjective assessment	Limiting illness	Malaise	Health problems
1 poorest	4.13	4.27	5.23	1.34	2.89	1.37 [ns]	3.50	1.19
2	2.28	2.21	2.19	1.12 [ns]	2.51	1.41 [ns]	3.09	1.34
3	1.50	1.26 [ns]	1.50 [ns]	1.05 [ns]	1.70	1.00 [ns]	2.25	1.19 [ns]
4	1.32 [ns]	1.16 [ns]	1.54	1.08 [ns]	1.61	1.23 [ns]	1.72	1.25
5 richest	1.00	1.00	1.00	1.00	1.00	1.00	1.00	1.00
X^2	117	77	89	8	82	6	90	11

[ns] Not significant at the five per cent level

Longitudinal Analysis

Having demonstrated a significant cross-sectional association between income and various measures of health, this part of the paper begins to explore the time dimension of the relationship. Logistic regression is used to calculate the odds ratios of reporting poor health for each of the health measures in various income categories at different points in time, while controlling for a range of other factors as specified. All results are presented for subjective health in order to keep the presentation of the analyses manageable, but any differences found using other measures of health are highlighted in the text. The analysis of BHPS is presented first, followed by the results for the NCDS.

BHPS

Table 5.6 shows the odds ratios for past income and health for reporting poor subjective assessments of health in wave 5 of the BHPS controlling for age and gender. For example, column 1 shows that women under 60 in the bottom fifth of the income distribution in 1991 are 2.3 times more likely to report their health as poor in 1995 as those in the top fifth. Comparing the results in similar association between health in wave 5 and both initial (wave 1) and current (wave 5) income. In the second column of Table 5.4, initial health is also included on the right hand side of the health equation and this greatly increases the predictive power of the regression. Having been unhealthy in 1991 is a very good predictor of being unhealthy in 1995. People under pension age with poor subjective health in wave 1 are around five times as likely to report poor subjective health in wave 5 as those originally in good health, while for pensioners the ratio is over nine.

More interestingly, and very strikingly, while including initial health at wave 1 in the regression reduces the relative odds ratios for the various income quintiles it comes a long way from wiping them out entirely. In other words, even controlling for health status in 1991, men in the poorest quintile in 1991 were still more than twice as likely to report only poor health in 1995 than were men who were in the top income quintile. This, certainly, is more suggestive of an effect of income on health than can be discerned from cross-sectional analyses. But it is only suggestive. It is of course possible that those observed with low income but good health in wave 1 of the survey actually have a history of poor health which didn't show up in the survey and which led to low income in 1991. Alternatively, historical factors such as educational attainment or childhood circumstances could be affecting both income and health at different times.

Table 5.6   Subjective assessment of health in wave 5: odds ratios for initial income and health

Independent variables	Adjusted Odds Ratios*	
	Wave 1 income only	Both wave 1 income and health
Women under 60		
Net family income quintiles		
1 - poor	2.32	1.88
2	1.93	1.66
3	1.2^{ns}	1.1^{ns}
4	1.0^{ns}	1.0^{ns}
5 - rich	1	1
initial health	-	4.75
X^2	51	239
Men under 65		
net family income quintiles		
1 - poor	2.68	2.27
2	2.34	2.01
3	1.62	1.42
4	1.51	1.51
5 - rich	1	1
initial health	-	5.55
X^2	100	295
Pensioners		
net family income quintiles		
1 - poor	2.66	1.96
2	1.97	1.5^{ns}
3	1.4^{ns}	1.3^{ns}
4	0.8^{ns}	0.8^{ns}
5 - rich	1	1
initial health	-	9.07
X^2	69	384

* The models control for age and gender as appropriate
ns Not significant at the ten per cent level

To investigate the effect of the length of time people experience poverty on their health, a number of models were developed with various measures of poverty over the course of the BHPS. In column 1 of Table 5.7, recent experience of poverty - based on the number of years spent on incomes below 50 per cent of the 1991 average - is added to the model containing initial income and health, age and gender. Having controlled for these variables, poverty experience only appears to be an independently significant factor for men under 65. For such men however, the more years they have spent in poverty the more likely they are to experience poor health in wave 5. For example, those men who spent all five years in poverty are 2.68 times more likely to have poor health than those who do not experience poverty by this definition.

The results vary slightly according to the health measure and definition of poverty employed. For example, experience of poverty is a significant factor for women's health under 60, for all of the other health measures. However, it is never reaches statistical significance for people over pension age. As with the lack of significance in the cross-sectional association between income and health, the latter could be a result of a 'healthy survivor' effect or that recent poverty experience is a the poor proxy for lifetime resources which may be the true determinant of health at older ages.

An alternative approach to looking at poverty - based on experience of financial strain over the previous five years - is shown in column 2. The table shows that this measure of subjective poverty experience is significant for all three population groups. For example, pensioners who have experienced financial strain throughout the five years of the survey are 1.7 times more likely to have poor health than those who have not had any financial problems. Experience of financial strain is significant for all health measures and all population groups. Moreover for each population group this model has the best goodness of fit, measured by the change in scaled deviance of all of the different approaches to measuring the relationship between income and poverty over time attempted here.

Table 5.7   Subjective assessment of health in wave 5: the additional effects of poverty experience and financial difficulties over time

Independent variables	Adjusted Odds Ratios*	
	Poverty experience[+]	Financial difficulties[++]
Women under 60		
Poverty experience[+]		
all years	1.21^{ns}	-
3 or 4 years	1.17^{ns}	-
1 or 2 years	1.31^{ns}	-
Financial difficulties[++]		
all years	-	2.16
3-4 years	-	1.89
1-2 years	-	1.49
X^2	240	261
Men under 65		
Poverty experience[+]		
all years	2.68	-
3 or 4 years	2.22	-
1 or 2 years	1.02^{ns}	-
Financial difficulties[++]		
all years	-	2.4
3-4 years	-	2.0
1-2 years	-	0.98^{ns}
X^2	310	335
Pensioners		
Poverty experience[+]		
all years	1.11^{ns}	-
3 or 4 years	0.99^{ns}	-
1 or 2 years	1.14^{ns}	-
Financial difficulties[++]		
all years	-	1.71
3-4 years	-	1.37
1-2 years	-	1.08^{ns}
X^2	385	395

* The models control for age and gender as appropriate and initial income and health
[+] Poverty is defined here as having less than half of average wave 1 income
[++] Financial strain is defined here as just getting by or experiencing difficulties
[ns] Not significant at the ten per cent level

NCDS

Results from NCDS complement those from the BHPS by looking over a longer timescale. While the most interesting results probably derive from the relationships between financial circumstances in childhood and later health we start by looking at the relationship between health at age 33 and income at age 23. It is important to note here that the dispersion of incomes at age 23 is much less than at older ages: the well-educated will not have had enough time to have started earning significantly more than people who are less well educated. This might partly explain why a much weaker relationship is observed between income at age 23 and health at age 33 than between contemporaneous income and health at age 33.

Despite this relationship being weaker for age 23 income, as Table 5.8 shows, there is still a clear association between income in the earlier period and health at the later date, a relationship which is reduced but not eliminated when health at age 23 is controlled for. Despite the long time gap men with *poor* health at age 23 are over seven times as likely to be in poor health at age 33 as those reporting *good* health at age 23 (the equivalent odds ratio for women is 6.62). It is perhaps an indication that those who are in poor health at such an early stage in their lives are very specific sub-sample of the population who are likely to be blighted by ill health for large chunks of their life.

Results for the health equations based on limiting illness and the malaise score were very similar, although the effect of health at age 23 is even stronger, particularly on the malaise score.

Table 5.8   Subjective assessment of health: odds ratios for poor health at age 33 given income and health at age 23

Income quintile	Men			Women		
	age 23 income only	age 23 health only	both income and health age 23	age 23 income only	age 23 health only	both income and health age 23
1 poor	2.10	-	1.79	2.48	-	1.98
2	1.36	-	1.24 ^{ns}	2.14	-	2.05
3	1.29 ^{ns}	-	1.23 ^{ns}	1.49	-	1.41
4	1.03 ^{ns}	-	0.99 ^{ns}	1.30 ^{ns}	-	1.29 ^{ns}
5 rich	1.00	-	1.00	1.00	-	1.00
age 23 health	-	7.34	6.95	-	6.62	6.28
X^2	40	248	271	54	277	310

^{ns} Not significant at the five per cent level.

The inter-relationship between income and health can be illustrated by reversing the models. Instead of having health as the dependent variable we can put income (defined as being in the poorest quintile at age 33) as the dependent variable with income and health at 23 as regressors. For men in particular the results are striking. The simple odds ratio shows that men who were in bad health at age 23 (on the subjective measure) were four times as likely to be in the bottom income quintile at age 33 as were men in good health at age 23. Even controlling for income at age 23 the odds ratio only falls to 3.65.

So, having low income at age 23 is a good predictor of being in poor health at age 33 (as Table 5.8 confirms), but at the same time being in poor health at age 23 is a good predictor of having low income at age 33. This illustrates the danger of drawing simple conclusions about the direction of causality.

The next stage of the analysis goes back further in time to investigate the relationship between health at age 33 and circumstances during childhood. Three measures of childhood circumstances are included in the models:

- financial difficulties - based on the number of times parents of cohort members said they had experienced financial hardship at the 11 and 16 year surveys;
- health - to take account of the fact that unhealthy children might be more likely to be unhealthy adults; and,
- father's social class at birth.

The final set of results based on these models is presented in Table 5.9. Once again, odds ratios are presented for each of the explanatory variables in our subjective general health equation. Any differences in the results based on the other measures of health are noted.

The results in Table 5.9 show how, on the basis of quite crude poverty measures, low income during childhood is strongly correlated with poor health in adulthood. The effect is stronger for those individuals with more 'persistent' experience of financial difficulty as a child. For example, women whose parents reported financial hardship once during their childhood are 1.6 times as likely to be in poor health at age 33 as are those with no reports of financial hardship; those with experience of two spells of childhood financial problems are more than twice as likely to be 'unhealthy' at age 33.

Table 5.9   Subjective assessment of health: odds ratios for poor health at age 33 given income and health at age 23

	Men	Women
Financial difficulties once age 11/16	1.32^{ns}	1.61
Financial difficulties twice age 11/16	1.98	2.15
Childhood health dummies:		
Physical condition disabling for future work	1.37	1.62
Physical condition not disabling for future work	1.07^{ns}	1.07^{ns}
Mental/emotional problem disabling for future work	2.35	2.58
Mental/emotional problem not disabling for future work	1.15^{ns}	1.58^{ns}
Father's social class at birth (p-value)	0.001	0.000
X^2	45	78

^{ns} Not significant at the five per cent level.

Note: Constant includes: no father's social class information (no father, unemployed, retired, etc.), no financial difficulties age 11 or 16, and no health problems (disabling or not) at age 16.

Childhood health is also an important determinant of adult health. In particular, where the respondent suffered from 'disabling' conditions as a child their probability of reporting fair or poor general health at age 33 is much higher (especially in the case of childhood mental/emotional problems).

For the other health measures, financial circumstances during childhood are found to be less important for limiting illness (women only) and number of health problems at age 33 (both men and women). In fact, it seems that childhood health is a more important indicator than family income during childhood of whether or not an individual suffers from a limiting illness in later life.

The results shown in Table 5.9 include measures of childhood health and father's social class as explanatory variables. In fact including these makes very little difference to the coefficients on the financial hardship variable. This suggests that childhood financial circumstances and childhood health both have an important, but separate, relationship with adult health. Similarly, one might expect that father's social class would be a better measure of average childhood socio-economic circumstances and, therefore, including this in the health equations would reduce, if not remove, the effect of financial difficulties. In fact, whilst including father's social class does slightly reduce the odds ratios on the financial difficulties variables, the strong relationship with adult health holds generally true.

The strong association between childhood financial circumstances and adult health is clearly apparent. One potential mediating factor in this relationship could be education. There is a large body of literature documenting the relationship between parental socioeconomic status and educational attainment, and it is not difficult to imagine that it is through education that income and/or parental social class impacts upon health in later life. For example, children from poorer families might have very limited access to quality schooling (because of the area in which they live, etc.), which might in turn feed through into lower awareness of health issues - such as available treatments and 'healthy' behaviours - and also poorer employment prospects, resulting in lower incomes and greater exposure to health risks in the work-place. Hence including education in any model of health and income should reduce the observed effect of income on health, and give us some information about transmission mechanisms. However, before reaching firmer conclusions about potentially causal mechanisms, we are conscious of the need to develop more enduring measures of socioeconomic status throughout childhood for inclusion in future statistical models.

Table 5.10 shows how the results - for the subjective health equation - are affected by including educational attainment in the health equation. The odds ratios for the education dummies are all relative to having no qualifications, so it is no surprise that they are all quite significantly less than one (i.e. individuals with any qualification are less likely to be unhealthy at age 33 than those with no qualifications). Comparing these results to Table 5.7 above, it is clear that the odds ratios associated with the financial difficulties variables do, in fact, become smaller when education dummies are included. Indeed, for men, being in financial hardship once during childhood no longer appears to matter for eventual health outcome once educational attainment is taken into account.

However, individuals who have experienced financial difficulties at both age 11 and 16 are still more than 1.5 times as likely to be in poor health at age 33 compared to those with no family financial problems during childhood.

Table 5.10   Fair/bad self-assessed general health: impact of including education dummies

	Men	Women
Financial difficulties once age 11/16	1.09^{ns}	1.40
Financial difficulties twice age 11/16	1.66^{ns}	1.58^{ns}
Childhood health dummies:		
Physical condition disabling for future work	1.23^{ns}	1.59
Physical condition not disabling for future work	1.19^{ns}	1.18^{ns}
Mental/emotional problem disabling for future work	1.99^{ns}	2.04^{ns}
Mental/emotional problem not disabling for future work	1.74^{ns}	1.38^{ns}
Education dummies:		
Other qualifications	0.65	0.74^{ns}
<5 O-levels/low-vocational	0.36	0.56
5+ O-levels/mid vocational	0.39	0.44
A levels	0.30	0.52
Highest vocational	0.22	0.32
Degree	0.28	0.25
X^2	98	110

^{ns} Not significant at the five per cent level.

Conclusions

The messages from this work so far are complex. Several things do come out of both sets of data though. The first is the remarkable persistence of ill health over time. The single best predictor of being ill now is having been ill five or even ten years earlier. And from this the value of longitudinal analysis is immediately evident. Those who are sick for long periods are highly unlikely to have anything other than low levels of income, and part of the cross-sectional income/health relationship is immediately clarified.

Secondly, while the relationship between past income and current health is a little less strong than that between current income and current health, it is still very significant. And it remains significant even when the available information on past health is taken into account. This suggests that there is more to the income health relationship than a simple cross-sectional correlation, but the possibility of co-determination by other factors remains. And it is important to note that the relationship is also strong the other way round. Being ill in the past is a good predictor of being poor now.

In the BHPS it is clear that additional measures of recent experience of poverty or hardship such as the amount of time spent in poverty or financial difficulty are important correlates of current health over and above the effect of initial health and income. From the NCDS the relationship between financial hardship suffered by the family during childhood and health at age 33 is strong. But the mediating role of education is very evident. There is certainly evidence that those who suffer poverty in childhood but who do well educationally go some way towards escaping the poor background/ill health cycle. Again the reasons for this are indeterminate because higher education leads not just to higher income during adulthood but it may also facilitate better access to information and encourage more healthy behaviours. But it is also important to note that even controlling for education there does still appear to be some continuing effect of poverty in childhood.

There remains, of course, much work to be done with these two datasets. The next stage of the analysis of BHPS will attempt to untangle the direct effect of some of the causes of low income and income change, such as unemployment or divorce and separation, on health and their indirect effect via income. We can also do much more towards disentangling the effects of parental income, childhood background and education on eventual health in the NCDS. That such work is both necessary and potentially very revealing is amply illustrated by the preliminary results presented here.

From a policy perspective, these results suggest that to reduce ill health in adulthood two strands of work are required. First, for long term benefits, efforts must be made to reduce financial hardship among vulnerable families with children and to improve educational opportunities for them. Secondly, that short run poverty must also be guarded against, which means ensuring vulnerable families are adequately protected against shocks to their income. For example, by providing adequate unemployment benefits or by ensuring fair and quick settlements in cases of separation and divorce and helping lone mothers who wish to return to work through retraining and the provision of decent child care.

Acknowledgements

The BHPS and NCDS datasets were made available by the ESRC Data Archive and originally collected by the ESRC Research Centre on Micro-Social Change at the University of Essex and the Social Statistics Research Unit at City University, respectively. We are grateful for their permission to use the data. However, neither the original collectors of the data nor the Archive bear any responsibility for the analyses or interpretations presented here.

Notes

1   This project is funded by the ESRC Health Variations Programme.
2   Although there are some notable exceptions, particularly from North America (see, for example, Hirdes and Forbes, 1989; Wolfson *et al.*, 1993; Miller and Korenman, 1994; Duncan, 1996), and British studies looking at the determinants of social class differences in health with a lifetime perspective (see, for example, Power *et al.*, 1991).
3   Further details about the NCDS are available in Power *et al* (1991) and Ferri (1993) and about the BHPS in Buck *et al.* (1994).
4   See, for example, West and Sweeting (1996).
5   See, for example, Richman (1978) and Rutter *et al.* (1976) for use of this index.
6   Actually in the BHPS a slightly crude version of net income is used which only takes account of tax on main employment income (see Webb, 1995).
7   In the analysis various proportions - from 30 to 70 - of average income were explored. However, this did not greatly affect the results and so half average income is used here for illustrative purposes.
8   This excludes the self-employed, who are not included in our sample here as we do not

have a net figure for self-employed earnings in NCDS5.
9   This includes 18 per cent unemployed, the rest being students, sick/disabled, housewives/househusbands and 'other' not working.

References

Arber, S. and Ginn, J. (1993), 'Gender and Inequalities in Health in Later Life', *Social Science and Medicine*, vol. 36, no. 1, pp. 33-46.

Blaxter, M. (1990), *Health and Lifestyles*, Tavistock/Routledge, London.

British Household Panel Survey. Economic and Social Research Council, Research Centre on Micro-Social Change, Colchester.

Buck, N., Gershuny, J., Rose, D. and Scott, J. (eds.) (1994), *Changing Households: The British Household Panel Survey 1990-92*, ESRC Centre for Micro-Social Change, University of Essex, Colchester.

Duncan, G. (1996), 'Income Dynamics and Health', *International Journal of Health Services*, vol. 26, no. 3, pp. 419-44.

Ferri, E. (ed) (1993), *Life at 33: The Fifth Follow-up of the National Child Development Study*, National Children's Bureau and City University, London.

Fox, J., Goldblatt, P. and Jones, P. (1990), 'Social Class Mortality Differentials: Artifact, Selection or Life Circumstances?' in Goldblatt (ed), *Longitudinal Study: Mortality and Social Organisation*, OPCS series LS no. 6, HMSO, London, pp. 164-90.

Hirdes, J.P. and Forbes, W.F. (1989), 'Estimates of the Relative Risk of Mortality Based on the Ontario Longitudinal Study of Aging', *Canadian Journal of Aging*, vol. 8, pp. 222-37.

Miller, J.E. and Korenman, S. (1994), 'Poverty and Children's Nutritional Status in the United States', *American Journal of Epidemiology*, vol. 140, no. 3, pp. 233-43.

Power, C., Manor, O. and Fox, J. (1991), *Health and Class: The Early Years*, Chapman & Hall, London.

Richman, N. (1978), 'Depression in Mothers of Young Children', *Journal of the Royal Society of Medicine*, vol. 71, pp. 489-93.

Rutter, M., Tizard, J., Yule, J. and Graham, P. (1976), 'Isle of Wight Studies: 1964-1974', *Psychological Medicine*, vol. 6, pp. 313-32.

Webb, S. (1995), *Poverty Dynamics in Great Britain: Preliminary Analysis of the BHPS*, Institute for Fiscal Studies, London.

West, P. and Sweeting, H. (1996), 'Nae Job, Nae Future: Young People and Health in the Context of Unemployment', *Health and Social Care in the Community*, vol. 4, no. 1, pp. 50-62.

Wolfson, M., Rowe, G. and Gentleman, J.F. (1993), 'Career Earnings and Death: A Longitudinal Analysis of Older Canadian Men', *Journal of Gerontology: Social Sciences*, vol. 48, pp. 167-79.

6 The Commuter's 'Experience' of Poverty: Towards a Post-Industrial Geography of Health

MARC CHRYSANTHOU

Introduction

An historically hegemonic discourse on poverty and health confirmed the excluded nature of the relatively deprived in society by focussing on them as 'the Poor'. This perspective is still manifest in policy documents, textbooks and articles. Unintentionally perhaps, the underlying political message conveyed is 'what should be done about the poor?' Or, 'How can we change their unhealthy lifestyles?' By contrast, more recent writings on social exclusion (Hutton, 1995; International Institute for Labour Studies, 1996; Geddes, 1997) articulate a non-separatist agenda of poverty research premised upon a link between affluence and poverty. This theorisation of poverty and affluence's interconnectedness asks broader political questions: Are 'the poor' poor because 'the rich' are rich? Do the affluent have a moral and political obligation to eliminate poverty? How does wider society exclude and stigmatise deprived populations?

However, the psycho-social or cognitive-affective dimension of this relationship, and how this affects political attitudes and health has been relatively neglected. Key questions here would include: What awareness do relatively disadvantaged and advantaged groups have of their own social locations and of each other? Does this differential awareness have implications for health status and/or political attitudes? (Wilkinson, 1996)

Similarly with geographical approaches to poverty and health, much research focuses on areas of poverty, for example, the inner-city, rural poverty, specific deprived localities. Again, this serves to recapitulate the spatial and political separateness of these areas; obscuring the 'systemic structural and hierarchical differentiation of space into affluent and poor localities (Cooke, 1989; Shields, 1991).

This chapter is a speculative attempt to contribute to an integrated geographical approach to poverty and affluence: one that recognises both the structural determination of poverty/affluence by space, time and money (Harvey, 1989) and the phenomenological dimension or lived experience of this objective framework (Chombard de Lauwe, 1956). Contrary to much poverty literature's focus on the deprived, the aim is to explore the cognitive-affective dimension of poverty from the perspective of the relatively affluent - or, broadly speaking, the middle class. Further, in contrast to the rather abstract, positivistic nature of research into class and health, or a statically-conceived notion of medical geography or social epidemiology, a 'postmodern' social geographical analysis - informed by an awareness of space, time, movement and speed (Baudrillard, 1983; Virilio, 1986; Harvey, 1989; Soja, 1989; Jameson, 1991; Sennett, 1994) - is employed to contend that geography is not 'simply' a spatial projection of social characteristics, but, along with geographical mobility and speed, an important contributory factor in explaining both health status and attitudes towards poverty.

Specifically, this postmodern analysis specifies an Ideal-Type - the Greater Manchester Commuter to explore the commuter's 'experience' of poverty. This experience, it is argued, is connected to two contemporary social and political trends: the persistence of class-based and poverty-related health inequalities (Moore and Harrisson, 1995) and the existence of a political culture in which poverty and inequality have been marginalised (Galbraith, 1993; Hutton, 1995). In relation to health inequalities, the argument is as follows: That the social geography of post-industrial Britain testifies to radically distinct spatial locations and movements (time-space routines) for disadvantaged and advantaged people; and that these time-space routines are intimately correlated with distinct lived experiences of the social world - including the awareness of one's relative position in society. Taken together, these two dimensions of spatial location/movement and experience affect health - detrimentally for the relatively poor, and positively for the relatively affluent. In relation to the politics of poverty, this dynamic social geography also has an impact on the relatively affluent's political perspective on poverty; specifically, to marginalise poverty as a political issue.

Landscapes of Health

The thesis of deindustrialisation describes a movement of capitalism into a new disorganised phase (Lash and Urry, 1987); a more flexible regime of accumulation (Harvey, 1989). In lay people's terms this refers to the demise of mass manufacturing - with a concomitant creation of mass unemployment - and its supersession by a more diverse service sector. The Greater Manchester conurbation testifies eloquently to the spatial implications of this economic restructuring - the winners and losers (Robson, 1988). On the one hand the entrapment of a residualised urban poor in inner-city 'Places on the margins' (Shields, 1991; Philo, 1995). On the other, 'village-sized fragments' of 'lifestyle clusters' dotted around the rim of the metropolis (Jencks, 1993). Taylor *et al.* (1996) in their panoramic book *A Tale of Two Cities* paint a vivid picture of Manchester (and Sheffield) in the throes of this postindustrial metamorphosis. Manchester's heart is surrounded by an inner-city ring containing areas of multiple deprivations. In the city-centre itself shoppers are increasingly exposed to the spectacle of homeless people and street-beggars. Miles further out in the Cheshire plains, the edges of the Peak District or West Yorkshire lie the affluent suburbs - the 'travel to work' region of affluent commuters. This 'basic geography of poverty' (McKendrick, 1997) travesties a more 'complex geography of poverty' (*ibid.*) of areas of extreme poverty and deprivation adjacent to areas of comparative affluence (Hall, 1995); resembling more a jigsaw or mosaic than a simplistic North-South or Centre-Periphery axis:

> This spatial and geographical proximity of very differently advantaged areas, with a very different 'quality of life', situated cheek-by-jowl with each other, separated by a single thoroughfare suggests a parallel between LA and Manchester.
> (Taylor *et al.,* 1996, p. 356)

The 'two cities' of Taylor *et al.*'s title - ostensibly a reference to Sheffield and Manchester, are also a reference to the radically different lived experiences within the same city of the poor and affluent as well as men and women, homeless and homeowners, car-drivers and pedestrians, young and old, heterosexual and gay, those with and without hope. However, the 'basic geography' of affluent commuterdom - Suburb/Inner City and Affluent/Poor - although over-simplified, does capture schematically social trends in living and working in the 1990s.

The basic and complex geographies of relative wealth and relative poverty correlate closely with a geography of health of the same area (While, 1989). On all the major variables used to measure ill-health Greater Manchester is consistently very much higher than the national average. Wide variations in incidence on all these measures exist across the 32 wards of the city, roughly on the north-south axis. A report *Health Inequalities in Manchester in the 1990s* (Stevens, 1993) documents particularly high levels of poverty and ill-health in the Central A, North C and South D sub-areas. While,

> The South of the City (except South D in Wythenshawe) houses the majority of the City's populations in professional, managerial and technical occupations, has more people working, more open space and people living there are generally healthier than in other parts of Manchester.
> (Stevens, 1993)

Locating Health

What is the nature of this close correlation between the geography of health and postindustrial urban geography? (Phillimore *et al.*, 1994). Obvious candidates as explanations would include differential material/structural factors (income, employment status, housing quality, poverty/affluence) lifestyle/behavioural factors (smoking, alcohol consumption, nutrition) (Moore and Harrisson, 1995; Carroll and Davey Smith, 1997). Recently, attention has been focussed on the contribution of psychosocial factors by Wilkinson's work (Wilkinson, 1996). Wilkinson's main thesis is that it is not absolute inequality that affects health in developed societies, but the psychosocial filtering of relative income inequality: 'What affects health is now no longer the differences in absolute standards, but social position within societies' (*ibid.*, p.75). Drawing on research evidence of higher stress and poorer health in lower-status baboons, vervet monkeys and civil servants, Wilkinson extrapolates that poorer people's awareness of their relatively low status in society creates chronic stress and low self-esteem, which become the psychosocial pathways through which relative poverty causes premature death and ill-health.

This social comparative model features in Oliver James *Britain on the Couch* (subtitled 'Why we're unhappier than we were in the 1950s despite being richer') (James, 1997). James suggests that maladjusted and excessive social comparison produces lower serotonin-levels which in turn produce unhappiness and despair. And, 'although it is true that in general, people with objectively low status, power and wealth are more at risk of suffering low-serotonin problems, it is also true that the higher echelons are now very much at risk as well' (*ibid.*, p. 14). This self-defeating social comparison is identified as a deadly component in the psychology of most of us living in an advanced industrial society whose organising principle and fundamental raison d'etre is the constant generation of false needs and insatiable desires.

Wilkinson's remedy for the poverty-ill health nexus is movement towards a society in which fairness, equality, dignity and social cohesion replace the prevailing health-damaging social values of inequality, insecurity and competitive individualism. As a psychiatrist, James defends the value of drug therapy and counselling as short-term treatments for low-serotonin, unhappy societies, but his recommendations for a long-term cure echo Wilkinson's social diagnosis: If people are to be healthier and happier in advanced capitalist societies, a communitarian ethos must somehow be cultivated to dispel the present aspirational individualism.

But what of geography? Is the spatial patterning of poverty/ill-health and affluence/health simply the geographical expression of differences in social power and resources? (MacIntyre *et al.*, 1993; Phillimore, 1993). Below, Wilkinson's psychosocial thesis is given a geographical twist and turned upside-down sociologically to explore three supplementary health theses. While not denying the contribution of absolute material factors or lifestyle factors as major health determinants, the health argument is that the geographical segregation of poverty and affluence in post-industrial society acts as a health-protective pathway. Firstly, the commuter's capacity to move through space and time, to exercise choice in residential location, contributes to psychological and emotional empowerment and well-being. Secondly, the commuter is insulated both physically and psychologically from unhealthy stimuli and environments. Thirdly, the commuter's 'experience' or exposure to inner-city poverty serves as a health-enhancing social comparison.

Just Visiting: A Commuter's Tale

Unlike modernist geographies - with their fixed coordinates, abstract projections, relatively stable identities and statically conceived locales - the dialectical conception of geography espoused by postmodern cartographers (Soja, 1989) can map the commuter's trajectories through space and time. Postmodernism's recognition of the unity of time and space, the micro-detail of 'le quotidien', the impact of speed on experience, and the fluid nature of identity-formation allow a theorisation of the between-two-worlds of the commuter (Rosenau, 1991).

Let us consider the world of the affluent, academic commuter. Although working in an inner-city University he or she may live twenty miles away on the edge of the Pennines or in the South Manchester suburbs; commuting by train or car. For example, Salford University is situated amidst one of the poorest areas in Greater Manchester - the setting for Walter Greenwood's *Love on the Dole* and Robert Roberts' *The Classic Slum*. Salford's industrial heyday is celebrated by the well-known urban landscape paintings of L.S. Lowry. Sitting in a high-rise office surrounded by the classic symptoms of urban deprivation (tower-blocks, graffiti, litter, high rates of crime, unemployment and poverty), elementary questions might spring into the academic's mind: How important is where one works in comparison to where one lives for one's health? How can a locale- or area-based theoretical approach to health account for the commuter's between-two-worlds mobility? (Cooke, 1989; Harloe *et al.*, 1990). Why do the majority of his or her academic colleagues choose to locate their homes in the suburbs or rural areas? Why, when perhaps one-third of these academics' lives is spent in a notoriously unhealthy external environment could one still extrapolate with some certainty that their longevity and health status would exceed those of people living in the tower-blocks across the dual carriageway? How does daily exposure to scenes of poverty and deprivation impact psychologically on affluent academic commuters? To these questions we now turn.

Though not historically novel, the phenomenon of the 'flight from the city' is a contemporary trend fuelled by people's desire to achieve a better 'quality of life' (Baldwin *et al.*, 1990). Since the nineteenth- century, Manchester's commercial and industrial leadership escaped into the suburbs to signify their elevated social status. In *Dunroamin*, their classic study of the popularisation of the 'suburban semi' from the 1930s, Oliver *et al.* (1994) relate how the middle-classes sought a sanctuary of the soul, a signifier of social status, and a haven of health away from the psychological stress and physical health hazards of the city (Fishman, 1987). This dream of a suburban utopia or 'subtopia' lives on in the 1990s. For many it is a dream:

> There is no question but that the overwhelming desire of the vast majority of the people with whom we discussed the issue was to 'live in a nice area' and, in particular, the suburbs.
> (Taylor *et al.*, 1996)

For others, it is an achievable reality:

For some 'new consumers', especially those who have some private wealth or occupation enabling professional work from home, this search for a better quality of life has led to a 'relocation' in some form of rural retreat. Others have been committed by necessity of career or by preference for urban living to take up residence in the suburbs, or in city-centre redevelopments.
(*Ibid.*, p.15)

Commentators view this accelerating social trend variously as evidence of 'urban antipathy', the 'Laura Ashley Factor', or a 'pernicious middle-class exodus'. A Malthusian tone is evident in their assessment of the long-term environmental and social impact of this suburban getaway in terms of the destruction of countryside and the depopulation of the city (Donnellan, 1997). The aspirational and salutogenic motivations behind this migration are allowed expression by the technology of telecommunications and computers (for those working from home) and (for those commuting to work) the symbol of the twentieth-century: the automobile. For Ross (1995) the car has become a ubiquitous and banal object. Its omnipresence in our psychic and cultural life bears witness to 'its seamless integration into the fabric of everyday life' (*ibid.*). For some the car has become an ironic reminder of the ambivalence of modernity: on its own, a signifier of freedom, individuality and power, en masse, it signifies frustration, conformity and pollution (Whitelegg, 1997). The 'resistible rise of the car' (Wolf, 1996) is difficult to halt while as an object of seduction, and a key lubricant of (post)modern lifestyles it appears 'irresistible'.

A survey carried out by Greater Manchester Passenger Transport Executive in 1990 estimated that 53,000 vehicles came into Manchester city centre every day. Sixty one per cent of all travel journeys to and from work in Manchester were by car, with another ten per cent being accounted for by passengers in cars. This daily migration to work and back also revealed a social class bias, with twenty five per cent being driven by ABs and 27 per cent by C1-C2s (Farrow, 1990, p.20).

Insulation

Car commuters receive health benefits, whilst at the same time screening themselves from the urban reality of poverty, and contact with poor people, by a strategy of social and geographic insulation. The decision to locate or relocate away from the city is a grand-scale, existential example of the 'strategies of avoidance' so memorably delineated by Goffman (1963) - strategies adopted on an everyday basis by pedestrians, bus and rail travellers to avoid assorted 'risky' urban scenarios (Taylor *et al.*, 1996). Physically, the boundaries of 'defensible space' (Newman, 1972) are the outer membranes of the house, the car, and the office. Commuters journey through 'urban condoms' (Sennett, 1995), the 'modern arteries and veins' of the city, like visitors to a safari park with their windows wound up. Despite the unforeseen 'externalities' wrought by the hegemonic car culture, the physical membrane of the car body still serves protective and liberating functions:

> With the actual decline in mobility brought on by mass car consumption, the inviolate shell of the car can still provide, though in a weakened form, the liberty from social constraint that speed once promised to provide.
> (Ross, 1995)

From the car-park, a risk-laden journey on foot is made to the 'sealed space' of the lift (Sennett, 1995) where a vertical journey whisks the commuter to a commodious office of on-line coffee and bottled mineral water (the local water supply being too risky). The commuter poses a challenge to Buttimer's conception of a human geography of place and space as being about 'ordinary people's experience of the geography which touches the skin in daily doings' (Buttimer and Seamon, 1980).

This physical insulation - 'very few people spend less than three-quarters of their lives in buildings and vehicles' (Day, 1990) - is integrated with a cognitive-affective insulation. As Sennett argues in *Flesh and Stone* (1994) - his account of the historical intertwining and segregation of bodies and cities - the modern metropolis bears witness to a Self/City divide, a rigid demarcation of inner experience and outer space. Highways form a physical expression of this divide; cutting off the poor neighbourhoods; preventing the formation of an impulse to care about the passing scene or the view from the high-rise window. As Sennett intones in his earlier work *The Conscience of the Eye* (1993), 'Caring about what one sees in the world leads to mobilizing one's creative powers'. Unlike the total immersion of the urban poor, the affluent consumer's exposure to the city is selective, well-protected and detached.

Geographic Mobility

By contrast with 'the dependency of actors condemned to geographical immobility' (Warde, 1989, p.278), the commuter possesses the capacity to move through space and time, thereby avoiding psychosocial identification with unhealthy places. The underpinning of this capacity to escape is the interlocking command of money, time and space (Harvey, 1989). As Lefebvre (1991) remarks, 'command over space is a fundamental and all-pervasive source of power in and over everyday life'. Vehicular technology may assist this command, but it is secondary to the social power that buys it. The 'time-space routines' (Seamon, 1980) of the geographically mobile allow full expression of the social and individual identities of the affluent. Compare the time-space mobility of the affluent with the 'joyrider's' symbolic covetousness of this power and identity. From this perspective we can regard:

> The significance of car theft and joyriding as a momentary escape for young men from the constraint of their own narrow households and neighbourhood, the almost nonexistent local labour markets, and constant self-denial involved in everyday poverty.
> (Taylor, 1997)

In terms of health, spatio-temporal constraint signifies stagnation whilst spatio-temporal freedom signifies unbounded growth. As Virilio (1986) reminds us, to be 'quick' - as in 'the quick and the dead are far between' - means to stay alive.

Social Comparison

A logical corollary of the thesis propounded by Wilkinson (1996) and James (1997) - that poor physical and mental health is strongly linked to stress caused by relative deprivation and comparatively lower status - is that higher status people (or baboons and monkeys for that matter) derive health benefits from their relative position. Although the exposure to urban poverty and deprivation that commuters receive is selective and tangential, it may be that their awareness - unconscious or conscious - of their privileged social and geographical location produces health benefits through a psychosocial pathway (literally linked to a geographical pathway). In Kevin Lynch's influential paper *The Image of the City* (1960), he describes the concept of an 'image repertoire' that urbanites use to interpret the urban geography around them. He reports that people carry an image of 'where I belong' in their mind's eye. This mental image is used to compare the differentiated urban space that they travel through; the less that the image and the reality correspond, the more indifferent they are to their immediate surroundings. One of the main findings of a Salford University Stress Audit (Eachus *et al.*, 1995) was the respondents' assertion of the importance of 'home' (*vis-à-vis* work) as an emotional or psychological refuge or escape. Although this refuge was ostensibly defined in contrast with their specific work environment (for example, the office), it could be that the situation of the University within an unhealthy, inner-city area also served as a mental spatial comparison in relation to a home within the suburbs. This insight captures the possibility of a health benefit conferred by the awareness of one's relative social and geographical position. Perceptions and judgments of 'nice' and 'no-go areas' are well-established folk knowledge recorded in the mental maps of commuters, city-dwellers, estate agents, and the police.

Given the choice (for example the social power) many people would - and do - choose to move away from areas of crime, deprivation, and pollution. This positive social and geographical statement is conversely a negative statement about what is rejected. If awareness of one's relative deprivation can have a negative health impact, then awareness of relative advantage can have a positive health effect. This awareness is stimulated on a daily basis by the time-space routine of the commuter.

The Politics of Experience

The affluent commuter is a 'surfer' of the waves of postindustrial, postmodernised society. Using this analogy, the car is a surfboard riding on waves generated at a deeper level by political and economic forces. These waves could possibly wipe some of their number out at any moment; leaving them struggling alongside those already in the cold, choppy water all around them. But as long as the wave carries them, they remain oblivious to the surrounding strugglers. How can they help anyway, they might ask? A convincing account of poverty and social exclusion needs to theorise 'the wave' of this analogy: 'the kind of meta-theory which can grasp the political economic processes (money-flows, international division of labour, and so on) that are becoming ever more universalising in their depth, intensity and reach over daily life' (Harvey, 1989). But, resuming the analogy, it also needs to theorise the surfers' experience - the cultural-ideological terrain of lived experience and its role in political and social transformation or reproduction. Critics of postmodernism's blindness to 'objective' reality or political and economic processes are themselves often blind to this phenomenological dimension. An integrated account of the commuter's experience requires both the objective spatial and social framework generated by politics, economics and technology and the subjectivities of social actors making sense of this framework from their particular locations.

There are political as well as health consequences arising from the commuter's 'experience' of poverty. The physical segregation recorded in the postindustrial geography is matched by a psychological apartheid. The mental maps used by the visiting commuter (Lynch, 1960) label external and unfamiliar landscapes of poverty as Terra Incognita, or simply The Other. Stereotypes and myths are forged in the absence of direct experience:

> The representation of Urban Others advanced by people living in Manchester's southern suburbs (9 or 10 miles from the centre of the city) tended to have a 'fantastic' and stereotypical quality, whilst the typifications from residents of the inner city ring itself or of 'mixed residential areas', had a more pragmatic, naturalistic, and sometimes even sympathetic quality.
> (Taylor *et al.*, 1996, p.173)

Differences are assumed to be 'mutually threatening rather than mutually stimulating' (Sennett, 1995). What Etzioni (1994) terms the 'spirit of community' is disintegrated by the acids of individualism, segregation, and middle-class economic contentment (Galbraith, 1993; Hutton, 1995). Clearly, the affluent and relatively affluent's awareness of and responses to poverty are conditioned by more than just spatio-temporal mobility: other factors would include middle-class economic insecurity, affluence perceived as just deserts, media images of 'welfare scroungers', and, more fundamentally, what Lyotard summarises as 'incredulity towards meta-narratives': the postmodern condition. (Lyotard, 1984). 'Poverty' as an issue is a casualty of a postmodern political culture of cynicism, suspicion, narcissism, and disenchantment with liberation or equality 'myths' (Lasch, 1991). 'Compassion fatigue' has set in (Ryle, 1996):

> Classless society, social justice - no one believes in them anymore. We're in the age of micro-narratives, the art of the fragment.
> (cited in Hebdige, 1988, p.160)

If the tenets of postmodernism hold any truth, then the commuter is absorbed in an individualised life-strategy; a strategy unconnected to any wider political project.

A Phenomenology of Speed

Space, time and mobility have been discussed as central concepts in the commuter's experience of poverty. However, a key dimension lacking from this exploration is that of speed. Speed is the blinkered god of (post)modern society: go faster, eat faster, get information more quickly, overtake your neighbour, earn a fast buck (Griffiths, 1995). While environmentalists try to convince us to jump on the brakes - to arrest the juggernaut of 'progress' - the warnings are lost in the rush of (post)modern life. To be slow is to be retarded, a slow learner, a has-been. The biblical injunction 'He who is first shall be last' lacks persuasive power in a secular age. The commuter is the archetypal person-in-a hurry. Speed is reflected in the social and spatial fabric of the city. If 'the between' of the 'between two worlds' of commuting is linked by the concepts of space, time and mobility, it is dissolved and transmuted by the concept of speed. It is this transmutation - the way that speed impacts on cognitive-affective functions - that needs to be explored.

From a geography of speed's perspective (Sennett, 1995) the city is not a place, it is a 'tapestry of trajectories' (Virilio, 1986, p.3). Virilio's Futurist-indebted fixation with speed points to a new conception of the city: 'The city has not been recognised as first and foremost a human dwelling place penetrated by channels of rapid communication' (Virilio, 1986 p.5). Salford University itself is bisected - literally cut in two - by a ceaselessly busy dual carriageway. The time-space routine of commuting enacts a daily penetration of the city, mainly by cars. The channels that permit this are the motorway and rail networks. For some commentators, notably Richard Sennett, the subordination of the city to the function of motion demeans the city as a human habitat and public arena; the Greek polis is shamefully reduced to symbolic equivalence with a railway terminus or motorway service station. From Marxist and Liberal traditions respectively, Jameson and Sennett argue that the car commuter is alienated from the city, but if we follow Virilio there is nothing to be alienated from.

The technical, vehicular prosthesis that commuters use to penetrate the city is the car. Yet the phenomenology of speedy, time-space routines - how it affects the commuter's identification with and emotional responses towards urban spaces - has been paid little attention by the social sciences:

> We do think that a sociology of these two cities (Sheffield and Manchester) as seen and understood by car drivers from the road ... would be an important addition to our understanding of how these cities and their various localities are understood, especially in an age in which such large proportions of car users infrequently leave their cars. In the late twentieth-century we need a sociology of the city seen from the car as well as a sociology of the publicly encountered street.
> (Taylor *et al.*, 1996, p.99)

The politics of the commuter's gaze is influenced by the phenomenon of speed. Sennett bemoans the fact that 'as urban space becomes a mere function of motion, it becomes less stimulating in itself; the driver wants to go through the space, not be aroused by it' (Sennett, 1994). The 'messy democracy' of street life is overruled by the politics of the gaze. The politics of universality, of community, of caring are effaced by the politics of self. Not only does s/he want to go through the space, but s/he wants to go through it quickly. However, the faster the commuter travels, the more s/he loses identification with the surroundings and lapses into a different modality of experience. For Baudrillard,

> Mobility without effort constitutes a kind of unreal happiness, a suspension of existence, an irresponsibility. Speed's effect by integrating space and time, is one of levelling the world to two dimensions, to an image; it loses depth and its becoming; in some ways it brings about a sublime immobility and a contemplative state. At more than one hundred miles an hour, there's a presumption of eternity.
> (Baudrillard, 1996)

Sennett's pessimism is far removed from Virilio and Baudrillard's joyful nihilism yet he shares their assessment of the impact of velocity on cognitive, aesthetic, emotional and moral sensibilities. Vehicular speed promotes indifference, irresponsibility, desensitisation, detachment, and Tocqueville's dreaded 'individualism'. The 'spirit of community' is undermined (Etzioni, 1994).The social fabric of the city is disintegrated by the isolated time-space routines of thousands of 'mercenary' commuters. The effect is one of polarisation:

With the realisation of dromocratic-type progress, humanity will stop being diverse. It will tend to divide only into hopeful populations (who are allowed the hope that they will reach in the future, someday, the speed that they are accumulating, which will give them access to the possible...) And despairing populations, blocked by the inferiority of their technological vehicles, living and subsisting in a finite world.
(Virilio, 1986, p.47)

Baudrillard's taunt, 'What are Chile, Biafra, the 'boat people', Bologna or Poland to us?' (Baudrillard, 1984) may serve as an indictment of the mediated status of knowledge in our information-saturated, image-drenched society, but it also captures the detached, fleeting gaze of the car commuter. Speed transforms the urban landscape viewed through the windscreen into the same cognitive-affective status as images on a television or computer screen. Both are 'spectacular' (Debord, 1970). The television viewer fatigued by images of poverty, pollution, ecological disaster can simply switch channels. The car driver can accelerate and turn up the car stereo. The political consequence of the daily foray into Baudrillard's 'hyperreality' (1981) is the 'waning of affect' that Jameson observes in postmodern culture (Jameson, 1991). Velocity acts as a solvent of social and political conscience: Whereas the pedestrian develops strategies of avoidance to navigate streets containing homeless people or beggars, the car driver simply speeds by; moving on before any ethico-political dilemma arises. 'Nihilism' (à la Baudrillard) is too crude and one-dimensional a description of affluent people's attitudes towards disadvantaged people, but perhaps Baudrillard is a prophet before his time. If current trends such as the computerisation of society, the medievalisation of the city, and the exodus of the affluent to the countryside continue, perhaps crossing the street to avoid a beggar will feature more commonly as a manoeuvre in a dystopian computer game (a quaint reminder of the way things were) than as a 'real life' urban strategy.

Conclusion

Using the suburban commuter as an exemplar, a dynamic social geography has been sketched to argue that the time-space routine of commuting (reflecting relative advantage in terms of time, space, money, mobility and speed) creates two main effects: Firstly, it bestows health advantages on the commuter through physical and psychosocial processes of isolation, geographic mobility and affirmative social comparison. Secondly, the suburban commuter's spatial separation reflects a geography of speed that contributes to political desensitisation to poverty.

Three interlocking themes have been expounded . One is that - for those who can afford them - time, space, mobility and speed hide consequences. The second is that this hiding of consequences may secure health benefits for those living time-space routines that avoid the residualised, deprived areas of post-industrial Britain. The third is that the time-space routine of commuting desensitises the commuter to the reality of urban poverty - indeed, it may even aggrandise political contentment. Of course, this portrayal of The Commuter is an ideal-type (a stereotype even). But, ironically for an experiential analysis, theoretical primacy has been accorded to the structural determinants of time, space and money rather than individual variations of biography, personality or political beliefs. One does not have to be a structuralist to agree that in some ways the roads of society drive us, or to see human beings in one sense as atoms hurtling down the bifurcated pathways of health/ill-health and wealth/poverty.

The political geography of the mind accompanying the social geography of poverty is far more variegated and contradictory than Galbraith's and Baudrillard's diagnoses of contentment and nihilism. It is precisely the 'reification' of this social geography of poverty and the invisible processes of global capitalism that tips the odds in favour of accommodation rather than confrontation.

Smith (1992) believes that 'the reawakening of interest in space and geography ...is central to a successful political renaissance' (1992, p.59). However, within the wider context of a much-vaunted disorientating 'crisis of representation' within advanced (post) industrial society - a three-fold crisis of ideology (what we believe), ontology (what is happening to society), and epistemology (how we can know about reality) (Chrysanthou, 1998) - a postmodern geography of the commuter contributes only a small part of the jigsaw that is contemporary political culture. This postmodern crisis of knowledge and belief has implications for responses and attitudes to poverty. In a cynical, individualised and disenchanted political culture, poverty is marginalised or, even worse, treated with suspicion or irony within inverted commas ('poverty'). Indeed the affluent commuter may be viewed as the personification of a widespread response to this crisis: While western civilisation might seem to be on the 'Road to Nowhere' (Hebdige, 1988), s/he knows where s/he is going. 'Bereft of coordinates' (Jameson, 1991) in relation to the Grand Map of the Enlightenment, the commuter skilfully navigates his or her well-travelled pathways of this crisis-strewn landscape.

For both Jameson (1988) and Wilkinson (1996), this social and spatial fragmentation cries out for wholeness. Jameson expounds a neo-Marxist aesthetic strategy of 'cognitive mapping' to restore a unified, coherent representation of the political and economic forces underlying the urban geography of poverty and affluence. Wilkinson calls for a more socially cohesive, more equal society through redistributive policies. This chapter has argued (somewhat pessimistically) that one barrier (one among many) to the implementation of either or both these strategies is the differential time-space routines of the affluent and the deprived. These differential pathways - embedded structurally and experientially - reflect and reaffirm the fragmentation and exclusion that anti-poverty strategists wish to overcome.

References

Baldwin, S., Godfrey, C., and Propper, C. (eds) (1990), *Quality of Life - Perspectives and Policies*, Routledge, London.
Baudrillard, J. (1981), *Simulations*, Semiotext(e), New York.
Baudrillard J (1983), *The Shadow of the Silent Minorities; or, the End of the Social and Other Essays*, Semiotext, New York.
Baudrillard, J. (1984), *On Nihilism On the Beach* 6, pp. 38-9.
Baudrillard, J. (1988), *America*, Verso, London.
Baudrillard, J. (1996), *The System of Objects*, Verso, London.
Buttimer, A. and Seamon, D. (eds) (1980), *The Human Experience of Space and Place*, Croom Helm, London.
Carroll, D. and Davey Smith, G. (1997), 'Health and Socio-economic Position - A Commentary', *Journal of Health Psychology* vol. 2, no. 3, pp. 275-82.
Chombard de Lauwe, P.H. (1956), *La vie quotidienne des familles ouvrieres*, Presses Universitaires de France, Paris.
Chrysanthou, M. (1998), 'Mapping the (Post)Modern Population: A Taxonomy of Public Health Research' unpublished paper.
Cooke, P. (1989), *Localities: The Changing Face of Urban Britain*, Unwin Hyman, London.
Day, C. (1990), *Places of the Soul*, Harper Collins, London.
Debord, G. (1970), *Society of the Spectacle*, Black and Red, Detroit.
Donnellan, C. (ed) (1997), *The Future of the Countryside*, Independence, Cambridge.
Etzioni A. (1994), *The Spirit of Community: The Reinvention of American Society*, Simon and Schuster, New York.
Farrow, E. (1990), *The Manchester Travel Survey (Summary Report)*, Greater Manchester Passenger Transport Executive.
Fishman, L. (1987), *BourGeois Utopias: The Rise and Fall of Suburbia*, Basic, New York.
Galbraith, J.K. (1993), *The Culture of Contentment*, Penguin, London.

Geddes, M. (1997), *Partnerships Against Poverty and Exclusion? Local Regeneration Strategies and Excluded Communities in the UK*, Policy Press, Bristol.

Goffman, E. (1963), *Behaviour in Public Places*, Free Press, Glencoe.

Griffiths, J. (1995), 'Life of Strife in the Fast Lane', *The Guardian* (Society Section) 23/8/95 pp. 4-5.

Hall, R.D. (1995), *Inner City Areas: The Same but Different: Area Differences in Manchester*. Unpublished Ph.D. thesis, University of Salford.

Harloe, M., Pickvance, C. and Urry, J. (eds) (1990), *Place, Policy and Politics: Do Localities matter?*, Unwin Hyman, London.

Harre, R. (ed.) (1986), *The Social Construction of Emotions*, Basil Blackwell, Oxford.

Harvey, D. (1989), *The Condition of Postmodernity*, Blackwell, Oxford.

Hebdige, D. (1988), *Hiding in the Light: On Images and Things*, Routledge, London.

Hutton, W. (1995), *The State We're In*, Vintage, London.

International Institute for Labour Studies (1996), *Social exclusion and anti-poverty strategies*, International Labour Office, Geneva.

James, O. (1997), *Britain On the Couch: Treating a Low Serotonin Society*, Century, London.

Jameson, F. (1988), 'Cognitive Mapping' in C. Nelson and L. Grossberg (eds), *Marxism and the Interpretation of Culture*, University of Illinois Press, Urbana.

Jameson, F. (1991), *Postmodernism, or, the Cultural Logic of Late Capitalism*, Verso, London.

Jencks, C. (1993), *Heteropolis: Los Angeles, the Riots and the Strange Beauty of Hetero-Architecture*, Academy Editions, London.

Lasch, C. (1991), *The Culture of Narcissism*, Norton, New York.

Lash, S. and Urry, J. (1987), *The End of Organized Capitalism*, Polity Press, Cambridge.

Lefebvre, H. (1974), *La Production de l'Espace* (English edition, Blackwell, Oxford, 1991).

Levine, D. (ed.) (1992), *Theories of Political Economy*, Cambridge University Press.

Lynch, K. (1960), *The Image of the City*, Massachusetts Institute of Technology, Boston.

Lyotard, J-F. (1984), *The Postmodern Condition*, Manchester University Press, Manchester.

MacIntyre, S., MacIver, S., and Sooman, J. (1993), 'Area, Class and Health: Should we be Focusing on Places or People?', *Journal of Social Policy*, vol. 22, no. 2, pp. 213-34.

McKendrick, J.H. (1997), *The Place of Poverty: Fantasy, Fixation or Fundamental Condition?* (publication forthcoming in *Journal of Poverty*).

Moore, R. and Harrisson, S. (1995), 'In Poor Health: Socio-economic Status and Health Chances - A Review of the Literature', *Social Sciences in Health*, vol. 1, no. 4, pp. 221-35.

Newman, O. (1972), *Defensible Space. Crime Prevention Through Urban Design*, New York, Macmillan.

Oliver *et al*. (1994), *The Foundations of Citizenship*, Harvester Wheatsheaf.

Phillimore, P. (1993), 'How Do Places Shape Health? Rethinking Locality and Lifestyle in North-East England', in S. Platt *et al*. (eds), *Locating Health*, Avebury, Aldershot, pp. 163-178.

Phillimore, P., Beattie, A. and Townsend, P. (1994), 'The Widening Gap. Inequality of Health in Northern England 1981-1991', *British Medical Journal*, vol. 308, no. 11, pp. 25-8.

Philo, C. (ed) (1995), *Off the Map. The Social Geography of Poverty in the UK*, Child Poverty Action Group, London.

Platt, S., Thomas, H., Scott, S. and Williams, G. (eds) (1993), *Locating Health*, Avebury, Aldershot.

Robson, B. (1988), *Those Inner Cities*, Clarendon Press, Oxford.

Rosenau, P.M. (1991), *Post-modernism and the Social Sciences*, Princeton University Press, Princeton.

Ross, K. (1995), *Fast Cars. Clean Bodies*, MIT Press, Cambridge.

Ryle, S. (1996), 'Nobody is coming to the aid of this party', *The Guardian*, 30/12/96, p.12.

Seamon, D. (1980), 'Body-Subject, Time-Space Routines, and Place-Ballets', in A. Buttimer and D. Seamon (eds), *The Human Experience of Space and Place*, Croom Helm, London, pp. 148-65.

Sennett, R. (1993), *The Conscience of the Eye*, Faber, London.

Sennett, R. (1994), *Flesh and Stone: The Body and the City in Western Civilization*, Faber, London.

Shields, R. (1991), *Places on the Margin: Alternative Geographies of Modernity*, Routledge, London.

Simmel, G. (1903), 'The Metropolis and Mental Life', in D. Levine (ed) (1971), *On Individuality and Social Form*, Illinois, Chicago.

Smith, N. (1992), 'Geography, Difference and the Politics of Scale', in J. Doherty., E. Graham and M. Malek (eds), *Postmodernism and the Social Sciences*, Macmillan, London, pp. 57-79.

Soja, E.W. (1989), *Postmodern Geographies: The Reassertion of Space in Critical Theory*, Verso, London.

Stevens, R. (ed) (1993), *Health Inequalities in Manchester in the 1990s*, Manchester City Council: Health for All Working Party.

Taylor, I. (1997), 'Running on Empty', *The Guardian* (Society Section) 14/5/97 pp. 2-3.

Taylor, I., Evans K, Fraser P. (1996), *A Tale of Two Cities*, Routledge, London.

Tocqueville de, A. (1904), *Ancien Regime*, Clarendon Press, Oxford [edited, with introduction and notes by G.W. Headlam].

Virilio, P. (1986), *Speed and Politics*, Semiotext(e), New York.

Virilio, P. (1991), *The Aesthetics of Disappearance*, Semiotext(e), New York.

Warde, A. (1989), 'Recipe for a Pudding: A Comment on Locality', *Antipode*, vol. 21, no. 3, pp. 274-81.

Wilkinson, R.G. (1996), *Unhealthy Societies - the Afflictions of Inequality*, Routledge, London.

While, A.E. (ed.) (1989), *Health in the Inner City*, Heinemann, Oxford.

Whitelegg, J. (1997), *Critical Mass : Transport, Environment and Society in the 21st Century*, Pluto, London.

Wolf, W. (1996), *Car Mania*, Pluto Press, London.

7 Examining the Relationship Between Material Conditions, Long-Term Problematic Drug Misuse and Social Exclusion: A New Strategy for Social Inclusion

JULIAN BUCHANAN and LEE YOUNG

Introduction

The intention of this paper is to examine the relationship between material conditions, long-term problematic drug misuse and social exclusion. It is the contention of the authors that, the issue of drug misuse, which many people see as one of the most serious social issues facing society, has been neglected as an area of interest for social scientists, one of the main reasons being, that drug addiction tends to be conceptualised as a medical problem, with social factors seen as peripheral. Whilst not ignoring the important contribution of medicine in the treatment and rehabilitation of drug addiction, this paper challenges the assumption that drug misuse is solely due to physiological or psychological pathology, the so-called 'addictive personality'.

Using the quantitative and qualitative data gained from structured interviews on Merseyside, England with 200 drug users between 1995-1997, the research examines the correlation between poverty, social exclusion and problematic drug use and suggests there is a relationship between:

- Structural changes in the 1980s' labour market
- The onset of large scale and long-term structural unemployment
- Widespread deprivation and poverty; and the
- Emergence of long term problematic drug misuse on a major national scale.

For the purposes of this paper, the term problematic drug misuse is used to refer primarily to heroin 'addiction'. Although drug misusers use various types of drugs, heroin was the primary drug of choice for the majority of young people in the mid-1980s (Pearson, 1987). It is significant that heroin is used clinically as a 'pain killer' (ISDD, 1991). When taken recreationally it gives users an initial sense of euphoria ('rush'), followed by a feeling of well being as all emotional, social and physical pain is numbed. Choosing a drug that kills pain is indicative of the social, economic and political circumstances that prevailed in the early to mid 1980s (Buchanan and Wyke, 1987). This generation of young people, their labour power no longer required, were victims of the Thatcherite revolution, in which they found themselves socially and economically excluded from the benefits of an apparently affluent society. The disturbing impact is highlighted by Stewart *et al.*:

> the mass youth unemployment for which the decades of the 1980s and 1990s will be historically famous, has eroded social restraints against offending and engendered a feeling of cynical apathy about the possibility of any kind of legitimate self improvement.
> (Stewart *et al.*, 1994, p.102)

Social and Economic Context

Although certainly not unique in 1990s Britain, Merseyside does to some extent represent graphically the legacy of nearly two decades of Thatcherite economic and social policy 'reforms'. Merseyside has been designated 'Objective One' status by the European Union, highlighting the serious social and economic decline the area has suffered. This is an acknowledgement that the region contains some of the poorest communities in Europe, with domestic product per head of population (one of the most significant indicators of poverty) falling below the European average. Merseyside is the only region in the UK to be designated as such.

As might be expected, the region contains many of the indicators normally associated with communities under stress – infrastructural dereliction, shrinking economic base, significant levels of long-term ill health and unemployment, poverty, crime and widespread problematic drug misuse (Liverpool City Council, 1991). Indeed, Home Office records shows that since the mid-1980s, Merseyside has regularly recorded the highest number of notified drug 'addicts' in the United Kingdom per head of population (Home Office, 1987-97).

Doctors are required to 'notify' the Home Office when they are treating an individual for drug addiction.

At the time of Mrs Thatcher's election in 1979 there were just over 1.2 million people registered unemployed in the United Kingdom (Timmins, 1995). Indeed, under Labour during '74-79, unemployment had reached a post-war high and the Tories had used the fear of unemployment as an effective election winning strategy. The point should not be lost, however, that the Labour Party were still committed in 1979 to a policy of full employment. In an effort to ameliorate the scourge of rising unemployment, the Labour Government introduced a number of measures such as the Temporary Employment Subsidy, the Job Release Scheme and the Youth Opportunities Programme. It is estimated that in 1978 such schemes were providing employment for some 400,000 people and at the time of their electoral defeat in 1979 unemployment was actually falling (*Ibid.,* 1996).

Once elected Mrs Thatcher, intent on reducing inflation, jettisoned the policy of full employment in favour of economic liberalism and began restructuring the welfare state, as a consequence unemployment rates soared to over three million by the early 1980s (Gallie *et al.,* 1995). In less than three years the policies of the Conservative Government were responsible for more than two million workers finding themselves as surplus to economic requirements. It should be noted, moreover, that these figures were the official headline rates and given that the Conservative government changed the definition of unemployment on 33 occasions (Oppenheim and Harker, 1996, p.48) the real rate of unemployment was possibly much higher.

The distribution of unemployment was not evenly spread either between or within regions. Areas that relied heavily on manufacturing industries such as shipbuilding, steel production, heavy engineering and coal mining – once the wealth producers of the nineteenth century, now found themselves blighted with severe employment shortages. With little regard for the social consequences, many of these industries were sold off to private enterprise or closed down. For places like Merseyside, with a reliance on such industries, New Right economic policy resulted in the loss of thousands of jobs, and many people became long-term unemployed. In the period 1981-91 Merseyside saw an overall 16 per cent loss of jobs, and by 1991 six electoral wards in Liverpool recorded levels of unemployment in excess of 31 per cent (Liverpool City Council, 1993). For some sections of Merseyside, then, the economic situation since the late 1970s has been, and remains, desperate with little sign of any upturn. Whole communities are without work, as industries have closed or been relocated.

Indeed, some people now in their mid 20s have never known full-time permanent employment since leaving school - a position apparently well understood by the present government:

> There is no more dreadful testimony to the last decade and a half than the position of the young unemployed and never employed. The lost generation is adrift from the working population, with no stake in society.
> (Straw and Michael, 1996)

In addition, to suffering this ignominy, those excluded from employment have seen their meagre living standards further eroded as welfare benefits have been reduced (Becker, 1991). Indeed, since 1988, many young people have had their benefits reduced or withdrawn completely. Life, for the majority of these people, resembles the 'solitary, poor, nasty, brutish and short' world described by 17th century philosopher Thomas Hobbes, Leviathan, 1651.

Heroin: An Alternative to Unemployment?

This depressing picture as a result of the Thatcherite programme has been imposed at a colossal social cost, in which 'society is dividing before our eyes opening up new social fissures' (Hutton, 1996, p.106). It is the backdrop against which those between 18-30 years of age have progressed from youth to adulthood. It is a bleak picture of despair with few opportunities available to improve ones life chances. Many of these people are victims of a set of economic and social policies that have no need for their labour, and regard them as surplus to requirements. Not only are they denied any opportunity to earn a living, the State also castigates them for being in such circumstances, labelling them as 'workshy', 'scroungers' and 'cheats'. Faced with such a hostile environment many young people in the early to mid-1980s turned to heroin as a means of blocking out the pain of an existence without opportunity or hope. Merseyside experienced epidemic proportions of problematic drug misuse (Newcombe and Parker, 1991). Sadly, writing in 1998, and in spite of the ubiquitous 'regeneration' strategies, for many people the situation shows little improvement with drug use and drug problems still increasing.

Right wing politicians and academics (Murray, 1996 and Dennis, 1997) have labelled drugs users, along with many other victims of the social and economic policies of the Thatcher era, as an 'underclass'. This thesis, a reworking of the 'cycle of deprivation' theory espoused by Sir Keith Joseph in the 1970s (Holman, 1975), suggests that an over generous post war welfare state was responsible for creating 'deviant' sub-cultures. Having rejected wider societal norms and values, these people are said to prefer a life of welfare benefits, criminal activity and anti-social behaviour. Within the confines of this paper it is not possible to debate the underclass thesis which the authors strongly reject. It is acknowledge however that many victims of the Thatcherite economic revolution - problematic drug misusers included - have through economic and social necessity developed alternative survival strategies.

Excluded from a shrinking labour market, for these people the chance of finding work is minuscule. Work gives people the opportunity to meet their needs, to satisfy their wants and have a personal identity and social status within a network of relationships (Commission for Social Justice, 1994). Denied this opportunity most problematic drug users have become part of an elaborate and well developed alternative economy involving petty crime and minor drug dealing. Having experienced poverty and deprivation for almost two decades, this alternative economy has become a major source of income and exchange of goods within deprived communities. The sale and purchase of stolen goods, is the only way that many families are able to partake in the trappings of an affluent society. It will require a major shift in social and economic policy to counteract this alternative economy.

Far from being lazy or workshy, problematic drug misusers work surprisingly hard to secure their daily supply of drugs. The need for heroin provides routine, purpose, structure, stress, rewards and most important of all it occupies the hours of each day. Figure 7.1 below describes the daily cycle of a typical problematic drug user.

1. The person wakes up anxious, concerned about generating sufficient funds, usually around £50-80 worth of heroin is needed to get them 'sorted'.
2. Without access to opiates they will begin to experience withdrawal symptoms of sickness, stomach cramps, aches and sweating, referred to as 'turkeying'.
3. The person 'plans' for the day ahead providing him or her with a focus.
4. The person goes out 'grafting', a euphemism for stealing. Many hundreds of pounds worth of goods will need to be stolen each day.
5. The stolen goods are sold at a fraction of their true value, often to people living in impoverished communities.

6. With cash in hand they seek a place to purchase heroin, - referred to as going to 'score'.
7. Once they have acquired a wrap of heroin they enjoy the pleasures of their hard work.
8. At this point having taken heroin the person will be able to sleep and rest.

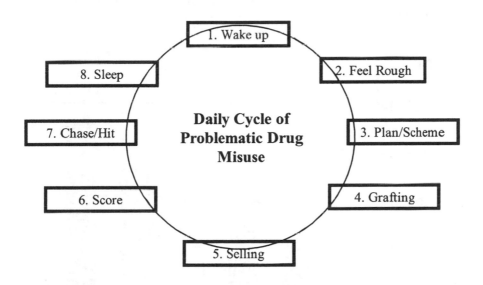

Figure 7.1   Daily cycle of problematic drug misuse

In many respects this daily routine provides similar experiences found in a demanding job – routine, purpose, goals, skills, identity, stresses and rewards. It occupies the hours of each day that would otherwise be mundane in comparison. The person can feel a sense of satisfaction at the end of the day having achieved what they set out to do, and like most people who work hard they appreciate the pleasures and rewards for their efforts. However, drug users are also driven by fear to continue this ritual. Unless they acquire opiates on a daily basis, they will suffer severe physiological and psychological withdrawal symptoms, leading to painful and sleepless nights.

This alternative existence is not confined to people who began taking drugs in the mid 1980s. Structural inequalities, lack of opportunities and poverty has continued to blight large sections of society and the number of people using drugs continues to increase, to the extent that drugs are becoming more readily available and part of youth culture generally. The British Crime Survey in 1996 identified nearly one in two of those aged between 16-29 years of age have at some point in their life, tried a prohibited drug (Home Office, 1997a). Clearly, the drug problem has become a major social issue, which is now permeating all sections of society. Home Office data (Home Office, 1997b) graphically illustrates the extent of the growing drugs problem in the United Kingdom.

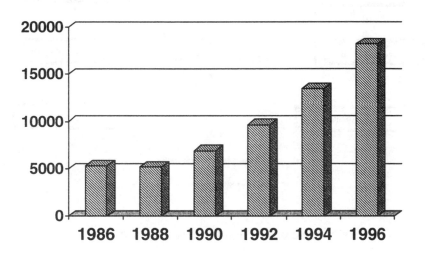

Figure 7.2   Number of new notifications of drug addicts to the Home Office, 1986-1996

Since the emergence of the heroin 'epidemic' the number of **new** 'addicts' has risen sharply since 1990. The total number of 'addicts' registered (new and re-notifications) has also shown a similar upward trend from 24,703 people in 1992, to 43,372 in 1996 (Home Office,1997b). Furthermore, the figures below indicate the growing number of individuals cautioned or found guilty for drug defined offences, again with a sharp rise from 1992 onwards. By 1995 the number of people cautioned or found guilty had risen to 93,631 (Home Office, 1997c).

Number of people cautioned or found guilty or dealt with for drug defined offences (Home Office, 1997c)	
1986	23895
1987	26278
1988	30.515
1989	38.415
1990	44922
1991	47616
1992	48927
1993	68480
1994	85691
1995	93631

Figure 7.3   Number of people cautioned or found guilty or dealt with for drug defined offences (Home Office, 1997c)

Profiling the Long Term Drug User on Merseyside, England

This section examines the relationship between social exclusion, poverty, and drug misuse. The findings, based upon quantitative and qualitative data, are gained from three separate research studies (Goldson *et al.,* 1995; Buchanan and Young, 1996; Buchanan and Young, 1998) carried out on Merseyside between 1995-1997. Of the 200 people interviewed, 134 men and 66 women, more than half were over 26 years old. Ninety nine per cent of the sample were currently unemployed. Only nine of the 200 interviewed identified themselves as black, this reflects the under representation of black people within drug services (Goldson *et al.,* 1995, p.19).

Heroin was identified as the main drug of addiction. Fifty-five per cent defined their drug use as stable and in control, a further 18 per cent said they were now drug free, while only 27 per cent of these long term problem drug users described their drug misuse as chaotic and out of control. This data challenges the image of all problem drug users being out of control and unable to function 'normally'. The majority of people had been taking illegal drugs for seven to 13 years, and therefore began their drug career between 1983 and 1989. This correlates with the 'drug epidemic' which became apparent in the mid-1980s. It is perhaps surprising that over 30 per cent began their drug career pre-1983 and continue to seek help. In the most recent study (Buchanan and Young, 1998) the average age of the drug misusers was 30 years old with an average length of drug use of 12 years, and therefore began using drugs in 1985. This again correlates with the time when opiate use became endemic to most major cities in the United Kingdom.

Some experts in the drug field have spoken about a ten-year drug misuse 'career cycle' - after which time drug misusers grow out of a drug centred existence and return to 'mainstream' society. These findings seriously question whether the notion of a ten-year cycle has relevance to today's drug misusers. In the 1960s it might have been possible for drug users to return to previous occupations, interests or lifestyles. However, the drug misusers involved in this research generally have no previous work experience to return to, and few if any, viable options are available to them. Faced with these circumstances it is difficult to see how drug misusers can gain access to mainstream opportunities.

Education is at the outset, a key factor in enabling individuals to have access to a wider range of opportunities. Significantly, 47 per cent of the research sample (n=200) did not continue their education beyond the age of fifteen. Furthermore 52 per cent of the sample have gained no qualifications, educational or vocational. Similar patterns emerge from research involving young offenders aged 17, 20 and 23 in 1991, 80 per cent left school without any qualifications, while15 per cent of the 23 year olds had never had a job (Stewart and Stewart, 1993). It is also interesting to note that the 1997 DfEE performance tables for Secondary Schools in England and Wales (DfEE Web Site, 1998) indicated that only 8 per cent of pupils failed to achieved at least one GCSE grade A* to G. This suggests that for the research sample, the process of social exclusion began a number of years before they started using drug. This exclusion continued into employment, with 14 per cent of the sample having never had a job, 54 per cent of the sample had been unemployed for more than five years.

It is argued that these people have been subject to marginalisation and exclusion prior to becoming drug users. However, once a drug using identity is ascribed, a process of stigmatisation, marginalisation and exclusion is initiated by wider society. This is legitimised by government policy that portrays drug users as an 'enemy within' and wages a 'war on drugs'. This sadly often results on a war on drug users (Ashton, 1992). This process is described in the following diagram:

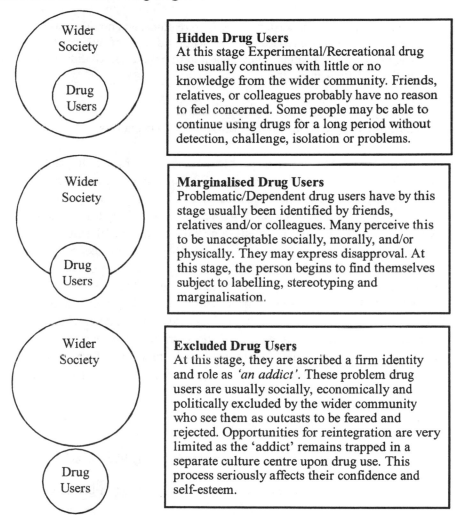

Hidden Drug Users
At this stage Experimental/Recreational drug use usually continues with little or no knowledge from the wider community. Friends, relatives, or colleagues probably have no reason to feel concerned. Some people may be able to continue using drugs for a long period without detection, challenge, isolation or problems.

Marginalised Drug Users
Problematic/Dependent drug users have by this stage usually been identified by friends, relatives and/or colleagues. Many perceive this to be unacceptable socially, morally, and/or physically. They may express disapproval. At this stage, the person begins to find themselves subject to labelling, stereotyping and marginalisation.

Excluded Drug Users
At this stage, they are ascribed a firm identity and role as *'an addict'*. These problem drug users are usually socially, economically and politically excluded by the wider community who see them as outcasts to be feared and rejected. Opportunities for reintegration are very limited as the 'addict' remains trapped in a separate culture centre upon drug use. This process seriously affects their confidence and self-esteem.

Figure 7.4   The marginalisation and exclusion of drug users

The distinct position and outlook of problem drug users who regularly use opiates was highlighted in a research report by Demos (Joseph Rowntree Foundation, 1997) which stated they:

> are generally more isolated than young recreational and non-drug users. Their comments emphasised a lack of close friends, a distrust of authority figures and feelings of stigmatisation. They appeared to have a less confident and more fatalistic outlook than others.

Developing a Strategy for Inclusion: A User Perspective

The issues that face long term problematic drug users are the same issues facing the long-term unemployed. The difference being, that drug users are subject to double discrimination and exclusion. Tackling this major social issue of exclusion is an enormous task that requires attention at a multiplicity of levels. No one single approach or strategy will prove to be 'the answer'. When fifty drug users themselves were asked what they felt they needed, interesting results emerged (Buchanan and Young, 1996). Three quarters of the sample expressed an interest in doing an educational course. The most popular choice being Basic Adult Education closely followed by English, Sociology and Psychology. These subjects possibly reflect a desire to understand and explore their own life experience as well as equip them better to engage in society. When asked why they chose these options, their statements illustrated the need to prove themselves, to be successful at something, and to be seen as capable in some way:

> It's something positive to show my child.

> I didn't really get anything from school so I'd really like another try.

> It would let me do things I've always been interested in but never had the chance.

> To prove to myself that I can do it.

Ninety-four per cent expressed an interest in recreational activities with netball, photography, snooker, football, stock car racing, outdoor pursuits and swimming being the activities most favoured. Interestingly, many of these activities are readily accessible in local communities, but the findings of the research indicate that drug users lack confidence and feel inhibited approaching organisations or groups of non-drug users.

Ninety-eight per cent expressed an interest in participating in a vocational training course. Catering, painting and decorating, hairdressing and furniture construction and restoration being the most preferred courses. Their aspirations are modest. They are practical courses that would provide them with some basics skills, which could be used informally within their local community, if they were unable to secure proper employment.

When asked what might prevent them from participating in educational, recreational or training courses they identified a range of factors:

Blockages to Progress

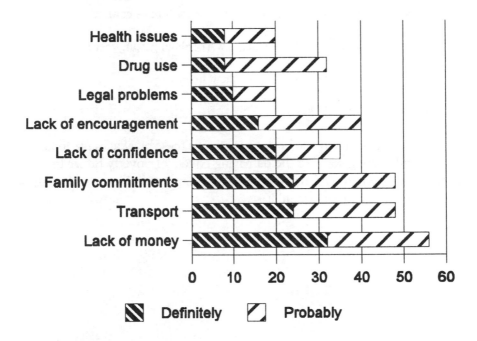

Figure 7.5 Blockages to progress

It might have been expected that drug misuse itself would have been the major problem, or indeed health related issues, however, the chart above indicates that it is issues related to poverty (finance, transport and family commitments) that pose the greatest hindrance to progress. It is interesting to note that the major 'blockage' is said to be a lack of money, when drug users themselves obtain a considerable amount of income through criminal activity. However, it would appear that problematic drug misusers regard the money they obtain through crime, solely as a means of satisfying their addiction. The shortage of money therefore, should be understood not simply as a financial issue, but an expression of the lack of opportunity to earn a legitimate income. The exclusion from the employment market also denies these people a 'normal' existence. Other factors such as a lack of encouragement and a lack of confidence could be seen as associated factors that are often the symptom of systemic marginalisation. The least problematic factors are those more likely to be directly associated with drug taking (legal, drugs and health issues). Comments from the drug users illustrate these points:

> It doesn't matter about anything else if you don't have confidence.

> If I had a bus pass I wouldn't need to worry about getting there.

> It is difficult to start these things without help.

> Dinner money would help.

When asked what could be done to remove these blockages the focus was again on alleviating some of the damaging effects of poverty rather than any major focus upon drug misuse. The need for finance, confidence and transport were highlighted as issues to address.

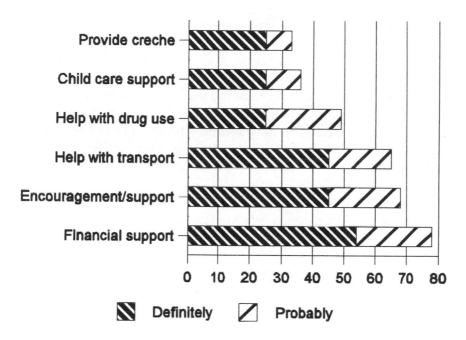

Figure 7.6   **Removing or lessening the blockages to progress**

When asked about what may assist them to stop using drugs, the sample mentioned employment more than any other option. Denied the opportunity of employment, their time was largely spent, watching television (36 per cent), or 'looking after the kids' (30 per cent), nearly two-thirds said that they would rather spend this time in paid employment. When asked about the notion of a structured day programme, to facilitate access to educational, vocational and recreational opportunities, each person interviewed believed it would have a significant impact in assisting in the process of rehabilitation and social inclusion.

It'll get people motivated to get up and do things.

There is nothing to do in the Bootle area for drug users or other young people.

Users need a higher profile, people need to be shown that (methadone) users can do the same things as others.

Second Chance Structured Day Programme

Following user led research (Goldson *et al.,* 1995), the Second Chance Structured day programme for recovering drug users was established in Liverpool city centre. The authors of this paper were commissioned to assess the impact of the programme upon the lives of the drug users and to provide ongoing action research. The study was undertaken between September 1995 and August 1997. The twelve week programme at Second Chance consists of the following:

- 6 week Vocational Module
- 4 week Personal Development Module
- 2 week Moving On Module

The research process comprised of in-depth interviews, at strategically identified points, with the aim of tracking a student's progress over a period of twelve months:

1. Six months prior to starting the programme
2. At the start of the programme;
3. At the completion of the programme
4. Follow-up interview three months after completing the programme.

In total one hundred students were interviewed over a two-year period. Of these 58 were available at the completion point. Twenty-two of these students were followed up three months after leaving Second Chance. Each student was asked the same set of questions on each occasion and asked to comment upon their development in relation to a number of pre-defined areas; Relationships, Confidence and Self-Esteem, Offending, Drug Use, Health, and Aspirations. In addition to qualitative comments, quantitative data was obtained using a five-point satisfaction rating: 0 (very poor), 25 (poor), 50 (okay), 75 (good) and 100 (very good). A summary of the finding are as follows;

Relationships

Thirty-six people who had children indicated a substantial improvement in their relationships with their children from an average satisfaction rating of 67 per cent at point of entry to an impressive 89 per cent rating at the point of completion. This was the greatest improvement achieved in any area measured during the period of the twelve-week programme. Potentially this has implications for agencies concerned to improve the quality of parent - child relationships.

> Since I've come here I've started to help my oldest with her homework and I'm reading to my youngest which I haven't done for a long time.

Confidence and Self Esteem

Prior to starting the programme students lacked confidence and felt less than 'okay' (44 per cent) when approaching a person who doesn't use illegal drugs. Encouragingly this had progressed to an average 69 per cent satisfaction rating at point of completion. The difficulty students' sense is well portrayed in the following comment;

> It is difficult you feel divorced from the mainstream, I want to get back into it.

Offending

The likelihood of drug related offending (100 per cent = highly likely) dropped significantly during the course of the programme in relation to theft and or deception. The average likelihood of offending was 35 per cent prior to entry. This dropped to 11 per cent at point of completion, and further to zero at the three month follow-up stage.

> I've changed dramatically. I've realised how far out of character it was for me. I'd have to start very heavy use to fall back into that.

Drug Use

Substantial improvement occurred in the expectations of students in respect of their desire and capacity to be drug free in twelve months time. Prior to entry it stood at 40 per cent (100 per cent = Highly Likely) and continued to increase at every stage to an average 85 per cent at the three month follow up stage.

It's my target. I understand that I can't continue to use heroin and get back into the mainstream. I'm getting older and I don't want to end up on the scrap heap.

It's given me a sense of focus. You need a reason to be drug free. You have a higher chance of employment.

Health

Students recorded improvements in relation to all aspects of health; *sleeping pattern, diet, weight and fitness*. The most impressive improvement was in respect of sleeping patterns which recorded a considerable and steady improvement from an average 36 per cent satisfaction rating to an average 63 per cent at the follow up stage. The following students' comments illustrate the process of improvement;

I was going to bed at dawn and getting up at midday and I was speeding all night. (prior)

It's got better as my health has improved. (start)

Good since I've been coming here, you get into a routine. (finish)

Aspirations

When caught up in a drug centred lifestyle the students had very little aspiration or expectations for themselves. However, this improved significantly as soon as they began at *Second Chance*. When asked how highly (100 per cent = very highly) they rated their ability and expectations of being able to 'hold down' a job the figure rose steadily throughout from a starting point of 32 per cent, to an eventual score of 83 per cent at the follow up stage. For many, new opportunities and developments increased confidence and opened new doors;

I came here to get my life sorted and I have done that plus I've got voluntary work with homeless people and I may get a job out of it and I've started a basic counselling course.

The detailed findings show that the vast majority of students reported improvements in virtually all areas of their lives as a direct result of taking part in *Second Chance*. Moreover, although 'getting a job' was the ultimate objective in taking part in *Second Chance* all students were realistic in their aspirations and appreciated their involvement in the programme was only the first of many more steps, towards achieving this objective. Confidence and self-esteem are crucial to this process and it is clear that *Second Chance* has a significant impact in this area of the students' lives. Indeed, in the three-month (post-programme) follow-up interviews, it was shown that confidence and self-esteem continued on an upward trajectory. This is a considerable achievement given the low starting point for the majority of students. The importance of this issue was highlighted in research carried out by Angela Devlin who interviewed people in prison to explore the relationship between social disadvantage and offending. In her conclusion she emphasised: *'The importance of praise and the fostering of self esteem cannot be over estimated'*. (Devlin, 1995, p.178)

Having spent three months at *Second Chance* a number of common themes emerged that illustrate an increased confidence, a stability and direction in life, an awareness of new opportunities, and a motivation to continue to progress:

*   47 per cent of students who completed specifically valued the positive contribution of the staff. A number of students were clearly impressed by the way in which they were treated with respect as fellow human beings and not as 'drug users'.

*   48 per cent of students made comments which illustrated that they valued the impact of the programme in regenerating their confidence, inspiring trust, developing social skills, relationships, hope and social integration.

*   31 per cent of the students appreciated the structure of the programme as it gave them a clear focus and order to their lives. This is an indication of their lack of involvement in mainstream social structures.

Students had a realistic notion of the limited chances of employment, but still tended to believe that attending *Second Chance* had to some extent made them more employable. *Second Chance* facilitated and enabled students to feel more confident, to have a sense of achievement, and to begin looking forward to a future not dictated or constrained by drugs. This is no mean feat, and provides a successful model for engaging with this serious social problem. Whilst it would be too much to expect such programmes to eradicate poverty, nevertheless, they are an important part of the strategy to address the issue of social exclusion. Only then, will it be possible for students to begin to socially integrate and take advantage of opportunities to improve their material conditions and quality of life. These issues are vital as they reflect the marginalisation and social exclusion experienced by the vast majority of problem drug users. There is therefore, a need for values that promote a socially inclusive society, rather than those that have divided society. This has been recognised by Vivien Stern who has long been promoting the rights and needs of offenders:

> Whilst the numbers of the socially excluded grow, the structures that exist to re-integrate them into society are being weakened. (Stern, 1996, p.15)

Strategies for Inclusion

Interestingly, while it is generally assumed that exclusion from the social, economic and cultural life of the community is a direct consequence of having become a problematic drug misuser, the research indicates that for the majority of the students interviewed, this process of social exclusion began prior to taking illegal drugs. Long-term drug use may be a response to social exclusion rather than the reason for their social exclusion. The major structural changes that have taken place in the labour market since the late 1970s, have effectively excluded this section of society from the economic activity and life of the community. The qualitative comments from students in the sample suggest that the long term impact of this dislocation has led to a negative internalised identity, epitomised by low self esteem, isolation, a lack of confidence and low expectations.

> I never even had the confidence to come to town before.

> They [wider society] look down on me as scum of the earth and as someone not to be associated with.

> No prospects for someone like me, I gave up years ago thinking I could get a job, I might as well reach for the moon.

These findings indicate that a strong relationship exists between a negative educational experience, limited educational achievement, and a lack of job opportunities, long term unemployment, poverty and problematic drug use. '*Steps to Reintegration*' outlines the phases and difficulties that drug-users experience in their attempts to reintegrate back into the wider non-drug using community. Importantly, it also shows the role and importance of structured day programmes, like *Second Chance*, in breaking this cycle as few agencies work at this level with a particular focus and understanding of the needs of long term drug users.

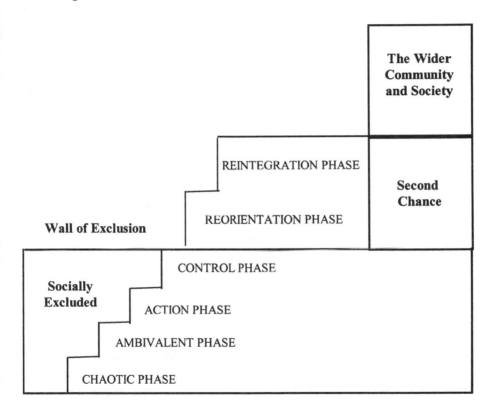

Figure 7.7   Steps to reintegration

Phases

1. *Chaotic:* The person has little insight and no real desire to change their pattern of drug taking.
2. *Ambivalent*: The person sometimes expresses some motivation to change their pattern of drug taking but quickly relapses to 'old' habits and thoughts;
3. *Action:* The person is clear about their future direction and makes a determined and positive effort to do something about their drug use.
4. *Control:* The person becomes stable and in control of their drug taking, they may even stop taking illegal drugs completely.

This process can for some people take many years with relapse occurring frequently at any phase in the process. However, having achieved the 'Control Phase' recovering drug users seek and need, reintegration in wider society but are usually prevented from gaining access, and are denied opportunities that are available to others. This discriminatory process can be described as a Wall of Exclusion. It is reinforced externally by societal prejudice and discrimination against drug users, who are publicly portrayed as the social enemy consisting of addicts, muggers, and burglars who are devious, dangerous, potentially violent people not to be trusted. When asked how they thought others saw them students commented;

People think you're scum.

They thought I was dirt.

They would look at me in disgust.

So strong and pervasive is this oppressive stereotype that the identity has, to some extent, become internalised and has led to a lack of confidence, low self-esteem, low expectations and a real deficit in terms of marketable skills.

By providing an empowering environment structured day programmes can support students through the difficult and challenging Reorientation Phase which enables students to develop qualifications, skills, self-knowledge and a belief in themselves as human beings with value and worth. Many Second Chance students appreciated the opportunity to develop social relationships for the first time in many years. They find this a refreshing change from what they describe as 'acquaintances' whose only real interest was in the 'substance' rather than the person. At Second Chance this rediscovery of social relationships involves facing up to emotions, recognising responsibilities, becoming accountable and learning to trust and be trusted, by others. It also involves experiencing acceptance, respect and trust which has for too long been denied to those labelled 'addicts'. Peter McDermott a writer and researcher on drug matters has first hand experience when he states;

> I can personally assure you that no matter how stable you are, or how useful your activism is, once you are 'outed' you will experience serious discrimination that can be very difficult to overcome. (McDermott, 1997, p.10)

Recovering drug users in this research, have shown a desire to constructively participate in society and engage in 'normal' every day activities from which they have largely been excluded. While major structural factors need tackling at a national level, structured day programmes like Second Chance do provide a new and important strategy to begin the process of social inclusion at a local level. Tony Blair recognised 'The most meaningful stake anyone can have in society is the ability to earn a living and support a family'. (Blair, 1996, p.11)

Conclusion

There are lessons to be learnt from the past two decades that have left many citizens with little or no opportunity to participate in society. The fragmentation of social cohesion is the most disturbing outcome of the major structural changes that took place under Thatcherism. Large sections of society were economically and therefore socially excluded. In the 1980s many young people, particularly non-academic school leavers, faced the prospect of life long unemployment, boredom and poverty. These are the circumstances in which heroin addiction reached epidemic proportions in the mid 1980s. Sadly, little has changed as the millennium approaches.

The majority of students who took part in this research were the young heroin users of the mid 1980s who have been socially excluded for most of their adult life. Attending Second Chance therefore, was for them a 'First Chance' to gain access to opportunities, and prove their capability to themselves, their families and the wider community. Significantly, the certificate they received for successfully completing the Second Chance programme was for many their first formal qualification. Recently, increasing recognition has been given to the need for the reintegration of excluded sections of the population. The Kennedy Report on further education suggested the Government should make a major shift in policy to focus upon the educational needs of people who left school with little or no qualifications (Kennedy, 1997). The important contribution then, of structured day programmes should not be understated, they play a crucial role in enabling marginalised groups to take up educational, training and employment opportunities. Without such programmes many of these people would not be in any position to participate in the governments 'welfare to work' initiatives, due to the corrosive impact that long-term social exclusion has had upon their confidence, self-esteem and identity. As one student acclaimed;

> It's the best thing that ever happened to me. It's a starting point for life without drugs.

* Second Chance is now called Transit.

References

Ashton, M. (1992), *Release White Paper on Reform of Drugs Laws*, Release Publications, London.

Becker, S. (ed.) (1991), *Windows of Opportunity: Public Policy and the Poor*, CPAG, London.

Blair, T. (1996), 'Battle for Britain' in *The Guardian*, 29th January 1996.

Bootle Maritime City Challenge (1993), *Baseline Monitoring Report,* Sefton MBC Economic Development Unit.

Buchanan, J. and Wyke, G. (1987), 'Drug Abuse, Probation Practice and the Specialist Worker', *Probation Journal*, vol. 34, no. 4, December, London, NAPO, pp. 123-26.

Buchanan, J. and Young, L. (1996), *Drugs Relapse Prevention: Giving Users a Voice*, Bootle Maritime City Challenge.

Buchanan, J. and Young, L. (1998), *The Impact of the Second Chance Structured Day Programme for Recovering Drug Users: A Student Perspective*, Social Partnership, Transit, Liverpool.

Commission for Social Justice (1994), *Social Justice: Strategies for National Renewal*, Vintage Press, London.

Dennis, N. (1997), *The Invention of Permanent Poverty*, Institute of Economic Affairs, London.

Devlin, A. (1995), *Criminal Classes*, Waterside Press, Winchester.

DfEE Web Site (1998), Performance Tables 1997 GCSE, www.open.gov.uk/dfee/dfeehome.htm.

Gallie D., Marsh, C. and Vogler, C. (eds) (1995), *Social Change and the Experience of Unemployment*, Oxford University Press, Oxford.

Goldson, B., Kennedy, J. and Young, L. (1995), *Second Chance Opportunities: A Service Users Perspective*, Liverpool Drug Prevention Initiative, Liverpool.

Holman, R (1975), 'Poverty: Consensus and Alternatives', in E. Butterworth and R. Holman (eds), *Social Welfare in Modern Britain*, Fontana/Collins, Glasgow.

Home Office (1987-97), Home Office Statistical Bulletin, Statistics of Drug Addicts Notified to the Home Office, United Kingdom, Government Statistical Service, London.

Home Office (1997a), *Study No.172 Drug Misuse Declared in 1996:latest results from the BCS*, London, Home Office.

Home Office (1997b), *Home Office Statistical Bulletin*, London, Government Statistical Service.

Home Office (1997c), *Statistics of Drug Seizures and Offenders Dealt With, United Kingdom, 1995 Supplementary Tables*, Government Statistical Service, London.

Hutton, W. (1996), *The State We're In*, Vintage Press, London.

ISDD (1991), *Drug Abuse Briefing,* Institute for the Study of Drug Dependence, London.

Joseph Rowntree Foundation (1997), *Findings Social Policy Research 133*, November 1997, Joseph Rowntree Foundation, York.

Kennedy, H. (1997), 'Learning Works' Report of the Kennedy Committee on Further Education.

Liverpool City Council (1991), *Liverpool Quality of Life Survey*, Corporate Policy and Information Unit, Liverpool.

Liverpool City Council (1993), *Census Key Statistics, Liverpool Wards,* Liverpool, Central Policy Unit, Liverpool.

McDermott (1997), 'Will Drug Users Respond to the Challenge' in *Drug Edition*, Issue 12, March 1997, Release, London.

Murray, C. (1996), *Charles Murray and the Underclass: The Developing Debate*, Institute of Economic Affairs, London.

Newcombe, R. and Parker, H. (1991), *Drug Misuse in Wirral: An Endemic Problem?* A Report for the Wirral Home Office Drug Prevention Team (unpublished).

Oppenheim, C. and Harker, L. (1996), *Poverty the Facts*, 3rd edition, Child Poverty Action Group, London.

Pearson ,G. (1987), *The New Heroin Users*, Basil Blackwell, Oxford.

Stern, V. (1996), 'Let the ex-cons back in' in *The Guardian,* 2nd May 1996.

Stewart, J., Smith, D., Stewart, G. with Fullwood, C. (1994), *Understanding Offending Behaviour*, Longman Press, London.

Stewart, G. and Stewart, J. (1993), *Social Circumstances of Younger Offenders Under Supervision*, ACOP, London.

Straw, J. and Michael, A. (1996), *Tackling the Causes of Crime*, October 1996, Home Office, London.

Timmins, N. (1995), *The Five Giants: A Biography of the Welfare State*, Fontana Press, London.

8 Material Deprivation Amongst Ethnic Minority and White Children: The Evidence of the Sample of Anonymised Records

ROBERT MOORE

Introduction

The black population is small and unevenly distributed, thus the surveys that have provided the traditional base for poverty studies have not picked up enough black people for a systematic analysis of their condition (Mack and Lansley, 1984; PSI, 1992). The *Labour Force Survey* (LFS), by contrast, is rich in data on employment, education, training and income, in addition it identifies respondents by ethnic group. Because the numbers of minority respondents in any one LFS are small, Haskey's studies of the minority populations (1988, 1990, 1991) were based on LFS data aggregated over three surveys. The 1990 study produced a total sample of just under 153,279 people, of whom 6,994 were from ethnic minorities and 4,936 recorded as West Indian, Indian, Pakistani or Bangladeshi. Of all the minority groups 2,238 were young people under the age of 15. Therefore we have excellent data on the economic circumstances of households but a relatively small sample of ethnic minority children. Tate (1997) describes the LFS as:

> a particularly good (and sometimes the only practical) source of household and family data on smaller population subgroups, for example ethnic minorities. (1997, p.90)

In the LFS children are treated as part of households and it is not clear from Tate's account whether children could be made the subject of a study based upon the LFS.

Many of the same points may be made about the *General Household Survey* (GHS). Lynda Clarke (1992) used aggregated data from the GHS to get a sample of 17,971 children but if they were disaggregated this would generate a minority sample of under 2,000 children and only the Indian and Pakistani samples would exceed 300. Clarke found 116,735 children in the Longitudinal Study (LS) and her sample was not divided by ethnic group but, subject to the problems of attrition mentioned below, only the smallest group of children (Chinese) would have been less than 300. It should be noted that these were all dependent children and some would have been over the age of 16. There is plainly considerable scope for developing the LS for studies of children.

The best survey of the ethnic minority population is the Policy Studies Institute (PSI) Fourth National Survey of Ethnic Minorities published as *Ethnic Minorities in Britain* (Modood *et al.*, 1997). This is very rich in its detail including data on income from all sources and the ownership of consumer-durables. The survey was of 3,291 households containing 5,196 adults and about 4,600 children (*ibid.* p.11). It was the former that were interviewed and were the main subjects of the study and there was a very high non-response to questions on income amongst South Asians. The *Family Resources Survey* may now offset the shortcomings of previous surveys and official statistics, although its numbers do not allow the study of small geographical areas (see Tadd and Berthoud, this volume). Traditional accounts of poverty see children as increasing the risk of poverty for adults, treating children as part of an adult household. Can we treat the child as the subject and the household as the potential problem for the child? Bradshaw notes that whilst we have:

> what constitutes an excellent national data base on family or household living standards, social conditions and social attitudes, children have not been the primary focus of attention.
> (1990, pp.3-4)

Later he notes that where we do have studies of children we do not have studies over time, they are cross sectional, not longitudinal (*ibid,* p.4).

The most notable longitudinal study of children has been the *National Child Development Survey*. More recently the OPCS (now ONS) LS has provided us with the data on one per cent of individuals in England and Wales upon which Clarke drew for her study. The LS gives us a sample which will enable researchers to discover, for example, the extent to which the same people suffer deprivation over time and others move in and out of deprivation.

The LS has a problem with higher attrition rates for minorities than for the 'white' population. Furthermore the 'ethnic' categories introduced in the 1991 census can only be applied backwards to sample members who appear in the 1981 and 1971 censuses.

Measuring Deprivation

For the first time in the history of the British census we have a Sample of Anonymised Records (SARs). This provides census data on a sample of 1 per cent of households and two per cent of individuals. To protect the anonymity of the samples the data are made available on a broad geographical scale, thus we have individual data for large districts and household data for the Regions. It is not possible to break the data down further.[1] This should be contrasted with the equally serious limitations of small scale and local studies from which it is not possible to generalise to wider populations. The census is not a poverty survey and contains no information on income so we lack any direct measures of poverty and deprivation, nevertheless the format of the SARs makes it possible to derive variables to conduct multivariate analysis, to select subsets of the population, pensioners, teenage households, women in employment, and to construct indexes of deprivation.

A wide range of methods are used to construct indexes to indicate the extent of material deprivation (Manchester Census Group/Local Authorities Research and Intelligence Association, 1993). Willmott and Hutchison used a z-score based upon unemployment, overcrowding, household amenities, ethnic composition, single parents and pensioners (PSI, *ibid*, p.5). Forrest and Gordon (1992) used separate z-scores to indicate material and social deprivation respectively, but they were, again, applied to local authority districts.

We have used the SARs to create an index of deprivation (Figure 8.1) that could be attached to individual children. It must be said that I would be amongst the first to criticise any sociologist who had *chosen* to use this index. In a memorable phrase David Donnison once said that you 'have to learn to itch where you can scratch'. The child-deprivation index was probably the best that could be created given the data available in the SARs. It was constructed from three variables: the number of employed persons in the household, car ownership and crowding in the household. In the following discussions 'high deprivation' refers to children scoring 3 or 4 on the deprivation index, 'very high deprivation' or 'highest deprivation' refers to those scoring 4.

Indicator	Yes	No
Access to car	0	1
Density above 1 person per room	1	0
Adults in employment	score 2 minus the number in employment	

Figure 8.1 Derivation of deprivation score

Why might these factors be combined to make an index of deprivation for children? Plainly children can not directly experience unemployment and ill-health as measured by the census as 'long term limiting illness' is impossible to apply to a child. The number of adults in employment will, however, directly impinge upon a child; with no adults working the household income will be low and may include a large element of means-tested benefits. Having a worker in the household connects a child with a world beyond home and school. Most importantly the worker brings an income into the household that makes it more likely that the parents can provide a varied diet, toys, books and outings.

In a crowded house a child may not have a room of its own, may get under parents' feet and have restricted opportunities to play indoors or to do homework. Accidents are more common among small children in crowded accommodation. Fights between siblings may arise from restrictions on movement and in shared rooms respiratory and gastro-intestinal infections may be transmitted. Murie (1983, pp.7-10) cites evidence on the impact of poor housing on educational performance and health of children reported from the 1960s and crowding leading to aggression or truancy. He also cites Rutter and Madge on the association between poor housing, delinquency and educational backwardness (pp.14-15).

Housing conditions have featured in nearly all measures of deprivation. This is partly because housing quality may contribute to deprivation and also because a large volume of housing data are available. Housing is a major social resource and its quality has been reported in censuses throughout the century. The non-availability of running water, inside toilets and baths have been taken as indicators of deprivation and their increased availability has been a measure of improved social conditions. The data and the improvements are connected because the allocation of funds to local authorities has been driven by formulae in large part derived from the census and demographic data. Deprivation is an important element in these indexes. A great deal of effort has therefore gone into measuring poor *areas*.

In considering the geography of deprivation housing tenure has been an important element because of the (increasing) association of council tenure with low economic status. But whilst areas of high council tenure may be relatively deprived one can not assume that an individual council tenant is poor. Some may be *at risk* of deprivation, others may not. Tenure did not seem an entirely suitable element to include in the index because not all persons living in council housing are living in deprivation. Because we are unwilling to treat council house living as a form of deprivation *per se* tenure has nonetheless been excluded from the index. Extreme parsimony was practised in deriving this index, the only housing factor being density of occupation. Although a 'bedroom standard' would have been better than a crude crowding measure it can not be derived from the census (Murie, 1983, pp.19-20; Dale *et al.*, 1996, p.17). Work on housing deprivation by Dale *et al.* (1996) uses a housing conditions index which overlaps with our deprivation index by including crowding and we will compare scores on our index with those of Dale *et al.*

Access to a car provides the opportunity to buy from shops outside the immediate neighbourhood and for visits. Without a car there are less outings, the town becomes larger and less well-known. Lack of access to a car may be no deprivation to someone in a city centre or with access to good public transport but it could compound poverty in a rural area. Similarly a woman and child in a household where a man monopolises access to a car may be more deprived than they seem. For a black family private transport may be the only safe means to travel, thus dependence on a good system of public transport may be a deprivation. Whilst a car may be very low on any poor household's list of priorities, the lack of access to a car shows a lack of a material possession that is widely owned. It is the only material possession counted in the census. Lack of a telephone, or lack of resources to use central heating would be better measures of deprivation, but neither are included in the census. The three elements of the index used are not unconnected; crowded housing may derive from low income or no income, as may lack of a car. These indicators of deprivation may therefore be combined to give a rough and ready index of deprivation for children but they are only proxies for material deprivation. The index describes a combination of social conditions in which most would choose not to live. Most importantly it is an index made up of factors likely to effect the child's physical and mental development and well-being. An important shortcoming in the index is that its method of construction prevents us from analysing the impact of the labour market on deprivation. Having built household employment into our definition of deprivation we are not able to consider, for example, the impact of unemployment on deprivation because the measurement of deprivation is not independent of unemployment. Ideally we need an index which includes lack of those possessions that were used to construct Mack and Lansley's 1984 *Breadline Britain* index. Then we could have treated lack of employed persons in a household as an independent variable. We have to itch where we can scratch. Townsend has recently discussed more elaborate and perhaps optimal methods of measuring poverty and deprivation but which could not be encompassed within the limited scope of any UK census (Townsend, 1993, chapters 2-4; and see also Townsend, 1996).

There is no reason to believe that the social conditions in which children live are identical to those of the whole population. For example children live in younger households, because it is young people who become parents. Because people have children the house is more crowded. Having a child causes household *per capita* income to decline. In addition children may remove a parent (usually the mother) from the labour market; an income is lost thereby, and less income has to go further. If a mother does continue to work she is likely to undertake part-time and low paid work. Childhood, in other words, is a period in which the risk of poverty is high.

Comparing any group of children with children in Great Britain would be misleading because there is no average 'British' child. We have used England as the baseline but in addition 'Poor England', the 21 local authority districts that appeared in the top 50 of Forrest and Gordon's tables for material deprivation *and* social deprivation (Forrest and Gordon, 1992, Tables 27 and 28). Their inclusion in the top 50 for each type of deprivation established the districts' deprived status beyond doubt. The differences between England and Poor England are very significant for white children but less so for ethnic minority children, as shown by the mean deprivation scores. Ethnic minority children are more deprived than white, wherever they live.

Table 8.1   Mean deprivation index scores; ethnic minority children

	Mean deprivation scores	
	Poor England	England
Black Caribbean	2.10	1.63
Indian	1.29	0.97
Pakistani	2.14	2.01
Bangladeshi	2.80	2.45
All children	1.4	0.9

Childhood is not one but a dynamic status. Children's 'careers' are dependent on the circumstances of the adults in their family or household. To be a child is to experience continuous change, it is a stage of the life-cycle in which circumstances are likely to change rapidly. The interplay of individual maturation and changing external circumstances can make the experience of being five quite different from being ten. The SARs only enable us to make a cross-sectional analysis of the children in 1991. The Longitudinal Study of the 1971 to 1991 censuses will enable us to explore longitudinal data effectively. We can only get a hint of the likely course of children's childhood by looking at the social circumstances of different age groups. This is not, of course, the same as looking at a cohort moving through childhood, but at three contemporary age groups at different but stages of their childhood.

Table 8.2 Deprivation by age bracket: white children, England

Deprivation score	0 - 5	6 - 10	11 - 15
0	31.3	44.1	54.5
1	39.7	31.5	26.5
2	13.7`	12.6	10.8
3	13.5	10.3	7.2
4	1.9	1.5	1.0
N = 100%	65,442	51,835	49,318

Table 8.3 Deprivation by age bracket: children not classified as white, England

Deprivation score	0 - 5	6 - 10	11 - 15
0	17.7	20.6	24.9
1	29.6	27.3	27.6
222.3	22.3	22.7	22.5
3	23.3	21.6	18.5
4	7.1	7.7	6.5
N = 100%	7,316	5,838	4,959

The distribution of children in the deprivation scores are as follows:

Table 8.4   Deprivation scores: all children, England and Poor England

Percentages

Score		0	1	2	3	4	N = 100%
All England	White	42.1	33.2	12.5	10.7	1.5	166,595
	Not White	20.6	28.3	22.5	21.5	7.1	18,113
Poor England	White	29.3	26.8	17.4	22.9	3.6	16,694
	Not White	33.6	23.1	25.7	27.3	10.3	6,331

We can see that whereas less than 12 per cent of white English children fall into the high category of deprivation, in Poor England over one-quarter do so. Just over three-quarters of white English children but 55 per cent of Poor England's children are in the two lowest deprivation scores. From white children's point of view the definition of Poor England is appropriate.

Deprivation declines with age; as a parent or parents change their pattern of child care and re-enter the labour market. Thirty per cent of white 0 to 5 year olds live in households with two earners and 50 per cent of 11 to 15 year olds. Is it possible that this finding was true only at the moment of the 1991 census? Tate (1997, Table 4) shows that older children are more likely to have both adults working, but a longitudinal sample would give us more specific answers in terms of adults leaving and joining the workforce during a child's childhood.

We now need to explore the data using the census 'ethnic' categories in order to examine the differences between children not recorded by their parents as 'white' in the census. With the exception of the next table white children are mainly excluded from the remainder of this paper.

Table 8.5 Deprivation scores: all children

Score	Percentages					N = 100%
	0	1	2	3	4	
White	42.1	33.2	12.5	10.7	1.5	166,595
Black Caribbean	17.7	21.1	24.4	31.4	5.4	2,048
Black African	14.4	19.1	24.0	29.0	13.5	1,063
Black Other	20.1	23.5	20.3	30.5	5.6	1,609
Indian	34.9	37.1	16.0	9.6	2.5	4,773
Pakistani	6.3	25.7	33.6	25.2	9.2	3,639
Bangladeshi	3.1	15.4	23.5	31.1	26.8	1,382
Chinese	30.7	36.5	17.1	12.5	3.1	654
Other Asian	24.5	38.9	19.2	13.8	3.6	890
Other other	25.9	29.7	19.4	21.2	3.7	2,055
All	40.0	32.8	13.5	11.7	2.0	184,708

As we saw in Table 8.5 all minorities are more highly represented than white children in the highest level of deprivation. Indian children however are found very slightly less than white children in the *two* most deprived categories (12.1 per cent to 12.2 per cent). The Bangladeshi children show an exceptionally high level with over a quarter scoring 4. Indian children score almost the same as white children for low deprivation as measured by the two lowest categories. Figure 8.2 provides profiles of the deprivation scores of the ethnic minorities. Let us consider each census ethnic category of children in turn.

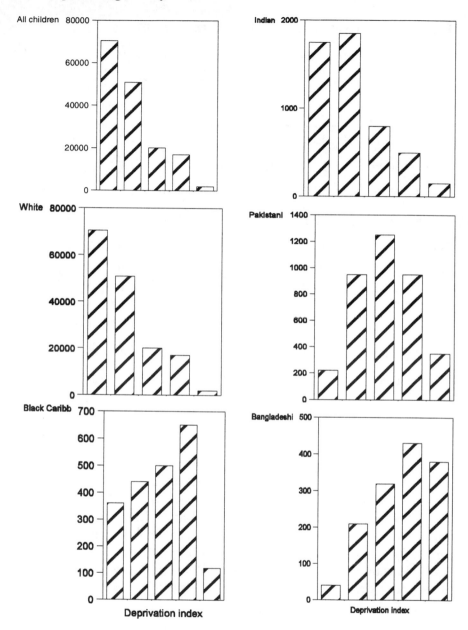

Figure 8.2   Deprivation scores by ethnic group, England

The data presented in the table and chart may be compared with data from other sources. In their survey of the ethnic minority population, Modood *et al.* (1997), found that Pakistani and Bangladeshi households were very substantially poorer than others, for example four-fifths had incomes below half average income. When pensioner and single parent households were excluded Pakistanis and Bangladeshis has four times the white poverty rate. Over one half of their households had no incomes from earners, unemployment was high and female economic activity rates low. Because of their recent arrival or interrupted employment records many were without National Insurance benefits and relied therefore on means tested benefits. Because when they were employed it was in low-paid occupation Pakistani and Bangladeshi households with an earner were worse off than white households with no earners (Modood *et al.* (1997), pp.153-158). Berthoud has shown from the FRS that 29 per cent of *working* Pakistani and Bangladeshi households relied upon means tested benefits (Berthoud, Table 3.5). The PSI survey also confirmed the incidence of over-crowding in Pakistani and Bangladeshi households. The impact of all these circumstances is mirrored by our data, with few Pakistani children in the lowest brackets and the Bangladeshis concentrated in higher deprivation. Their mean scores were 2.14 and 2.8 respectively, compared with 1.44 for the white children.

The PSI survey divided the census category 'Indian' into Indians and African Asians, a sensible distinction not observed by the census. We will see below that there is a difference in the incidence of deprivation between African-born and other Indians. PSI discovered that Indians and African Asians had slightly higher incomes but larger households than the white population, by 'higher' they meant fewer in the lower incomes, slightly more in the upper income brackets and therefore a slightly higher average. The FRS suggested that whilst median Indian incomes may not be as high as white, Indian *household* incomes are higher (Tadd, Table 1; Berthoud, Tables 1.5. and 3.3). We see in the data above that the Indian children's deprivation may be sharply contrasted with that of Pakistanis and Bangladeshis. Caribbean household incomes were between those of the Indian and white households, but there were fewer adults in Caribbean households to share this income (*ibid.*, p.157). Although relatively few fall into the highest deprivation category the Caribbean children are skewed towards higher deprivation with a much lower proportion than white children in the two lowest brackets. This is not entirely explained by the PSI study which nonetheless found widespread poverty amongst Caribbean households. A very high proportion of Caribbean households are single (female) parent households and the PSI study found that 70 per cent of such households had incomes below half average incomes. This is the same proportion as white families but because the incidence is higher is goes part of the way to explain the scores in Table 8.5 and Chart 8.1. We begin this SARs-based analysis with Caribbean children.

Black Caribbean Children

The black Caribbean population is concentrated in London and the West Midlands; 36.9 per cent in Inner London, 21.5 per cent in Outer London and over 16 per cent in the West Midlands. 96.7 per cent of the children were born in the UK. Nearly 43 per cent with high deprivation scores are in Inner London and 15.6 per cent in Outer London, they are over-represented in the black Caribbean population of Inner London and under-represented in Outer London, suggesting that when a family escapes deprivation it escapes from Inner London. The PSI survey also noted spatial factors in that better-off Caribbean households were found in areas with lower densities of minorities and therefore fewer lower incomes (*ibid.*, p.162).

Of those in the highest deprivation, 76.6 per cent live in one parent families (compared with 12 per cent of those in least deprivation) and 76 per cent of those in high deprivation live in female headed families. By contrast 72 per cent of children with the lowest deprivation score live with a married couple and another seven per cent live with a cohabiting couple. But we should not overlook the fact that 18.9 per cent of the children at the highest level of deprivation were living with a married couple, roughly one in five.

Black Caribbean children live in households with slight more long-term sick persons than white children (13.5 per cent compared with 11.4 per cent) and the proportion is slightly greater among the most deprived. (17 per cent). Only three per cent of Black Caribbean children live in households with a least one person of pensionable age.

Family type and the stage of family development will plainly affect adult labour market chances, detrimentally where the child is young and living with a single parent. This is born out by the fact that a two adult and or male headed family is more likely to have an adult in work. Whilst it is true for all black Caribbean children it is especially true for children in single parent families that there is a greater likelihood that a family member will be in employment when the child is older. Thus one half (55 per cent) of the 0 to 5 year old children have at least one adult in employment but two-thirds (69 per cent) of the 11 to

15 year olds. For single adult families the proportion with an adult in work rises from 38 per cent to 52 per cent. What is perhaps most notable is that over one-third (36 per cent) of the black Caribbean children in single adult households have that adult in the labour market and working. Non-manual workers are more commonly found as the heads of the families of highly deprived children, suggesting that these are women in low-paid non-manual jobs. This conjecture is supported by the PSI study which showed that 69 per cent of Caribbean women worked in non-manual occupations and 61 per cent of Caribbean women worked in the public sector and especially in hospitals (39 per cent of Caribbean women) (Modood, 1997, pp.110-11). These are topics or further exploration.

The association between deprivation and housing is clear with less than five per cent of those in high deprivation living semi-detached houses (none in detached), 55 per cent in flats and 39 per cent in terraced housing. Eighty-nine per cent of those with the two highest deprivation scores live in public rented housing (local authority or housing association). Over one half of the flat dwellers are found in London and a further 19 per cent in the West Midlands. Housing associations are important providers of housing for Black Caribbean children, with 12 per cent living in this tenure.

Indian Children

Table 8.5 shows that Indian children have a different incidence of deprivation from black Caribbean children. Only seven per cent live in Inner London and 30 per cent in Outer London. The most deprived are over-represented in the Inner London child population, under represented in Outer London and slightly over-represented in the West Midlands and the North West. Nearly 95 per cent (94.7 per cent) were born in the UK and 3.3 per cent in India. Only 2.5 per cent fall into the highest deprivation category. However, those born in Africa show a lower incidence of deprivation than those born in India. The 'East African Asians' have had different economic trajectories from Indian 'Indians' in the UK but it is not possible to pick up these differences for the children in the SARs because the data do not include birthplace of the head of the family.

Ninety-three per cent of Indian children live in two parent families, 92 per cent in male-headed families. Only six per cent of Indian children live in lone parent families of whom one half (46.2 per cent) are found in high deprivation. Three-quarters of the small proportion of children who are in this high deprivation category live in two parent families. Large numbers of residents in the household also seem to increase the chances of deprivation, although this may be an artefact of the deprivation index because however affluent the family we can not expect the number of rooms in a house simply to increase *pro rata* as the number of residents increases.

A fifth of all Indian children live in a household with at least one person with a long term limiting illness and two-fifths of the most deprived. These long term ill residents will almost certainly have defined themselves as being outside the labour market, if they are not already of pensionable age. More than one in ten of Indian children live in a household with a pensioner resident, which may be a factor contributing to crowding, but interestingly enough a lower proportion of the most deprived have a pensioner resident. Although we may only speculate, a possible explanation for this is that pensioners may be contributing to family expenditure and/or providing child care which enables other adults to work. Could a pensioner in the household thus provide some protection against deprivation for Indian children?

Eighty per cent of Indian children live in a family with head in employment, two per cent more than white children. Because we have included the number of employed persons in the construction of our index it is never the case that a child can appear at the highest deprivation score and have a member of the household working. This is the single factor most likely to keep them out of the highest deprivation by definition. In terms of work, male non-manual employment lifts the Indian child out of the high deprivation category. Eleven per cent with manual worker-headed families are in high deprivation categories compared with 3.2 per cent of non-manual. Seventy-eight per cent of children in high deprivation have a family head in manual employment. Unlike the black Caribbean children, Indian children in high deprivation are much more likely to have a family head in a manual occupation than a non-manual occupation. Given the over all high level of employment there is very little increase in employment and decline in deprivation across the three age brackets for Indian children.

Twelve per cent of the Indian children live in flats with the remainder equally divided between terraced and other houses. Three-quarters in the highest deprivation live in terraced houses. Eighty-six per cent of all Indian children live in owner-occupied dwellings but of those in the highest deprivation 43 per cent live in public rented accommodation.

Pakistani Children

Just over two per cent of these children live in London and the South East, 23 per cent in Humberside and Yorkshire, 17 per cent in the North West. 88.5 per cent were born in the UK and 11 per cent in Pakistan. Nine per cent are in the highest deprivation and one-third (34.4 per cent) are in high deprivation with no significant differences across the age brackets. 85 per cent of those in high deprivation were born in the UK, 14 per cent in Pakistan. Those in the highest deprivation are under-represented in Outer London and over-represented in the Pakistani child population of Yorkshire and the West Midlands.

Ninety per cent live with married couples and 9.3 per cent with lone parents. Males head 88 per cent of families and 84 per cent of those in the highest deprivation. Fifty-four per cent of female headed families have a high deprivation score (31 per cent of male headed). Two-thirds of Pakistani children live in households with six or more residents.

A third of all Pakistani children live in a household with at least one person who suffers long-term limiting illness and over 40 per cent of those who are in the highest deprivation bracket. One in 12 of the latter have a pensioner in the household but slightly fewer in children's households over all. The PSI survey also showed high rates of disability amongst Pakistani men and many who had effectively retired from the labour market in mid-life (Modood, 1997, p.85).

Fifty-five per cent of the children live in a family where the head is employed and, as we would expect, two-thirds of those families where the head is unemployed or economically inactive are in high deprivation. Eighty-two per cent of the heads of family in high deprivation describe themselves as manual workers. There is no change in the employment level of adults across the children's age brackets. Children in high deprivation are more likely to have a family head in manual occupations, nearly 90 per cent, irrespective of the gender of the family head.

Seventy-one per cent of Pakistani children live in terraced houses (81 per cent of those in high deprivation). Eighty-two per cent live in owner-occupied dwellings including 64.5 per cent of those in high deprivation. Only 11 per cent live in council and housing association rented housing but of these 20 per cent of these are in high deprivation. When we look at council housing alone, 57 per cent of Pakistani children living in council housing are in high deprivation.

Bangladeshi Children

Bangladeshi children are highly concentrated in the south east; 42.5 per cent live in Inner London (23 per cent in the Borough of Tower Hamlets) and over 64 per cent in London and the south east with a further 12.9 per cent in the West Midlands and 10.6 per cent in the North West. Two-thirds (67.1 per cent) were born in the UK and 32.1 per cent in Bangladesh. Fifty-eight per cent are in high deprivation, 70 per cent of those born in Bangladesh. Those in high deprivation are over-represented in the child population concentrated in Inner London and under-represented in Outer London and the south east.

One-third of all Bangladeshi children live in households where there is at least one person with a long term limiting illness, reflecting the findings of the PSI survey, and one in 20 of all children in households with a pensioner.

Deprivation *increases* across the age brackets but not at a statistically significant level, so all we may say with any confidence is that the incidence of deprivation does not decrease. Ninety per cent of children live with married couples and 9.4 per cent with lone parent, over three-quarters of the latter are in high deprivation, although we should bear in mind that 56 per cent of children in two parent families are also in high deprivation. Eighty-six per cent of Bangladeshi children's families are headed by a male and two-thirds of the female headed are in high deprivation. Only 39.4 per cent live in families where the head works, with the remainder divided equally between unemployment and economic inactivity. The family heads are overwhelmingly manual workers (74 per cent) of whom 59 per cent are in high deprivation compared with 17 per cent of non-manual workers. Eighty-two per cent of those families with an unemployed head are in high deprivation. Over 75 per cent of family heads describe themselves as manual workers, and nearly 90 per cent of the heads of family of the highly deprived children, irrespective of the gender of the family head.

Seventy-three per cent live in large households. Fifty-three per cent reside in terraced houses, 35 per cent in flats (49 per cent of those in the highest deprivation). Forty-seven per cent live in public rented accommodation and 45 per cent in owner occupied. Forty-two per cent of the latter are in high deprivation but 75 per cent of those living in public rented housing. Just over seven per cent of Bangladeshi children are housed by housing associations, making them the only 'Asian' group for whom the associations are significant providers. Given that both the private and local authority providers in Inner London have been reluctant to house minorities (Tower Hamlets pioneering the use of 'voluntary homelessness' to avoid making provision) it is perhaps not surprising to find that 70 per cent of the housing association tenured households are in Tower Hamlets.

Dale *et al.* in the final chapter of their 1996 discussion of housing deprivation and social change, use an index of housing conditions based upon the 1991 census data; the index was based upon tenure, density, household amenities and whether or not the accommodation was self-contained (Dale *et al.*, 1996, para.9.6). The higher the score, the better the housing conditions. The maximum score was nine and minimum zero. An analysis of the housing conditions score for all ethnic groups, by household structure (*ibid.*, Table 9.9) shows that:

> ... averaging across all types of household, those of White ethnicity have the highest mean value on the index of housing conditions, followed closely by Indian households. Bangladeshi and Black African household have the lowest mean values.
> (Dale *et al.*, 1996, p.114)

We would expect a significant degree of congruence between the scores on the housing conditions index and the index of deprivation because housing density contributes one-fifth of the latter score and up to one-fifth of the former. So it would be absurd, for example, to attempt to correlate the two scores. But do the two scores tell the same story?

Table 8.6   Scores and rank order on mean deprivation score and housing conditions index, all children, England

	Deprivation Index score (1)	Housing condition index (2)	Rank order (1)	Rank order (2)
White	0.96	6.58	1	1
Black Caribbean	1.86	5.95	3	3
Indian	1.08	6.44	2	2
Pakistani	2.05	5.51	4	4
Bangladeshi	2.63	5.23	5	5

The rank orders are the same for both indexes.

Discussion

This is probably the first attempt to describe deprivation amongst ethnic minority *children* in England by taking the children as the subject of the study. There are many gaps in the data, we would prefer to know more about income and about the ownership of possessions included in the *Breadline Britain* study or the PSI's *Ethnic Minorities in Britain*. The available data only enabled us to make a relatively simple analysis using indirect measures of deprivation. We should bear in mind that this analysis has been a tough test for the SARs. Had we looked at adults we could have explored their economic status, their hours worked and an imputed income. Their education level and the industry in which they worked would have given us a better idea of the likely basis of poverty or affluence. Vital data are missing from the SARs for children. Because children are outside the labour market and almost entirely without earned or unearned incomes we need more data about the adults in the households in which children live. Additional household data are needed in individual data files of the SARs. Thus if income is included in the 2001 census, in the SARs we will need household income in order to study children effectively. Although it might be more costly to calculate, there would be little threat to confidentiality if house-hold income was attached to individual files, thus enabling us to have a direct means of comparing the economic resources in children's households.

The SARs enable us to compare on the national scale the incidence of deprivation amongst children. They do not enable us to make any statements about the absolute levels of deprivation, or about relative levels of deprivation. In the late 1980s about one-third of children were living in poverty (Oppenheim, 1993, p.52) but only 14 per cent of the SARs children were in the highest two categories of the deprivation index. The index certainly under-estimates poverty because households on very low incomes might just escape the higher deprivation scores. We have referred above to the example where the index puts into the lower deprivation scores those children living in families where two earners bring home less than a poverty wage. The index should not therefore be treated as a reliable measure of poverty in any absolute sense. As low wages become an increasingly significant cause of poverty and deprivation any index constructed from the data currently available will become more un-reliable, and must become so unless the SARs can be enhanced by including household income.

Our indexes suggest that the incidence of deprivation is higher amongst non-white children, with the exception of Indian children. It is even higher than amongst the white children in the most deprived parts of England. Black Caribbean children are three times as likely to be in high deprivation as white children, Pakistani children nearly three times as likely and Bangladeshi children nearly five times. These ratios are consistent with the findings of the PSI survey. These ratios could perhaps be taken into account when surveys produce minority samples too small for analysis.

We have confirmed Inner London as an area where the incidence of deprivation is high and especially high amongst Bangladeshi children, and even higher amongst newer arrivals. For Pakistani and Bangladeshi children we note the high incidence of long term limiting illness and adult absence from the labour market, with a larger number of pensioners in children's households than would be found in the population of children at large.

Tenure has been an overworked indicator in research, owner occupation includes rich and poor living in a wide range of quality and types of dwelling. We confirm however that owner occupation is the normal tenure for a majority of Asian children in the high deprivation category, with the exception of Bangladeshis. Our index ranks the Black Caribbean, Indian, Pakistani and Bangladeshi children in the same order as Dale *et al.*'s 1996 housing conditions index.

How do the SARs compare with other data? The value of the LS in the study of child deprivation has yet to be demonstrated, but the data suffer from the same deficiencies as the census (crucially, no income data). The PSI survey is the only survey specifically targeted at the minority populations. It has a small sample compared to the SARs, and is much less suitable for generating data at the regional and sub-regional levels. The advantage of the SARs is that it is a very large sample that can be used at smaller scale geographical levels. Even more importantly they can be used for the analysis of data for smaller sub-samples of the population. The SARs also offer a very easy way to work, the deprivation indexes and the kind of analysis presented here can be produced the day after the SARs are published. They require no lengthy and expensive research administration and field work on the part of the analyst. The price is a limited data set, the effects of this have been explored in this paper. The benefits of using the SARs, especially when the data can be used alongside the richer data of other surveys, are nevertheless plain to see.

Note

1   All the census data, including the SARs, are Crown copyright.

References

Amin, K. (1992), *Poverty in Black and Mite. Deprivation and Ethnic Minorities*, CPAG/Runnymede Trust.

Berthoud, R. and Brown, J.C. (1981), *Poverty and the Development of Anti-poverty Policy in the United Kingdom*, Heineman.

Berthoud *et al* (1985), *Challenges to Social Policy*, Gower.

Berthoud, R. and Ford, R. (1996), *Relative Needs: Variations in the living standards of different types of household*, Policy Studies Institute, London.

Bradshaw, J. (1990), *Child Poverty and Deprivation in the UK*, National Children's Bureau for the United Nations Children's Fund.

Clarke, L. (1992), 'Children's Family Circumstances: Recent Trends in Great Britain', *European Journal of Population*, vol. 8, pp. 309-40.

Dale, A. Williams, M. and Dodgeon, B. (1996), *Housing Deprivation and Social Change*, HMSO, London.

Donnison (1982), *The Politics of Poverty*, Martin Robertson, Oxford.

Forrest, R. and Gordon, D. (1992), *People and Places: A 1991 Census Atlas of England*, SAUS.

General Household Survey. OPCS, HMSO, London.

Haskey, J. (1988), 'The Ethnic Minority Populations of Great Britain: Their Size and Characteristics', *Population Trends*, vol. 54, pp. 29-31.

Haskey, J. (1989), 'Families and Households of the Ethnic Minority and White Populations of Great Britain', *Population Trends*, vol. 57, pp. 8-19.

Haskey, J. (1990), 'The Ethnic Minority Populations of Great Britain: Estimates by Ethnic Group and Country of Birth', *Populations Trends*, no. 60, pp. 35-8.

Haskey, J. (1998), *The Fragmented Family: Does it Matter?*, IEA Health and Welfare Unit, London.

HMSO (1993), *Labour Force Survey 1990/91*.

Jones, T. (1993), *Britain's Ethnic Minorities: An analysis of the Labour Force Survey*, PSI, London.

Labour Force Survey. OPCS, HMSO, London.

Mack, J. and Lansley, S. (1984), *Poor Britain*, George Allen and Unwin.

Modood, T. *et al.* (1997), *The Fourth National Survey of Ethnic Minorities: Ethnic Minorities in Britain: Diversity and Disadvantage*, PSI, London.

Modood, T. and Acland, T. (1998), *Race and Higher Education: Experiences, Challenges and Policy Implications*, PSI, London.

Moore, R. (1982), *The Question of Race in the 1986 Census*, House of Commons, Home Affairs Committee, Second Report, Vol. 11, HC 33-11.

Moore, R. (1995), 'Children and Deprivation in Liverpool', University of Liverpool, Department of Sociology, unpublished.

Manchester Census Group Local Authorities Research and Intelligence Association (1993), *Indicators of Local Poverty and Deprivation. Methodological Issues*, MCG/LARIA.

Murie, A. (1983), *Housing Inequality and Deprivation*, Heinemann, London.

Lambert, S. and Streater, J. (1980), *National Child Development Survey*, Macmillan, London.

Oppenheim, C. (1993), *Poverty, The Facts*, CPAG, London.

Policy Studies Institute (1992) *Urban Trends 1*, PSI, London.

Tate, P. (1997) 'Data on Household and Families from the Labour Force Survey', *Labour Market Trends*, vol. 105, no. 3, pp. 89-98.

Townsend P. (1993), *The International Analysis of Poverty*, Harvester Wheatsheaf.

Townsend P. (1996), *A Poor Future*, Lemos and Crane.

9 'Shortchanging' Black and Minority Ethnic Elders[1]

MARGARET BONEHAM

Introduction

'Shortchanging', the title of this paper implies that inequalities in society extend to a particular group of older people who may be vulnerable in old age. It has been argued that many older people from black and minority ethnic groups are at a special risk of being shortchanged in that they experience both the financial and emotional pressures of living in an ageist and a racist society. The term 'double jeopardy' has been used to summarise the position of such older people. It developed as a result of research undertaken in the United States which first focused on the disadvantages of income and ill health experienced by minority elders in the 1960s and 1970s (National Urban League, 1964; Dowd and Bengtson, 1978). This paper will review and evaluate the evidence that they may experience the double disadvantage of age and race. It will explore the position in Britain as it reflects the complexity of diverse communities which are rather crudely placed under the broad umbrella of 'black and minority ethnic'. Is there evidence of widespread poverty? Are some groups more vulnerable than others? Is the most appropriate policy response the improvement of access by providing benefits advice in several languages?

Furthermore is it possible to identify apparently 'commonsense' assumptions about older people from black and minority ethnic groups made by those in health and welfare services? A recurring theme in historical research is that older minority ethnic people have been seen *as* a problem rather than as *having* problems. Those in power are able to distance themselves from issues concerning the health and welfare of such individuals by adopting attitudes based on generalisations and stereotypes. Using a social constructionist approach, as Clarke and Cochrane argue (1998) an unpacking can take place of assumptions attached to a range of apparently 'deviant' groups such as single mothers and members of minority ethnic groups. The usefulness of this concept will be explored in relation to poverty, ethnicity and age.

Background

In order to ascertain the extent of 'shortchange' in the long term, it is important to examine demographic trends. The older people under discussion are heterogeneous: residents of Britain over 60 years of age who were born in China, West Indies, West and East Africa, India, Bangladesh, Pakistan all of whom have migrated to the UK plus others of African and West Indian ancestry who were born in Britain (Black British). The current numbers of what will be termed minority ethnic elders is small - about 3.2 per cent of the total according to the 1991 census who were over 65 years old, compared with 16.8 per cent of the white population (Pearce and White, 1994). However in the next decades as the minority population grows that proportion will increase rapidly. This is shown in the population pyramids for different ethnic groups which indicate a narrow apex for instance for Asian groups indicating at present a small elderly population compared with the white populations (Heath and Dale, 1994, p.7). However, there is a substantial proportion of middle aged and young groups whose ageing can be anticipated. Surveys completed by the Policy Studies Institute (PSI) comparing data from 1982 with 1994 suggest already a small increase of older people within South Asian and Caribbean groups (Berthoud, 1997, p.20).

It appears that the amount of limiting long term illness is at present higher than in white groups (apart from Chinese and Black African groups) (Blakemore and Boneham, 1994). This is a reflection of a lifetime of disadvantage in employment conditions and poor housing. The conclusions should be treated with caution as it must be remembered that numbers of over 75s are small and there are issues concerning the extent to which different ethnic groups interpreted the question accurately. Nevertheless vulnerability to limiting long term illness is a problem which restricts a person's daily activities. Unemployment rates are likely to be higher and influence a persons ability to save and their eligibility to a pension.

Particular reference will be made throughout to a research study known as the Health and Ethnicity Project (HEP) which focused on the unmet need for health and welfare services amongst black and minority ethnic older people living in inner city Liverpool. Whilst the main intention of the study was psychiatric it also revealed some interesting findings concerning the social and economic circumstances of 418 older people from African, Caribbean, Chinese and Black British groups. There was a preponderance what might be termed 'young old' males (65-74 year olds) which reflects the numbers of migrant seamen, factory and restaurant workers who have come to Liverpool since the 1920s, especially in the 1950s and 1960s. The author of this paper was research coordinator of the project between 1991 and 1993. The Institute of Human Ageing and the Department of Psychiatry at Liverpool University obtained Inner City Partnership funds for the study. Its aim was to explore a neglected area - mental illness in older black and minority ethnic people and reasons for the low take up of existing services. In order to do so it was decided to measure the extent of depression and dementia in such groups, to investigate the potential barriers to service use and to make recommendations to the Health Authority. One of the reasons for the lack of data in this area is the difficulty of obtaining a representative sample. There are problems in the use of traditional methods such as the electoral register which gives no indication of age or of those who would identify themselves as 'Black British' individuals. These older people were identified in HEP through a combination of methods: FHSA lists, liaison with community sources and religious organisations, snowballing and a door knock in areas of minority ethnic population. (For a fuller explanation of the method and results see McCracken, Boneham *et al.*, 1998). Forty per cent of those on the FHSA lists could never be contacted (derelict house, restaurant, no such place) and despite extensive effort these individuals could not be traced. Only 87 people refused (17 per cent of those approached). A total of 418 people were successfully interviewed in Phase 1 and 71 who were diagnosed with depression or dementia were reinterviewed in Phase 2. As well as being questioned with a Geriatric Mental Health State schedule respondents were also asked about activities of daily living, migration, links with their country of birth, family circumstances, housing and perceptions of services. Some of these findings will be referred to in the following discussion, which initially turns to some general themes.

Absolute Poverty

The evidence which suggests basic income inequalities is fairly extensive (see Figure 9.1). It is apparent that older people from minority ethnic groups are at greater risk of absolute poverty because of a combination of processes which place them at an unfair disadvantage. Inequalities in working life between low and high paid are compounded in old age in various ways. On three levels there are issues of relevance: low income, use of credit and access to welfare benefits.

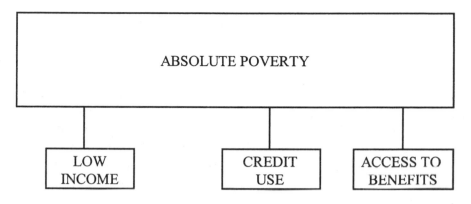

Figure 9.1   Basic income inequalities of minority ethnic older people

Low Income

Reports suggesting economic disadvantage are numerous (for example, Haringey CRC, 1979; Bhalla and Blakemore, 1980; Barker, 1984). Private and occupational pensions are only open to those who are in permanent and well paid jobs. Many have not accumulated a record of contributions for pensions because employers have neglected to undertake this task. As a result of racism and labour market disadvantage many older Asian and African Caribbean workers are likely to have been made redundant early, to have had a poor chance of promotion, poor working conditions in manual jobs with a low earning capacity (Blakemore and Boneham, 1994).

However, it is important to make clear that this is not a homogeneous group. Within the broad category of minority older people some are worse off than others. There are those who have never been in paid work at all who are therefore reliant on family savings. These include a majority of Asian women, some African Caribbean women or those entering the UK as retired. Also in general Bangladeshi and Pakistani communities appear to have especially low incomes compared with any other minority groups. This is due to higher rates of unemployment amongst men in the group, women with low rates of economic activity. Those in employment have low wages and there are larger family sizes with higher numbers of children and more adults (Berthoud, 1997).

In all, the apparently 'commonsense' assumption has been made by employers that members of black and ethnic minority groups are lacking in skills, fit only for the worst jobs and ineligible for promotion, even in fact to basic entitlements to future pensions. Thus, they have not been seen as 'proper' citizens of Britain but more as an expendable work force.

Credit Use

Another area of concern in this review is the high level of borrowing apparent in minority ethnic groups and the extent of bad practice (Herbert and Kempson, 1996). Those on low incomes may have a need for credit. High street credit is inaccessible because potential borrowers are considered a bad risk or there are language difficulties. There is no detailed data available on older people and it is possible that credit use does decrease with age (Herbert and Kempson, 1996). However, sending remittances home is common in particular where at least one adult in a family has been born abroad. The Fourth PSI study found sending support to family outside the household was apparent in a fifth or sixth of Indians, African Asians and Bangladeshis, a third of Pakistanis and Chinese, but well over a third of Caribbeans (Berthoud, 1997, p.166).

In the Health and Ethnicity Project, of the 418 older people interviewed 30 per cent responded that they sent letters regularly to relatives in their country of birth and 26 per cent sent money or parcels abroad (McCracken, Boneham *et al.,* 1998).

The use of foreign exchange agents who provide loans to cover remittances is widespread in the Pakistani community. Israr, a retired textile worker recalls:

> since coming to the UK in 1961, I have always used the services of an local agent.
> (Herbert and Kempson, 1996, p. 54)

In Kempson's study a minority of these agents were using forceful tactics to make sure that money was repaid. Unlicensed money lenders were found in the Oldham Bangladeshi community, granting only high interest loans or harassing clients for payment. The presence of 'go betweens' charging high fees for arranging credit was also found. Clearly this is an area where minority elders are vulnerable to exploitation from within the communities themselves and is a result of extremely limited choices. The answer may lie in ensuring that other options are available to those who need to use credit by broadening access to other traditional sources or encouraging community based savings (Herbert and Kempson, 1996).

Thus a 'commonsense' stereotype has been manifest in the policies of financial institutions that ethnic minority groups are unreliable and this has had long term consequences for older people.

Access to Benefits

There are important issues raised by several reports on the problems of access to benefits (National Association of Citizens Advice Bureaux, 1991; Bloch, 1993; Age Concern, 1996). For instance there is the case of an elderly woman mentioned in a recent conference of an elderly woman whose husband had gone to Pakistan. She received letters from the Benefits Agency she could not understand and so placed them in the bin. When her money stopped she reluctantly went for help to the CAB. It was a routine enquiry which needed organising and she returned to being on benefit. It emphasises the difficulty of ongoing communication (Albeson, 1996). Indeed the barriers to receiving entitlements are numerous, ranging from language difficulties, problems arising from differing naming systems, institutional racism, fear of officialdom, lack of knowledge of the benefits system, worries over passport checks.

Policies themselves may be based on stereotypes. The habitual residence rule acts against minority elders. Even people who have satisfied all the immigration rules, are citizens of Britain and have leave to stay can be refused income support if it is found that they are not 'habitually resident in the UK'. So elderly Asian people are refused extra help if they return to Bangladesh or Pakistan for a long break (Albeson, 1996). The process operating here is again the presumption that minority ethnic elders are not full citizens of Britain because they show ties to another country as well as this one. This is even if they have lived all their working lives in Britain and qualify for a retirement pension.

Law's recent study found there to be considerable non claiming, under claiming and delayed claiming in Chinese and Bangladeshi households (Law, Hylton, Karmani and Deacon, 1994). They found that the stigma of accepting means tested benefits was strong in these and Pakistani households. There are interesting contrasts from a religious perspective noted by the authors: among Bangladeshi Muslims some viewed benefit as 'Lillah' or charity for the poor and thus only for the destitute, whilst others saw it as 'Haq' or a right to which they were entitled. Older members of the community were more likely to take the latter view. However the idea of shame was widespread among Chinese households.

To look at the 'commonsense' assumption here, it has been presumed by welfare and health agencies in the past, that those who do not access a service do not need it. This ignores the many other reasons for a low take up. The growing research evidence suggesting a lack of sensitivity to cultural differences is forcing those agencies to question their policies.

In conclusion, many older people are 'shortchanged' in that they can be said to lack the income for even the basic necessities of life: due to low income or non existent savings, problems with acquiring credit and difficulties in accessing welfare benefits. However it must be acknowledged that 'double jeopardy' is not always the most appropriate image. There is a small group of middle income older people in the Asian and African communities who are not in poverty who were in skilled occupations when working. They are certainly not vulnerable victims of economic circumstance. Yet there is still a process of marginalisation. It has also been shown that they are not much better off and that their chances of promotion at work were limited by racial discrimination. Furthermore unlike the white elderly in similar economic circumstances the more affluent older minority ethnic elders have remained in the inner city and not joined the 'white flight' to lower density suburbs (Blakemore and Boneham, 1994). It appears that family ties and fear of racism may influence migration patterns at least in the case of these ethnic groups. They therefore remain in disadvantaged environments and share a poverty of experience with less affluent neighbours.

Relative Poverty

At this point the evidence will be considered which emphasises the psychological and social dimension to poverty (see Figure 9.2). Minority ethnic elders also may lack the ability to participate fully in life according to the norms and expectations of the rest of society. This is a definition of relative poverty: of being poor in relation to others. Claire Blackburn writes:

> poverty is an experience - an experience of 'doing without' - that touches every part of life and family health care.
> (Blackburn, 1991, p. 12)

Feelings of loss of a future or financial security can mean psychological stress is added to material disadvantage. Powerlessness and exclusion can cause depression and influence intergenerational family relationships. The environmental context in which poverty is experienced has a profound impact on the well being of minority older people. All this contributes to a sense of 'shortchange'.

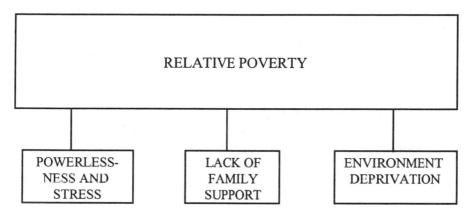

Figure 9.2   Social and psychological dimensions to poverty faced by minority ethnic older people

Powerlessness and Stress

It has been argued that 'knowledge is power' and that minority older people realise that without it they cannot access the services that they require (Aslam, 1995, p.22). It has already been demonstrated that information services are geared up to the needs of the majority population rendering the minority excluded and in poverty. The Archbishop of Canterbury's Commission on Faith in the City stated that:

> Poverty is not only about shortage of money. It is about how people are treated and how they regard themselves; about powerlessness, exclusion and loss of dignity.
> (Archbishop of Canterbury Commission, 1985, p.195)

Poverty impedes choice and induces powerlessness. There is a restriction imposed by lack of finance which means choice for any elderly person on low income may mean either to eat or to have heating. Lack of control works against feelings of positive self esteem and may mean a lack of motivation and lack of expectations. Certainly poverty marginalises the older person and enforces isolation. It reinforces discrimination and rejection by the host society. The individual experience of living in a climate of hostility brings about a 'poverty of spirit' which creates a sense of 'shortchange'. Fisher's theory of 'locus of control' suggests people who do have control are less at risk of experiencing helplessness and depressive illness than those who have no control (Fisher in Blackburn, 1991, p.45).

In the Health and Ethnicity project mentioned earlier 71 older people out of the 418 interviewed in inner city Liverpool were diagnosed as suffering from a mental illness (Boneham *et al.*, 1997). The prevalence levels for depression were 15 per cent. These rates are as high as for white elderly in other similar community studies and yet contact with mental health services is very low. These 44 men and 27 women were interviewed in Phase 2 of the study as they were diagnosed as suffering from dementia or depression. Racism was an element in their illness. A major factor in anxiety levels for those with depression was worry over finances, both their own and that of their immediate family.

An example will illustrate from personal case notes:

> An elderly seaman from Sierra Leone is very concerned about his bills - will go to the CAB about a note demanding £16 per week to repay a social fund loan. He is trying to obtain attendance allowance and still feels he is entitled to a war pension which he does not get.

The 'commonsense' assumption throughout is that minority elders do not experience stress as a result of low income or racism; if they did so they would get in touch with services or that the extended family would look after them. Neither presumption is accurate. There is unmet need and family support is not inevitable.

Family Support

Family may be the main source of support if in individual is in receipt of a low income. A large proportion of older Asians live with their relatives and strongly value these warm contacts. Berthoud argues that 'the fact that so many minority (and especially Asian) people in their sixties lived with their adult children places them in a good position to receive family care if they need it in their seventies or eighties' (Berthoud,1997, p.55). However it does not follow that all family members have the time , expertise or finances to care for elderly relatives. A caring worry free future cannot be seen as inevitable. Other research indicates that whilst not in complete decline the extended family is under pressure; social change is apparent. The first large group of British born Asians bringing up their children in the UK are creating new family patterns. They are revising their attitudes towards the extended family, with daughters in law who were the traditional carers taking up part time employment and even showing a tendency to reject close links with older people (Blakemore and Boneham, 1994). In Leamington Spa a small group of older Sikh women were experiencing isolation and loneliness, when on first contact they had appeared relatively well integrated in the extended family unit (Boneham, 1989). Other community surveys demonstrate a wandering in the streets by older Asian men which is only part done out of preference and a means of socialising. In fact older men may not be wanted at home and certainly do not exercise the control over resources they might once have had when they were the breadwinner.

When looking at other ethnic groups the picture is also of a far from inevitable family support system. A third only of African Caribbean elderly lived with an adult child in the recent PSI study (Berthoud, 1997, p.44). In the Health and Ethnicity Project in Liverpool only 54 per cent of cases of depression saw relatives at least monthly compared with 72 per cent of non cases. This differed markedly from the sister study to HEP, known as ALPHA a longitudinal of all elderly in Liverpool, where 90 per cent of both depressed and non depressed saw relatives monthly. The conclusion drawn was that lack of social contact was associated with depression and that there were simply fewer relatives in this country to provide support for some minority elders. (McCracken *et al.*, 1998).

An interesting pattern emerges if we explore the nature of the financial relationship between family members. Herbert and Kempson refer to the borrowing and financial dependency between mother and daughter.

> I usually go to my mum and try and borrow a little bit of money off her and then pay her back . My mum helps to support me a lot in that way. My mum is an old age pensioner and she's got my sister's kid to bring up; she's 13. She's living on the breadline herself but we kind of help one another.
> (Herbert and Kempson, 1996, p.35)

Perhaps that financial relationship helped the older person to feel needed and strengthened an emotional bond. Social networks are complex and the elderly person's role of care giver rather than helpless recipient may be valued as extremely important. However it is not a cosy picture of inevitable support by children towards their elders as the latter become more frail and vulnerable. It is more a situation of group interdependency in a situation of adversity. The process is one of reinforcing group identity in a weak financial situation, one which may be compounded by poor housing.

Environmental Issues

The poorest in society are often located in the most deprived housing in inner city areas or deprived estates. Ethnic minority households are in general disproportionately represented in the worst pre 1919 terrace housing. Indeed high levels of rent arrears are reported in particular amongst Caribbean groups and general worries over money (Berthoud, 1997, p.180). This has a variety of implications for the quality of life of older people from these communities. Housing design is likely to be flawed so there is more cost in upkeep because of poor insulation and high fuel bills. Ownership of a car or a deep freeze is problematic so there is a heavy reliance on the local store which has a monopoly and so provides expensive food. Local services are withdrawn such as post offices and banks making choice even more restricted (Philo, 1995).

The experience of minority ethnic elders in Liverpool 8 confirms this view. Respondents in Phase 2 of the Health and Ethnicity Project came from the most deprived wards of liverpool 1,3,8 and 17 comprising the wards of Abercromby, Granby, and Smithdown where the Jarman Index of deprivation is highest for the city (50- 62). Twenty-seven of the 71 minority elders who were interviewed by the author were living in 19th century Victorian terrace housing either alone or in multiple occupation. Some of the streets were partially demolished. Respondents sometimes lived in a few isolated houses between boarded up buildings with rubbish skips standing at the end of the block. Ten of the respondents mentioned housing as a major factor to their depression. Problems expressed ranged from desperate desire to move away because of isolation and fear of burglary to worries over dampness, the payment of rent and general upkeep.

In 18 per cent of instances the heating would have been adequate but use was limited because of financial difficulties (Boneham *et al.*, 1997). Environmental problems such as damp, cold and high noise levels are known to be linked to high levels of anxiety and depression. In other parts of the city it has been shown that improvements in housing have led to lower levels of symptom recording and higher levels of expressed feelings of security and well being (Galen, 1990).

Why do minority ethnic elders not move out or improve their housing situations? Severe financial constraints and fear of racism in other parts of the city may be the key.

Another issue concerning numbers is that of disparities between urban and rural groups. There is clearly a concentration of black and ethnic minority people in certain urban areas of the UK as the 1991 census reveals with 44.6 per cent in Greater London, 14.1 per cent on the West Midlands (Owen, 1994). However, those older people from more rural populations may suffer no less from poverty and the effects of inequality. Whilst living in much smaller minority populations with little access to transport and specialised services there will be isolation and barriers to receiving services. The process operating in this instance is that of arguing from a 'commonsense' stance that the fewer the numbers of individuals in need the less important it is to respond. Writers such as Patel argue that if service providers play the numbers game and dismiss small groups as not justifying expenditure on specialist workers then their isolation is compounded and this might be viewed as institutionalised racism. (Patel, 1995).

To improve the situation for minority older people in genuine need it is clear that access to benefits are in need of improvement. The processes of marginalisation could be reversed by inclusive policies. These take time to implement and rely on commitment in order to counteract previous discrimination. Recommendations that have emerged from various research findings include the targeting of take up initiatives amongst the least frequent users. There seems to be general agreement that translation of materials into various languages is only part of the solution. Such material has to be made available in areas commonly used by older people (for example, doctors' surgeries, hospitals, churches and temples). Outreach work with minority communities over a period of time is vital. Bridges of trust have to be built to overcome stigma and ignorance. Take up levels are best raised where informal community links are forged with preferably the appointment of development officers (Aslam, 1996; Law et al., 1994; Boneham et al., 1997). Anti racist policies in Benefits Agencies will only be introduced and monitored if there is commitment at management level. The promotion of more ethnic minority staff to such levels, as Law argues (Law et al.,1994), is part of the mechanism by which urgent change will take place. Funding for initiatives remains one of the biggest barriers.

There is an awareness of this issue on a European level. The European Network on Ageing and Ethnicity held a conference in 1996 entitled 'Hidden Walls' in which they explored the social exclusion of age and race as experienced by older migrants living in Denmark, Germany, Britain and France. They called for international legislation to combat age and race discrimination, in particular to fully address the implications of the past recruitment of migrant labour to low skilled employment and to take account of the number of those who have come to Europe as a result of the colonial past of the country of resettlement or as refugees displaced by war and political repression. These are all groups recognised to be at great risk of poverty because they are often excluded from mainstream services.

In conclusion it is clear from the preceding discussion that many black and minority ethnic older people are indeed 'shortchanged' and that the double jeopardy hypothesis is to some extent proved. Apparently 'commonsense' judgements made by employers, landlords, Benefits Agencies, Social Services and Health agencies have reinforced stereotypes concerning minority elders by categorising them as 'different', a 'problem' and not part of the nation of Britain. These myths can be challenged and their consequences addressed but only if diversity of experience is acknowledged. Some older people from different cultural backgrounds are more vulnerable than others: Pakistani and Bangladeshsi older people, women who have not been economically active, Chinese and other elders living in rural areas, small communities not in conurbations where special funding is particularly difficult to justify, older African men living in the seaports without close family support. Thus gender, location, migration background and education levels are all relevant factors in understanding patterns of poverty and ethnicity amongst older residents of Britain.

Note

1   The title of this paper is taken from a conference held on October 6th 1995 organised by Age Concern, London called 'Shortchanging Ethnic Elders'.

References

Age Concern (1996), *Perspectives on Poverty and Ethnic Minority Elders*, Age Concern, London.
Albeson, J. (1996), pp.14-18 in *Perspectives on Poverty*.
Archbishop of Canterbury Commission (1985) *Faith in the City*, C of E Commissioners, London.
Aslam, N. (1996), pp.22 -25 in *Perspectives on Poverty*.
Barker, J. (1984), *Research Perspectives on Ageing - Black and Asian Old People in Britain*, Age Concern, Surrey.
Berthoud, R. (1997), in Madood *et al. Ethnic Minorities in Britain: Diversity and Disadvantage*, PSI, London, pp.1-59, 150-183.
Bhalla, A. and Blakemore, K. (1980), *The Elders of Ethnic Minority Groups*, AFFOR,

Birmingham.

Blackburn, C. (1991), *Poverty and Health - Working with Families*, Oxford University Press.

Blakemore, K. and Boneham, M. (1994), *Age, Race and Ethnicity*, Open University, Milton Keynes.

Bloch, A. (1993), *Access to Benefits - The Information Needs of Ethnic Minority Groups*, PSI, London.

Boneham, M. (1989), 'Ethnicity and Ageing in Britain: A Study of Elderly Sikh Women in a Midlands Town', *New Community*, vol. 15, no. 3, pp.447-49.

Boneham, M. *et al.* (1997), 'Elderly People From Ethnic Minorities in Liverpool: Mental Illness, Unmet Need and Barriers to Service Use', *Health and Social care in the Community*, May, vol. 5, pp.173-81.

Clarke, J. and Cochrane, A. (1998), 'The Social Construction of Social Problems', in E. Saraga (ed), *Embodying the Social: Constructions of Difference*, Routledge/Open University, London, pp.3-43.

Dowd, J. and Bengtson, V. (1978), 'Aging in Minority Populations - an Examination of the Double Jeopardy Hypothesis', *Journal of Gerontology*, vol. 33, pp.427-36.

Fisher, S. (1984), 'Stress and Perceptions of Control', in Blackburn 1991 (ed), Lawrence Erlbaum Associates, London, p.45.

Galen Research and Consultancy (1990), *Better Health, Better Housing*, Galen Research, Leicester.

Haringey CRC (1979), *The Ethnic Elderly*, CRC, London.

Heath, S. and Dale, A. (1994), 'Household and Family Formation in Great Britain: the Ethnic Dimension', *Population Trends*, Autumn, pp.5-13,

Herbert, A. and Kempson, E. (1996), *Credit Use and Ethnic Minorities*, PSI, London.

Law, I., Hylton, C., Karmani, A. and Deacon, A. (1994), 'Racial equality and social service delivery: A study of the perceptions and experiences of black minority ethnic people eligible for benefit in Leeds', Sociology and Social Policy Working Paper 10.

McCracken, C., Boneham, M., Copeland, J.R.M., Williams, K.E., Wilson, K., Scott, A., McKIbbon, P. and Cleave, N. (1998), 'The Prevalence of Dementia and Depression Amongst Black and Ethnic Minorities', *British Journal of Psychiatry*, vol. 171, pp.269-73.

Modood T and Webner P (1997), *The Politics of Multiculturalism in the New Europe: racism, identity and community*, Zed Books.

Modood, T., Berthoud, R. *et al.* (1997), *Ethnic Minorities in Britain: Diversity and Disadvantage*, PSI, London.

National Association of Citizens Advice Bureaux (1991), *Barriers to Benefits*, NACAB, London.

National Urban League (1964), *Double Jeopardy, the Older Negro in America Today*, National Urban League, New York.

Oppenheim C and Harker L (1996) *Poverty: the facts*, CPAG.

Owen, D. (1994), 'Spatial Variations in Ethnic Minority Group Populations in Great Britain', *Population Trends*, Winter, pp.23-33.

Patel M (1996) *Black Housing Associations and Private Finance: a good practice guide*, FBHO, London.

Patel, M. (1996), pp.2-5 in *Perspectives on Poverty*.

Pearce, D. and White, I. (1994), '1991 Census of Great Britain: Summary of Results', *Population Trends*, Winter, pp.34-39.

Philo, C. (ed.) (1995), *The Social Geography of Poverty in the UK*, CPAG, London.

10 New Labour, New Poor
ROY CARR-HILL[1] and BOB LAVERS

Introduction

According to the Social Security Green Paper published in the middle of the 1980s, 'Want in the sense of absolute deprivation - has been largely eliminated' (*Reform of Social Security*, Background Paper, vol. 3, para 48, HMSO, 1985). This statement conflicts with the experience of many of those living on social security.

In attempting to measure the level of deprivation in society, there are three main approaches:

* relative deprivation approach: based on a survey in which respondents are asked to specify which of a list of items they believe are minimum necessary essentials, and then asked whether or not they themselves have access to them. This approach, first used in Britain by Mack and Lansley (1985), has been used in a number of over-serviced countries and in at least one developing country (Carr-Hill, 1994);
* attitudinal approach: again based on a survey, in which respondents are asked to make estimates of the income levels which they consider 'just enough to make ends meet', 'insufficient' or on which they could only 'manage with some difficulty';
* budget standards: using data about society's current standard and patterns of behaviour and combine them into a detailed costing of the components of a minimally adequate level of living. The budget approach is 'a hybrid between empirical and prescriptive budget methods using nutritional science but ignoring social science evidence of customary diets and consumption patterns, this approach avoids prescribing of the minimum level of living'.

Use of Budget Standards

Some budget studies have been used primarily to demonstrate what an *inadequate* income looks like. Seebohm Rowntree, in his surveys of poverty, did not specify what was enough to live on decently: his aim was to demonstrate, to all those people who thought that all deprivation was caused by mismanagement of an otherwise adequate income, that a significant proportion of the poor in York were deprived simply because they had too little money for their physical need alone. Similarly, Mollie Orshansky, the US Economist who in 1965 constructed the budget which became the official US poverty line, wrote that 'if it is not possible to state unequivocally "how much is enough", it should be possible to assert with confidence how much, on average, is too little'. Neither author had defined poverty; they showed the numbers who were well below any poverty line.

All the budgets distinguish between what are called 'budget standard costs' and 'variable costs'. The budget standard costs comprise food, clothing, personal care, household goods and services and leisure. The variable costs comprise housing, council tax, fuel, transport, NHS charges, insurance, debts/fines/maintenance orders, job-related costs, seeking-work costs, pets, alcohol, tobacco and charitable donations.

There are two main versions of the budget approach, which more or less correspond to this division. The first, which is the method used by Seebohm Rowntree and, more recently, by the Family Budget Unit (FBU) which endeavours to include and cost a family's whole purchases given the prevailing patterns of consumption amongst the poor at the time. The FBU has attempted to cost all the components of a typical family budget in the 1990s, first at a *modest but adequate* (MBA) level, at a lower level called *low cost but acceptable* (LCA). For its LCA budgets, moreover, the FBU distinguishes between variable costs (like housing, fuel, transport and children) and standard costs over which the families have more control (like food and clothing). The second used for example, by the US National Research Council Panel on Poverty and Family Assistance, restricts the budget to core items like food, clothing, utilities, the costs of which are rounded up by a multiplier.

Rowntree's Contribution

Rowntree conducted three surveys of York residents, in 1899, 1936 and 1950. One important aspect of these surveys was concerned with defining the primary poverty line in terms of the cost of the bare essentials required to enable a person to survive physically. The methods used and results of these surveys are described in Rowntree (1901), Rowntree (1941) and Rowntree and Lavers (1951) and the items included as described in Annex I. Rowntree (1903) restricted his budget to core costs (food, clothing, rent, fuel and light) only at a poverty level. Parker (1998) says Rowntree relied on a margin for needs other than food, clothing and shelter. But in the 1899 Report (p.109), he gives detailed calculations for the fuel required and his additional estimate of 2d a week per person is based mainly on the cost of soap and lighting (see Annex I).

Despite the fact that Rowntree clearly set out to construct complete family budgets (see Annex I), we have restricted ourselves to the dietaries because of the change in the way in which housing, fuel and clothing are provided and used would make comparisons very difficult to interpret. Thus:

- *housing rent* - calculated as 4s0d in 1899, 9s6d in 1936 and 15s0d in 1950. Clearly the idea that one could rent a four bedrooms and bathroom for *as little as* £10 a week (applying the same multiplier as for food) is totally unrealistic because of the changes in the housing market;
- *fuel and light* - the amounts allowed in the budgets were 1s10d in 1899, 4s4d in 1936 and 7s7d in 1950. These were based on buying coal for the living room and originally, candlelight and then restricted lighting. Again, our standards are now very different; although in this case the minimum cost would be of the same order (the rough equivalent is £6 per week);
- *clothing* - the amounts allowed in the budgets were 2s3d in 1899, 8s0d in 1936, and £1 7s 9d in 1950. The idea that we would be spending *as much as* £14 a week on clothing is also ridiculous;
- *household and personal sundries* - the items included in the lists given in *Poverty and Progress* and *Poverty and the Welfare State* would be only a small part of the set that would be used now. This reminds us, that the 'consumer society' is only a relatively recent capitalist attempt to sustain an inherently unstable system.

It is quite possible that these differences would compensate for each other but that would make comparisons very difficult to interpret. The restricted aim here is to present estimates of the cost today of Rowntree's dietaries and to trace the growth in this cost over the last 100 years.

Rationale for the Paper

Obviously, all the budgets are developed as a comment on policies towards income redistribution and welfare. As our focus in this paper is on the adequacy of the current level of social security benefits, this chapter measures the existing benefit levels against those identified by Seebohm Rowntree.

There are five more or less distinct ways of exploring the adequacy of benefits (Bradshaw and Lynes, 1995): historical trends, examining the equivalence scales, whether the scales in fact meet basic needs, comparing the incomes and living standards of beneficiaries with others, and cross country comparisons.

There are three reasons for adopting the historical approach used in this paper: first, in the context of this centenary, it is of historical interest to see how much the 'poorer than workhouse' diet of a century ago would cost today; second, given the debates over the reform of the Welfare State, the current cost of the dietary prescribed at the inception of the Welfare State should be an element in those debates; third, it is sometimes easier to understand the implications of over-time trends than to agree on the assumptions implicit in a current budget standard.

Organisation of this Paper

We begin in section 2 by examining the cost of the 1899 dietary, which was evidently frugal in the extreme. As a result of the advances which took place in knowledge about nutrition generally, and vitamins and mineral salts in particular, the 1936 dietary differed substantially from that of 1899. Since Rowntree published full details about the dietary adopted in the survey of 1950, and since this differed only marginally from that used in 1936, section three discusses the cost of the 1950 dietary.

We are concerned mainly with the cost of food, which, in the early part of the century amounted to 60 per cent of the total cost for a family of five (man, woman and three children between the ages of three and 16), of surviving at the minimum standard, the remaining 40 per cent being made up of expenditure on rent, clothing and household sundries (these proportions had become more or less reversed by 1950); however in the last section we investigate changes in the standard of living in general for those living at subsistence level.

Rowntree's 1899 Dietary

It was Rowntree's intention to arrive at an estimate of minimum necessary expenditure for the maintenance of merely physical health (Rowntree, 1903, p.87).

Constructing the Dietary

These items were discussed under three heads: food, rent and household sundries (see Annex I discussed above).

He based his dietary, consisting of specified quantities of items of food intended to satisfy the body; basic protein and calorie requirements, and an order issued by the Local Government Board regulating workhouse diets throughout England and Wales in 1901. A number of alternative rations were specified for each meal. Rowntree says that 'although the Local Government Board paid due regard to economy, some are considerably more expensive than others'; and that 'only the cheaper rations have been chosen [and] no butchers meat is included. *The standard here adopted is therefore less generous than that which would be required by the Local Government Board'* (p.99 his italics). Examples of the rations for a Sunday and for a typical weekday are given as Annex IIA and the quantifies specified over a week for men (M) and women (W) and children (C) in Annex IIB. The dietary was therefore to be so rudimentary as to be 'less generous' than that required for the residents of workhouses.

Rowntree later says that 'These prices refer solely to the cost of the food: they include none of the necessary expenditure associated with food' (p.105). Also 'The poor do not possess knowledge ... to select a diet as nutritious and as economical ... as the standard'.

Our Estimates for Different Years

Using the detailed menus specified by Rowntree for a family of two adults and three children for each meal on every day of the week (see the examples and quantities given in Annex II), we estimated the equivalent cost in 1985 and in 1998 at the local cheap supermarkets in York and where cheaper, the open air market.

The estimates of the current cost of Rowntree's dietary are, of course, based on many simplifying assumptions: bread, biscuits and cake, for example, would usually have been made at home at the turn of the century, but today we have used shop prices for these items. The alternative of pricing the ingredients of foods prepared in the home, which we attempted with the various puddings in 1985 (see Lavers and Carr-Hill, 1985), would involve slightly different assumptions but make little differences to the final index.

Using this data we calculated the cost in 1985 of the 1899 dietary and repeated the exercise today in 1998 of the price of this particular basket of goods; and for each of the years in which Rowntree conducted a survey, we drew on the prices of selected items given by Rowntree himself in his surveys (where prices were not given because those items were not in the dietary for that year it has been assumed that the relative prices of such items behaved in the same way as those of the items for which information is available for all years). The results are given in Table 10.1: for purposes of comparison we also show in Table 10.1 the approximate value of the retail price index for all items based on the year 1899 (taken from Deane and Cole, 1962).

Table 10.1 The cost of the 1899 dietary, its price index and the approximate RPI for 1899 = 100

Year	Cost of 1899 Dietary (£)	Index of Cost	RPI
1899	0.64	100	100
1936	1.13	177	193
1950	1.76	275	385
1985	24.62	3847	4698
1998	24.83	3880	7558

Source: Rowntree (1901); Rowntree (1941) and Rowntree and Lavers (1951); Deane and Cole *British Economic Growth*, 1688-1959, 1962.

The estimates suggest that in 1985 a family of five would have needed to spend almost £25 a week on food just to maintain an 1899 'poorer than workhouse diet'; and that, in 1998, the cost would be only slightly more than this. It is, however, noticeable that the index of the cost of the 1899 dietary has risen much slower than the Retail Price Index (RPI), so that in 1998 the RPI is nearly twice the Index of Cost.

The Second Dietary

The second dietary was constructed in 1936 and modified in 1950 to take account of minor changes in consumption patterns, some of which resulted from food rationing.

Constructing the Second Dietary

The 1936 dietary, was based upon the recommendations of a BMA committee (BMA, 1933) 'to determine the minimum weekly expenditure on food-stuffs which must be incurred by families of varying size of health and working capacity are to be maintained, and to construct specimen diets'. In *The Human Needs of Labour* Rowntree (1937) reports the total cost for a family of five of £1.03. When we came to estimate the cost of the 1950 dietary (see Annex III) in 1936 prices, however, we arrived at the higher value of £1.18 (see Table 10.2, column 1). The differences between the 1936 and 1950 dietaries involved only replacing skimmed condensed by full cream milk and sugar, deducting some bacon and cheese, dripping and suet, but adding margarine (see Rowntree and Lavers, 1951, p.10). The main contribution to the price difference was the milk.

The dietary is for a man, wife, and three children under 14. A woman was thought to require 83 per cent as much food as a man, and the requirements of children to vary according to sex and age. The dietary has a 'man value' of 3.78. In calculating the necessary expenditure for food we allow 12s. 6.5½d. for a man, 10s. 5d for a woman, and 8s 1½d. for each child.[2]

Rowntree's second modified dietary was drawn up in the early part of October 1950. He says that 'The price of the different items are based on information gathered by an investigator who visited a number of shops which cater for working class people' (PWS, p.13). We followed the same procedure, using the discount supermarkets Aldi and Netto whose doors are rarely darkened by the middle class. The former which only accepts cash, probably is the closest reflection to the indoor shopping environment half a century ago.

Our Estimates

On this basis, the price of the 1950 Dietary, i.e. that prevailing at the inception of the Welfare State, suggests that the same minimal basket of goods would cost £31.15 today. In the previous exercise in 1985, the estimated cost was £30.95 - only 20 pence less. We attribute the small difference from 1985 to the spread of relatively aggressive competition between supermarkets regardless of quality.[3]

Table 10.2 The cost of the 1950 dietary, its price index Rowntree's subsistence income level, the equivalent subsistence income, based on the relative weight assigned to food in the RPI, and the scales of social security benefit excluding rent

Year	Cost of 1950 Dietary	Index of Cost of 1950 Dietary	Rowntree Actual Subsistence Income[a]	Outdoor Relief National Assistance/ SB/IS	Equivalent Subsistence Income Level[b]
	£	£	£	£	£
1899	0.97	100	1.08	-	-
1936	1.18	142	2.65	1.90	-
1950	2.17	244	5.76	4.43	6.20
1985	30.95	3191	-	90.00	106.75
1998	31.15	3216	-	139.00	137.00

a Rowntree includes rent in his discussion of the poverty line in 1899 and 1936; in 1950 he estimated the subsistence income at £5.01 excluding rent but we have added on the median rent of 15s paid by class 'A' and class 'B' families (see PWS, p.85), which was also the average rent for five rooms plus a bathroom.

b 1950 estimates based on the weight of food in the average RPI (350/100); 1985 and 1998 estimates based on weight of food in expenditure patterns of lowest income quintiles in Family Expenditure Surveys for those years (29 per cent and 22.7 per cent respectively).

The Equivalent Subsistence Income

Also shown in Table 10.2 are some relevant comparisons which enable us to estimate changes in the broader cost of living of families at a subsistence level. Rowntree's estimate of the minimum expenditure, including that on housing, necessary to enable a family with three children to subsist is given in column 4. The cost of the 1950 dietary (£2.17) was only part of what Rowntree adjudged to be the poverty line. For the same family of two adults and three children, we have estimated an overall figure of £5.76 including rent. The fifth column gives the scale of social security benefit prevailing in the same years. Our estimates of what a family of five would require if they subsisted on Rowntree's 1950 dietary is given in the last column. These have been derived as follows.

If we assume that families today as Rowntree's Class 'A' and 'B' families with income *under* his poverty line devote the same proportion of total expenditure to food as the average lowest income quintile family, this yields what call the equivalent subsistence income level. A scaling up from the 1998 figure of £31.15 (the cost of the 1950 basket today) in line with the ratio of the cost of Rowntree's dietary to his subsistence income would give a figure of *around* £83. (A similar calculation for the cost of the 1899 dietary yields a figure of £66.)

However, whilst the proportion Rowntree allowed for food in 1950 (38 per cent) was quite close to the weight given to food in the RPI basket of goods (350/1000), it must be remembered that the RPI is the *average* weight assigned to food across families of all incomes (excluding pensioners). The latest Family Expenditure Survey (1996/97) shows that households containing two adults plus children (mean number of persons per household in this group = 4.1) in the lowest gross income quintile of those households *(under £259 weekly) spend 22.7 per cent of this* budget on food.[4] The inverse of this proportion, applied to our Rowntree subsistence diet price equivalent of £31.15 would give total subsistence income levels of £137 a week. (A similar calculation for the cost of the 1899 dietary yields a figure of £109). The present Supplementary Benefit levels allow about £139 for a family of five, (£79.00 + £17.30 + £17.30 + £25.35) plus a Family Premium of £11.05 rent and rates are paid in full up to a limit set locally.

Discussion

Relevance for Today

Rowntree (1903) quotes an economist as follows: 'What an employer gets out of his workmen will depend very much on what he first gets into him. Not only are bone and muscle to be built up and kept up by food, but every stroke of the arm involves an expenditure of nervous energy which is to be supplied only through the alimentary canal. What a man can do in 24 hours will depend very much on ... what he has had to eat the 24 hours previous.'

He goes on to say that these factors have now (in 1903) acquired 'an urgency that is not easy to exaggerate in consequence of the stress and keenness of international competition' and that 'the conditions of commercial "success" are absent when there is inadequate nourishment'.

Given the stress in current debates about competitiveness in education and training Rowntree's comments are salutory; we should first of all make sure that people have enough to eat. Moreover, a parallel line of reasoning about stress in the workplace would imply a concern with decent living conditions.

Rowntree (1951), in commenting on the allowance he made for clothing, says 'No allowance made for any gifts of old clothing which may be received. In fixing minimum wages, we have no right to assume charitable gifts, which are at best exceedingly precarious' Rowntree (1937, p.95).

This also has very contemporary relevance with the debates over the impact of the lottery on charitable income.

Has 'Absolute' Poverty Gone Away?

In most developed economies, the provision of benefits sufficient to purchase physical necessities - food, clothing, warmth and shelter - is an accepted principle of good government. But 'social necessities' - personal care, household goods, household services and leisure - tend to be excluded. However, the recent approaches to budget standards have sought to answer the further question, how much is enough for decency, for human dignity, a reasonable sum to live on.

These are important debates. But because of the political salience of the poverty line in an unequal society, there is no technically correct way either to measure poverty now (wherever that is) or to measure trends over time. Clearly technical skill is important but it is only evaluated in a political context. We can therefore:

- demand a basic level of technical competence;
- express the assumptions in each approach clearly;
- demonstrate the implications of each particular approach.

Like others in this collection, this is what we have attempted to do in this paper.

Our choice of relying on historical dietaries rather than constructing one incorporating contemporary nutritional knowledge - as, for example, have Grant and Stitt (1993) and the Family Budget Unit - is, of course, unusual. But whilst we cannot claim to have measured absolute poverty, assessing the extent to which current income support levels are adequate in terms of minimum diets fixed 100 and 50 years ago, goes some way in that direction.

Our analysis shows that families dependent on social security have a standard of living no higher than that enjoyed by similar families in 1950, shortly after the establishment of the welfare state. Indeed current levels of Supplementary Benefit are only just enough to provide what Rowntree thought of as a basic minimum in 1936 (and only 25 per cent more than his 'poorer than workhouse' diet of 1899). Perhaps the title should have been 'New Labour, Old Poor.'

Notes

1   Reader in Social Statistics, Centre for Health Economics, University of York.
2   The relation between the food requirements of men, women and children was based on tables prepared by Cathcart and Murray, which he says, were then generally accepted. See his footnote on p.13 of Rowntree 1951.
3   Note that recent comparisons of prices in UK and European supermarkets would suggest we still have a long way to go - hence 'relatively'.
4   Assuming the lowest quintile members follow Polonius's advice to Laertes (Hamlet, I.3), 'Neither a borrower, nor a lender be, for loan oft loses both itself and friend. And borrowing dulls the edge of husbandry', Andrews, R. and Gibson, R. (eds.) Cambridge School Edition, 1994, p. 35.

References

Bradshaw, J. and Lynes, T. (1995), *Benefits Uprating Policy and Living Standards*, Social Policy Report No. 1, Social Policy Research Unit, University of York.
Bradshaw, J. (ed) (1993), *Household Budgets and Living Standards*, Joseph Rowntree Foundation, York.
Bradshaw, J. and Holmes, H. (1984), *Living on the Edge: A Study of the Living Standards of Families on Benefit in Tyne and Wear*, Tyneside Child Poverty Action Group.
Bradshaw, J. and Holmes, H. (1989), *A Study of Living Standards of Families on Benefit in Tyne and Wear*, CPAG, London.
British Medical Association (1933), *Report of Committee on the Expenditure on Food Necessary to Maintain Health and Working Capacity*, November, BMA, London.
British Medical Association (1950), *Report of the Committee on Nutrition*, BMA, London.
Brown, J. (1994), *Children on Income Support*, Board of Social Responsibility, London.
Carr-Hill, R (1994), *Measuring Poverty in Côte d'Ivoire*, Background Paper for World Bank Programme to Alleviate Impact of Devaluation.
Cooke, K. and Baldwin, S. (1984), *How Much is Enough: A Review of Supplementary Benefit Scale Rates*, Family Policy Studies Centre, London.
Deane, P. and Cole, W.A. (1962), *British Economic Growth 1688-1959*, Greg Revivals, UK.
Department of Social Security (1985), *Reform of Social Security*, Background Paper, vol. 3,

para 48, HMSO, London.

Family Budget Unit, King's College, London.

Family Expenditure Survey 1996/97. Central Statistical Office. HMSO.

Gosschalk, B. and Frayman, H. (1991), *The Changing Nature of Deprivation in Britain: an Inner Cities Perspective*, unpublished.

Grant, D. and Stitt, S. (1993), *Rowntree: Poverty Revisited*, Avebury, London.

HMSO *Monthly Digest of Statistics*, HMSO, London.

Lavers, R.J. and Carr-Hill, R.A. (1985), 'Staying Alive in 1985', *Low Pay Review*, vol. 23, p.14.

Mack, J. and Lansley, S. (1985), *Poor Britain*, George Allen and Unwin, London.

Oppenheim, C. (1990), *Poverty, the Facts*, Child Poverty Action Group, London.

Parker, H.C. (ed) (1998), *Low Cost but Acceptable: A Minimum Income Standard for the UK*, Family Budget Unit, London.

Rowntree, S.B. (1903), *Poverty: A Study of Town Life*, Macmillan, London and New York.

Rowntree, S.B. (1937), *The Human Needs of Labour*, Longmans, London, New York and Toronto.

Rowntree, S.B. (1941), *Poverty and Progress: A Second Social Survey of York*, Longman Green, London, New York and Toronto.

Rowntree, S.B. and Lavers, G.R. (1951), *Poverty and the Welfare State*, Longman Green, London, New York and Toronto.

Veit-Wilson, J. (1994), *Dignity not Poverty: A Minimum Income Standard for the UK*, The Commission on Social Justice, Paper 6, IPPR, London.

Annex 10.I Rowntree's (frugal) approach to constructing budget standard poverty lines

The constituent components of Rowntree's poverty lines in the three survey years were:

Table A10.1 The constituents of Rowntree's poverty lines

	1899		1936		1950		
	s	d	s	d	£	s	d
Food	12	9	20	6	2	7	4
Clothing	2	3	8	0	1	7	9
Rent	4	0	5	6	-	15	0
Fuel and Light	1	10	4	4	-	7	7
Household Sundries	10	-	1	8	-	6	0
Personal Sundries	-	-	9	0	-	11	6
	30	0	49	0	5	15	2

He notes that:

Rent: It was not possible to specify a necessary minimum. Instead the *actual sums paid for rent have been taken as the necessary minimum rent expenditure.*

We can see how limited the 'margins' are by examining the amounts for household and personal sundries.

Household Sundries: This was taken to include clothing, light, fuel, and so on. Estimates for clothing were based on interviews and the amount of fuel tended to be standard as this related to keeping a fire in the living room only, regardless of the size of the family (or home).

It was, however, difficult to specify the average sums required for other household necessities because most households would say that 'If we **have** to buy anything extra, such as pots or pans, we have to spend less on food that's all'. So he allowed 2d per person per week (a 'margin' of less than four per cent) most of which was specified so that the real unspecified 'margin' was less than one per cent.

The amount had only doubled by 1936 to 1s 8d. It was slightly more in 1950 and Rowntree and Lavers gave details of what would be included.

Table A10.2 Details of spending on household sundries

Household sundries	1950	
	s	d
Linen (towels, sheets etc.)	2	1
Saucepans, cooking utensils		6½
Cleaning Materials: Brushes and dust pans, polish and soda		9
Soaps	1	11
Toothbrushes & Toothpaste		4½
	5	8

Personal Sundries

There were no allowances for personal sundries in 1899. The amounts seem to constitute a relatively large margin in 1936 and 1950; however the detailed breakdown suggests otherwise.

Personal Sundries in 1936 and 1950 are detailed in the following table.

Table A10.3 Details of spending on personal sundries in 1936 and 1950

	1936		1950	
	s	d	s	d
Unemployment and Health Insurance	1	7	1	0
Contribution to sick and burial clubs	1	0	1	0
Trade Union subscription		6		9
Travelling to and from work	1	0	1	0
Stamps, writing paper		6	1	0
Daily newspaper		7		8
Wireless		6		5
All else (beer, tobacco, presents, holidays, books, travelling)	3	4	6	8
	9	0	12	6

Annex 10.IIA   1899 Dietary: The typical meal

		Breakfast	Dinner	Supper
Sunday	M/W child 8-14	Bread, Margarine, Tea	Boiled Bacon & Pease Pudding	Bread, Marg. Cocoa
	Child 3-8	Bread, Milk	Boiled Bacon & Potatoes & Skim Milk	Bread & New Milk
Typical Weekday	M/W	Bread, Porridge, Treacle	Boiled Bacon or Cheese, Bread, Potatoes	Bread, Vegetable Broth, Cheese
	Child 8-14	Bread, New Milk, Porridge, Sugar	Potatoes with Milk, Bread, Cheese	Plain Cake, Milk (or Cocoa)
	Child 3-8	Bread, New Milk, Porridge, Sugar	Boiled Bacon, Potatoes, Skim Milk	Bread, New Milk

Men and women were expected in addition to have a lunch of 4oz bread and 1½oz of cheese; Children, 2oz bread, ½oz butter, 2oz cake or biscuits.

Annex 10.IIB   1899 dietary quantities for men, women, children

	Unit	M	W	8-14	3-8
Bread	lb	7 ³/₈	6½	5	4¾
Margarine	oz	1	1	1	0
Boiled Bacon	oz	9	9	9	3
Pease Pudding	oz	12	8	0	0
Porridge	pint	12	8	4½	3
Tea	pint	1	1	¾	0
Cocoa	pint	1	1	2¼	0
Potatoes with milk	lb	1½	1¼	1	¾
Potatoes	lb	1½	1	1	¾
Cheese	oz	24	19	8	2
Vegetable Broth	pint	4	4	2	½
Skim milk	pint	4	3	2¼	2
New milk	pint	0	0	3	6½
Dumpling	oz	8	6	6	4
Treacle	oz	1½	1	0	0
Suet pudding	oz	8	6	12	0
Gruel	pint	1½	1	0	0
Cake	lb	0	0	2	¾
Butter	oz	0	0	3	3

Annex 10.III 1950 dietary

	s	d	1998 prices (£)
Breast of mutton - 2½ lb. at 8d. per lb. (imported)	1	8	2.70
Minced beef - 2lb. at 1s 4d. per lb.	2	8	2.20
Shin of beef - 1½lb. at 1s 6d. per lb.	2	3	2.03[1]
Liver 1lb. at 1s 6d. per lb.	1	6	0.39
Beef sausages 1lb. at 1s 3d. per lb.	1	3	0.99
Bacon 1¼ lb. at 1s 11d. per lb. (cheapest cut)	2	4¾	1.36
Cheese 10oz at 1s 2d. per lb.		8¾	0.88
Fresh full cream milk 14 pints at 5d. per pint	5	10	2.38
Herrings 1½ lb. at 8d. per lb.	1	0	2.04 (kipper price)
Kippers 1lb. at 1s. per lb.	1	0	1.36
Sugar 3lb. 2oz at 5d. per lb.	1	3½	0.78
Potatoes 14lb. at 9lb. for 1s.	1	6½	0.84
Bread 23½ lb. - 13½ loaves at 5½d. each	6	2¼	3.65 (wholemeal)
Oatmeal - 2lb. at 6d. per lb.	1	0	0.40
Margarine - 2½lb. at 10d. per lb.	2	1	0.63
Cooking fat - 10oz at 1s. per lb.		7½	0.14 (lard)
Flour - 1¼lb. at 9½d. per 3lb. bag		4	0.04
Jam - 1lb. at 1s. 2d. per lb.	1	2	0.39
Treacle - 1lb. at 10d. (in tins)		10	0.69 (golden syrup)
Cocoa - ¼lb. at 8½d. per ¼lb.		8½	0.24
Rice - 10 oz at 9d. per lb.		5½	0.19
Sago - ¼lb. at 9d. per lb.		2¼	0.07 (rice price)
Barley - 2oz at 9d. per lb.		1	0.04 (pearl barley)
Peas - ½lb. at 10½d. per lb.		5¼	0.16 (tinned)
Lentils - ¾lb. at 10½d. per lb.		8	0.46
Stoned dates - ½lb. at 10½d. per lb.		5¼	0.70
Swedes - 6lb. at 2½d. per lb.	1	3	0.96
Onions - 4½lb. at 5d. per lb.	1	10½	0.94
Apples - 4lb. at 5d. per lb.	1	8	1.40
Egg - 1 at 3½d.		3½	0.07
Extra vegetables and fruit	1	6	1.12[2]
Tea - ½lb at 3s. 4d. per lb.	1	8	0.35
Extras, including salt, seasoning etc.		9	0.56
	47	4	31.15

→

Low Cost But Acceptable

Warmth and Shelter	A healthy palatable diet
Social Integration	Avoidance of chronic diseases

Access to good
quality health care

Access to good
quality education

↓

Social   Justice

[1] Unfortunately, unable to obtain legal price for this in March 1998 - so have substituted stewing steak.

[2] Estimated as average of apple and onion price now.

11 'Spare Some Change for a Bite to Eat?' From Primary Poverty to Social Exclusion: The Role of Nutrition and Food

ELIZABETH DOWLER and SUZI LEATHER

Food is an expression of who a person is, what they are worth, and of their ability to provide for basic needs. It is a focus for social exchange. Food is also a major contribution to basic survival and long-term health. For these and other reasons, the cost and contribution of food have been used as direct indicators of poverty, and as essential components of cost of living indices. This chapter has three aims: to examine briefly the history of food in poverty measurement; to review the role of food and nutrition in poverty analysis; and to provide pointers to contemporary research and policy responses.

A Century of Food and Nutrition in Poverty

Seebohm Rowntree was probably the first to use ideas about nutritional requirements in a systematic way to define a minimal subsistence cost of living or poverty line. Rowntree did not of course use this poverty line to *identify* who was poor - that was done visually and on a relative poverty basis (comparing the living conditions of working class people in York with living conditions conventionally recognised and approved) (Veit-Wilson, 1986). The poverty line was used to separate people identified as poor into those who had insufficient income to purchase basic survival necessities, and those whose income was sufficient to buy basic necessities but who were unable so to do for other reasons (not necessarily inefficiency). In calculating basic needs Rowntree deliberately chose a diet so economical and unattractive that none should accuse him of setting too high a nutrition standard and therefore too generous a poverty line.[1] It was a theoretical dietary, not based on what people actually purchased to eat, or how much such a diet actually cost, or how it was eaten (what combinations of food). Its purpose was recognised as '*merely physical efficiency*', not to estimate a minimum income people could or would actually live on (Veit-Wilson, 1994).

Nonetheless, subsequent poverty head-count surveys between 1914 and the late 1930s by Arthur Bowley among others, did in fact use this 'primary poverty' measure to indicate minimal subsistence costs. It thus acquired a validity, which translated into allowances for the

> temporarily or permanently non-productive section of the population, the aged, widowed, orphaned, sick and unemployed, [...] fixed so as not to exceed the poverty line standard. Less could be given, but not more. [...] Rowntree's intolerably low minimum of 1901 was transformed into the unattainable maximum in the troubled twenties and hungry thirties.
> (Woolf, 1946, p.74)

Rowntree himself, of course, calculated a new 'human needs' standard (published in 1918 and 1937) which was still not meant as an optimum diet, level of housing, or any other need, but which approximated the International Labour Office's (1938) second level of 'decency without comfort' (Woolf, 1946), and close to the then level of minimum wages being fixed by trade boards.

The context of this work throughout the thirties, as at the turn of the century, was the increasing anxieties among the public, science professionals and the government about hunger, malnutrition, appropriate levels of living and the role of the state. Food and nutrition issues had been seen as essential to the remit of the 1904 Committee on Physical Deterioration, reviewing the means of producing men (*sic*) capable both of defending the empire and working productively to further it. During the 1930s nutrition was again perceived as a widespread problem among the poor, and the scientific profession was again annexed to determining minimal living costs. For instance, the 1933 'Hungry England' report, which was commissioned following a series of letters from concerned professionals (health and otherwise), was produced by scientific experts appointed by the *Week-End Review* (a journal associated with the Political and Economic Planning 'think-tank'), and drew on contemporary physiological standards of dietary needs (Smith, 1995).

John Boyd Orr built on these anxieties in his 1930s survey of the causes and extent of poverty, and the consequences for nutritional conditions. However, Boyd Orr's approach was quite different from that of Rowntree, Bowley and others. Rowntree had used prevailing nutritional standards to define a *minimal* subsistence level; Boyd Orr drew on what was then known as the 'newer knowledge of nutrition' (which largely referred to work on vitamins),[2] and employed what he called '*optimum* requirements' (our italics). These were based on the *'physiological or ideal, viz., a state of well-being such that no improvement can be effected by a change in the diet'* (Boyd Orr, 1936, p.12).[3] Arguably this alternative approach aimed to measure the level of income below which people could not participate in the customary way of life in society, in this instance, eating the kind of diet considered normal. Boyd Orr estimated the level of income needed at about 20-30s. per person, where 10s. per head is spent on food (Boyd Orr, 1936). In marked contrast, the British Medical Association (BMA) (advised by Bowley *et al.*) had said in 1933 that

> it could be done on 5s. 11d. for a man, 4s. 11d. for a woman, between 2s. 8 d. and 5s. 4d. for a child and about 22s. for the standard family of a couple and three children.
> (Woolf, 1946, p.75)

In addition, the BMA diet had assumed about 50 per cent of income to be spent on food; Boyd Orr and Rowntree (1936) estimated the proportion to be about 39 per cent.

These differences in minimal income required, which depend on the underlying subsistence paradigm, the food price data used, and assumptions about, or measurement of, proportion of income spent on food, proved critical in the establishment of how much money a family needed to live on. There was much public debate about the issues, because their outcome affected the levels of social assistance being established as well as wage levels. The BMA view prevailed, both in terms of the paradigm and of the actual costs.[4] The issues were also of course about understanding causality, and therefore responsibility, for poverty and nutritional deprivation. The Unemployment Assistance Board, for instance, claimed their levels were adequate for social life '*enough for all foreseeable needs, not only food and rent but renewals of clothing and household equipment*' (Veit-Wilson, 1994, p.101); but in private the Board acknowledged that '*there is no absolute criterion or scientific basis of need*' and that, rather, the principles of less-eligibility still applied (Veit-Wilson, ibid).

This difference between the public and private positions of the policy community was continued in the workings and report of the Beveridge Committee. While it was recognised internally that the processes were rather less incontestable and fixed, the public stance was that scientific justification existed for the establishment of poverty lines through application of costings to objective dietary standards. The Beveridge Report used the lower poverty line from Bowley and the BMA, with a minimal price uprating for cost of living changes since 1933, and a probable under-estimate of the cost of necessities other than food (i.e. an over-estimate of the proportion of income spent on food) in calculating the scales for benefit levels. Writers conjecture a number of reasons for this choice: that Beveridge did not in fact really understand the conceptual differences between the two Rowntree standards (one as a bare survival, one as basic realistic needs costs); that ideas about minimal subsistence were inconsistent and confused, sometimes by the same person at different times; that economists were keener on models and averages than observations of practice and allowances for variation; that residual principles of less-eligibility still applied (for example, Woolf, 1946; Veit-Wilson, 1994). In practice, however, the Beveridge Report enshrined the original Rowntree 'shock the public' poverty level as that on which people ought to be able to live with prudent budgeting. Those who could not were then at some level incompetent, and responsible for their own poor nutritional state (Walker and Church, 1978; Rivers, 1979). This level had severe consequences for the health and well-being of those forced by circumstance to live on state benefit levels for more than a brief period.

During the 1950s and 1960s few investigated food as part of poverty. It was not until the late 1970s that nutritionists started making measurements of the diets and nutritional conditions of poor households in the UK. Walker and Church (1978) for instance, looked at food expenditure and nutritional outcomes for lone parents living on Supplementary Benefit, and reviewed the theoretical impossibility that parents whose income was exclusively state benefits would be able to purchase sufficient food for their children to grow properly. They continued the tradition of using government standards as a benchmark for judging the adequacy of intakes. Since then, a few other nutritionists have maintained that approach, either making use of national survey results or collecting smaller samples of empirical data. Their work is summarised in Dowler and Rushton (1994), Leather (1996) and Craig and Dowler (1997). In most of these studies, researchers have measured nutritional conditions in households identified as living on low income or as poor through a variety of social indicators, including receipt of means tested benefits, location, or social class based on occupation (for example, Nelson and Naismith, 1979; Lasker and Mascie-Taylor, 1989). In some instances the aim has been to investigate the relationship between benefit receipt, income and nutrition (though few have successfully measured income); sometimes such research has challenged the adequacy of benefit levels (for example, Dowler and Calvert, 1995). There has been no national survey of nutrition and diet in low income households since the Second World War, though MAFF is now proposing to undertake such a survey during the next few years (Dowler *et al.*, 1998).

A separate strand of research has continued the 'dietary costing' tradition: to cost a basket of goods and compare the results with (usually) benefit levels. These studies are summarised in Dowler and Rushton, 1994; NCC, 1995; Nelson *et al.*, this volume. Some have used a theoretical basket, constructed from national survey data on food and nutrient intakes so as to meet reference levels for specified household types and average supermarket prices (for example, Nelson *et al.*, 1993). Others have used a list of basic food items and taken prices typical of shops patronised by poor households (for example, NCH, 1991). Yet others have specifically compared the cost of a list of basic food items in contrasting richer and poorer areas (for example, Mooney, 1990; Piachaud and Webb, 1996). In 1992, the Ministry of Agriculture, Fisheries and Food simulated a low income 'healthy diet' from the *National Food Survey* data; the week's food cost £10 per head.[5] Not only is this in itself probably more than most low income households spend on food, the pattern of food usage it required was completely unrecognisable and impractical: '*in essence, poor consumers would be expected to adopt a totally different eating culture from the rest of the population*' (Leather, 1992, p.76). This, as Leather argues, is discriminatory, and brings us on to food as part of social exclusion and deprivation.

It was Townsend, in his seminal poverty study, who brought food back into the picture of general deprivation. People who are poor

> lack the types of diet, clothing, housing, household facilities and fuel, and environmental, educational, working and social conditions, activities and facilities which are customary, or at least widely encouraged and approved, in the societies to which they belong.
> (Townsend, 1979, p.413)

In the deprivation index subsequently constructed from Londoners' views of 'necessities', Townsend included a dietary deprivation index (Townsend, 1987):

- having had at least one day in last fortnight with insufficient to eat;
- having no fresh meat or fish most days;
- having no special meat or roast most weeks;
- having no fresh fruit most days;
- having gone short of food at least once in last 12 months to meet a family member's needs.

Mack and Lansley (1990) in the *Breadline Britain* survey took the process one stage further and asked survey respondents whether or not they agreed items were 'necessities'. They constructed a deprivation index from the responses. Not being able to provide three meals a day for children or two for adults; not having fresh fruit; and not having a meat, fish or vegetarian dish every other day, were deemed 'necessities' by more than 77 per cent of interviewees, and were among the first 16 ranked criteria of deprivation. Callan and colleagues (1993) used an Irish data set to explore the relationship between income and deprivation indices in order to identify the poor - defined as those excluded from their society due to lack of resources. Food indicators which figured among 'necessities' identified by survey respondents were: to be able to have a meal with meat, chicken or fish every other day; to be able to have a roast meat joint once a week; not to have had a day during the previous fortnight when the respondent had had no substantial meal; and whether the household had had to go into debt in the past year to meet ordinary living expenses, including food.

In other words, these indices of deprivation and exclusion are based on what society's members regard as appropriate or normal essentials for everyday life. They represent a rather different approach from experts deciding what minimal nutrient or energy needs should be, what kinds of food-stuffs people should eat to obtain them, and what level of pricing people should search for.

This approach has parallels in the US, where indicators of household food security, both as perceived by household members, and in terms of practice and behaviour (such as going without food, or types of food), have been incorporated into national nutritional surveys (Radimer *et al.*, 1990). Household food security as such is not measured in Britain, although a number of qualitative surveys document the mechanisms low income householders use to try and ensure they obtain or consume food (Leather, 1992; Dobson *et al.*, 1994; Kempson, 1996).   For instance, people manage by eating different foods, or less food, or by eating with friends or family, or by using free food in day-centres and soup kitchens.   People also simply go hungry; parents in particular often describe going without food, or eating more simply than their children, to protect their dependents and release cash for paying bills and other necessities.   People living in such circumstances are usually well aware of potential health consequences, but they prioritise keeping a roof over their head and/or their family together (Dowler, 1998).

The Role of Food and Nutrition in Poverty Measurement

We could begin by asking what it is about food and nutrition that can aid or hinder poverty critiques.   Clearly part of the answer is that nutritional data (that is, data on consumption of food constituents) contribute to a materialist analysis: costings of basic necessities can be constructed and used in definition and measurement.   Essentially, a minimal nutrient intake (in the most basic versions, of calories alone) is defined, usually as an average for a population, and quantities of foodstuffs to supply such a daily intake calculated.   These foodstuffs are costed, and an allowance is added for additional basic needs costs (housing, clothing, fuel, and so on).   Alternatively, assumptions are made about the proportion of income spent on food, and the theoretical cost of minimal food is scaled up accordingly.   The result is used as a minimal cost of living, or absolute poverty datum line (for example, Reutlinger and Selowsky, 1976; Dandekar, 1981; Lipton, 1982; among many; reviewed in Dowler, 1996).[6]   Seebohm Rowntree was probably the first to use ideas about requirements in a systematic way to define a minimal subsistence cost of living or poverty line, and the results were very powerful.   That his dietary was based on contemporary, rigorous science, strengthened the findings and conclusions.

The figures obtained are seen as objective because they use scientific criteria of minimal requirements for survival, rather than observing what people living on low incomes actually purchase, which is said to have potential for including elements of 'human inefficiency'.   Such objectivity is in fact spurious; there is no universal standard for energy or any nutrient which unequivocally separates sufficiency from insufficiency.   Most requirement figures are probability statements based on the likelihood of avoiding deficiency or (less often) achieving health, if a given amount is consumed. They are usually drawn up for different age, gender, body weight and activity categories. But they are not objectively established minima or optima but socially constructed standards for a given place and circumstance (Dallison, 1996). Smith (1995), for instance, gives a cogent account of the private arguments and public debates surrounding the publication of dietary standards for energy and protein in 1934 by the Ministry of Health's Advisory Committee on Nutrition and the Nutrition Committee of the British Medical Association. The 1934 publication represented a revision, albeit minor, of accepted dietary standards that

> was not the result of the production of any new experimental or survey data..[but rather..] the outcome of a process involving professional rivalry and public controversy, followed by the emergence of common interests in preventing the reoccurrence of that controversy.
> (Smith, 1995, p.281)

The standards were an important contribution to the discussion on levels of unemployment assistance, and of the extent and causes of ill-health and malnutrition. At issue then was whether the 'standards' should be set for the average person or for the unemployed - the latter having lower requirements. The present view of international committees of experts is that the choice of cut-offs for energy needs still depends what basis of body size and activity is used (Payne, 1992; Shetty et al., 1996, among others).[7]

There is also no objective standard for sources of nutrients - no-one eats a diet devised by a least-cost analysis program (see MAFF £10 diet above), nor one costed at theoretical minimal prices. Indeed, the problem with many costing exercises is the source of price/quantity data and its uprating over time. Rowntree used the average retail prices for food in York except where the Co-operative price was cheaper, prevailing rent costs and a very small, possibly guessed, allowance for the cost of all other 'necessities'. The 1933 BMA recommended diet with costings seemed to have been based on the lowest prices obtainable for the worst qualities of every item, and at a time when the food index was lower than at any time since the 1914-18 war (Woolf, 1946). Numerous contemporary survey sources show the diet recommended (which, like the MAFF £10 diet 60 years later, bore little resemblance to what people actually ate) would, in fact, have to cost 10-20 per cent more than the BMA Report claimed (Woolf, 1946). Nearer to our present time, the National Children's Home, in a 1991 food cost survey, used prices typical of shops which their clients, known to be poor, usually used (NCH, 1991); they were accused of subjectivity and non-scientific rigour, although the publication of the survey results had widespread effects.

The approach of both Boyd Orr and the Budget Standards Unit was quite different: to look at what level of income is necessary to meet these requirements, or what people have to spend to obtain basic goods. While this is more humane and realistic it still begs the question of who decides on the translation between nutrients and foods (and what quality and commodities to include - for example, 'own brand' vs. branded goods vs. 'low-cost') and ignores the social and cultural constraints of poverty, induced by demography, geography and social exclusion.

We mentioned the least-cost-diet issue: it is a world-wide general observation that poorer households maximise the nutrients and energy they can obtain for as little cost as possible, and that richer households, while they spend more on food than poorer, spend a lower proportion of income to purchase energy (calories), thus buying 'less efficiently'. The food economic behaviour of those living on a 'survival' level has been subject to much study (for example, Lipton, 1982; Berhman, 1988) outside industrialised, developed countries. One of the paradoxes is that even the poorest households do not appear merely to purchase to meet physiological requirements alone, but try and satisfy cultural demands for taste or tradition in food type or preparation methods. What is more, if a household's economic circumstances change for the better, members are often observed to buy more expensive foods than hitherto, which are sometimes less calorie dense than commodities bought previously, but which carry higher status (such as meat), or are more tasty (such as fruit) (Berhman, 1988).

This discussion highlights one obvious point: people consume (in both economic and nutritional senses) food not nutrients. Rowntree originally costed nutrients from standards defined by experts; more recent poverty work cited above has used particular commodities ('meat' or 'fruit') or meal patterns ('having a hot meal') as a reflection of normal, accepted practice. A practice, furthermore, which is legitimated by reference to society in general rather than to an expert group. Berhman (1988) in discussing the observed looseness of the relationship between nutrients and income, argues that the economic data demonstrate people seeking and purchasing increased food variety as income rises, as opposed to behaving as nutrient utility optimising agents. He claims that variety of food-stuffs must in itself be a desirable aspect of life; variety is a trait or consumption good which people are prepared to purchase for its own sake. Indeed, current UK recommendations for a diet conducive to health include reference to variety and to specific food commodities - for example, to consume five or more portions of fruit and vegetables daily. There is as yet no official recognition of either the actual practice, or measurement of the ability to purchase a varied dietary base/sufficient fruit and vegetables, as indicators of poverty.

This issue of 'ability to purchase' refers to food access, which encompasses economy and location. That is, access includes the amount of money a household or individual chooses to spend on food, which depends on how much money they have and the priority they give to food rather than other needs. Secondly, access refers to the kinds of shops people can reach or choose to patronise, the price of foods and other essentials in those shops, and the range of commodities available. The locational element has become increasingly important in the UK over the last two decades: one consequence of the increasing polarisation of income and deprivation in the UK is the effect on food retailing. The spatial concentration of poverty is debatable, but poor people do tend to live in inner cities and/or large local authority estates; food shops have struggled to survive in these places, partly because residents spend less but mostly because the food retailing market has concentrated. Street markets and small, specialised high street food shops are disappearing; to some extent discount operators fill this retail gap, offering very low prices on a limited product range. Superstores (>25,000 sq.ft) have increased fourfold, mostly located outside town centres and designed primarily for car access (Department of Health, 1996).[8] The poorest are less likely to have cars, and public transport to better shopping centres is often inadequate. Food recommended for health tends to costs more in the shops found where poorer people live than in the superstores (Piachaud and Webb, 1996). The poor have increasingly been denied food access on both counts.

One consequence of science being used to justify minimal poverty lines is that any gap between costed basic needs and actual purchasing patterns, let alone health/nutritional outcomes, can readily be laid at the door of human inefficiency. It has been said that people do not know how to manage their budget, shop sensibly, or behave appropriately (they smoke, drink alc· ⁱ ·nd so on) and, by and large, are therefore seen as responsible for their own plight. This issue becomes particularly acute when the poverty lines are implicit in levels of social assistance, as they are in the UK, where the principles of 'less eligibility' seem to have been lost, or are no longer explicit. Governments are always trying to reduce public expenditure, and there is therefore pressure on the state to set its minimal subsistence level as low as possible if it also triggers welfare payments, and to assert its sufficiency for food as for other goods.[9] Those who cannot manage to live healthily at these levels can then be described as inefficient or incompetent, and their conditions not the responsibility of the state (Leather, 1996; Dowler and Dobson, 1997).

Where Now? Food and Nutrition in Poverty Definition and Response

With current interest in defining minimum wages and welfare reform as policy instruments against poverty, there will clearly continue to be a need for some sort of costing of the food element of basic goods. There needs to be a shift of position from that of the previous UK government of continuing to defend the sufficiency of social assistance levels; their inadequacy has continually been demonstrated (see Kempson, 1996, and in relation to food, see Leather, 1996; Craig and Dowler, 1997 for summaries; Dowler and Calvert, 1997). Leather (1992, 1996) among others has called for the process of calculation to be more transparent. One mechanism would the budget standards approach (Bradshaw, 1993). Where the food element of benefits levels is concerned, a food budget standard (Nelson *et al.*, 1993) would encourage transparency over the technical aspects of choice of nutrient standards or foods, and of prices, as well as the cost of other basic goods. Also it would clarify what goods and practice the money is intended to cover and should recognise the differential sufficiency for the long and short term. A somewhat different policy response from the past would be to ring-fence the food element in benefit levels; for instance, when fines or mandatory deductions are made for debts or arrears, sufficient money to enable the household to purchase sufficient food must be left (Leather, 1996).

There is also mileage in systematising food usage indicators. For instance, indicators could be constructed which measure food commodity variety or diversity in individuals' or households' diets; the practice or ability to obtain five fruits and vegetables for daily consumption; the ability to provide a meal for a visitor, or for some given festival. Dobson and colleagues noted that an enforced commensality was a (much regretted) feature of food choice in low income households: everyone had to eat the same thing at the same time, with no possibility of individual choice or experimentation (Dobson *et al.*, 1994). One could construct an indicator based on whether and how often parents went without food to feed their children, or were unable to provide fresh food.[10] Household spending on food often has to be flexible when many other items in the household budget are at fixed costs. Not only is household integrity sustained at the expense of the well-being and long-term health of its members; but also 'food being cut back' is itself a powerful marker of the inadequacy of income, since low income households are often given little choice about paying rent or utilities' costs. Some of the US household food security indicators take account of reductions in food purchase to meet other pressing needs. Patronage of free food banks/day centres is another marker of insufficient income, and has been used as a measure of food poverty at individual and household level in the US and Canada (Riches, 1997). Finally, current research on operationalising access indicators is being carried out, in terms of local shop food price and time/distance indices.[11]

Any indicator has to be interpreted against reference standards of some kind, whether quantitative or qualitative. We have already highlighted that any choice of standards is not a purely scientific process, as Plant says:

> Physical survival and autonomy are basic needs and the goods which satisfy them: food, health care, education, welfare - are basic, indispensable goods. So if the purpose of a liberal society is [..] to allow citizens to pursue their own good in their own way, the [effective] exercise of citizenship [..] requires a certain set of basic needs and basic goods.
> (Plant, 1983)

However, he also argues that:

> there is no apolitical way of deciding what needs are basic, and any level at which the claims to needs are to be met will reflect social values and democratic processes. This is a moral question for political debate, not one which can be derived from a purely administrative approach.
> (ibid)

Indeed, any costing of basic needs must include not only physiological requirements (as before) but also the social: food needs to be seen as a legitimate marker of social exclusion (for example, Leather, 1996; Lang, 1997; Dowler, 1998). Those who cannot afford to eat in ways acceptable to society; for whom food shopping is a stressful experience because they have insufficient money, or the shops they can reach are inadequately stocked with poor quality goods; whose children cannot have a packed lunch similar to their friends'; who cannot invite friends or family to a meal - these are people excluded from the 'minimum acceptable way of life'. In other words, the social, cultural and psychological functions of food have to be acknowledged in any assessment of basic needs or of social exclusion.

This brings us on to the basis of justification for, and therefore evaluation of, policy intervention for the food and nutritional needs of the poor. Nutrition as understood and practised in much of the twentieth century has been located either in welfarism (redressing the adverse consequences of market distribution) or human capital development (improving productivity, or ensuring education is effective, or reducing public health differentials - see below). Either approach can be based on assumptions about poor entitlements and/or nutritional or housekeeping ignorance, and policy responses range from welfare food handouts to education in appropriate knowledge and skills. In recent years nutritional problems and policy intervention have begun to emerge on the policy agenda as aspects of social justice or human rights (Dowler, 1996; Köhler *et al.*, 1997).[12] As Leather argues:

> access to a standard of diet which will create and sustain health is constitutive of citizenship. [..] People have the right to an adequate supply of food. Government policy should be to recognise this right in law; to guarantee an income adequate to meet basic food needs; and to ensure easy access to, and diversity of choice of, [food].
> (Leather, 1996 unpublished)[13]

The incoming government has not recognised the right to adequate food for health or social well-being. It has however, set itself to address inequalities and social exclusion. Space precludes a full analysis of the role and impact of nutrition in the policy responses and the potential impact of such policies on nutrition conditions of the poor. In the international nutrition scene there has been some interest in using nutritional measurements as indicators of the development process itself (ICN, 1992), acknowledging that economic development processes, or economic structural adjustment, have differential impact on nutritional conditions: the poor do badly. While there is some interest in the UK in using nutrition outcome indicators to evaluate food and nutrition projects specifically aimed at low income groups, there is not, as yet, interest in using nutritional indicators to assess the cost of the economic growth strategies of the last two decades for those who have borne the brunt of them, or as part of general poverty assessment.

The new government has also made strong public commitment to addressing inequalities in health, and we briefly draw attention to two acknowledgments of the role of food and nutrition. The first is the *Acheson Enquiry into Inequalities in Health* (Committee of Experts headed by Sir Donald Acheson, a former Chief Medical Officer; report due in March 1998). There were a number of specialised presentations (written and verbal) to this committee, of which nutrition was one. The nutrition submission was written by the former chair of the Low Income (and Diet) Project Team, a sub-group of the Nutrition Task Force to *Health of the Nation* under the previous government; and one of the present authors (Suzi Leather) was the external expert asked to review and comment. The Low Income Project Team had been set up to 'disseminate examples of good local practice which might enable those on low incomes to ensure they eat healthy diet'. This remit had come from a grudging recognition that those on low incomes (not 'the poor') 'may experience particular difficulties in obtaining a healthy and varied diet' (Department of Health, 1996, p.32). The remit explicitly excluded discussion of benefit levels, and asserted that 'the needs of [low income households] could not be met by national actions' (ibid.). In other words, responsibility for the problem and response was firmly located at local or individual levels; measures to alleviate nutritional deprivation were completely separate from those addressing income. In practice, the Low Income Project Team set itself a wider task, of proposing effective intervention in government, private and public spheres, and a self constituted group - the Standing Conference on Food and Low Income - has promoted their report and its policy proposals since (Nelson, 1997). These call for research and collaborative intervention at all levels of government (national and local), with the private and voluntary sectors and research community, to promote national recognition that economic and geographic access to food are key issues.

Therefore the choice of chair and a member of the Low Income Project Team to present nutrition's case to the Acheson Committee is instructive. It remains to be seen whether and how the Committee's Report takes the nutritional recommendations on board.

The second policy initiative is the Green Paper *Our Healthier Nation* (Department of Health, 1998). In this document, the social causes of ill health, and the inequalities which stem from them, are acknowledged and used as the basis for recommendations. Improving food and nutrition is recognised as an important contribution to improving health (Davey Smith and Brunner, 1997; James *et al.*, 1997). Problems of food access are given as an example (being able to reach decent supermarkets by public transport). These are promising signs that the structural and social components of poor nutrition are being taken seriously. However, as many have been quick to point out, there is no new money to support the policy recommendations: local public/private sector partnerships and lottery applications are promoted, as are community based initiatives, of which a food co-operative run by volunteers is given as a successful example.

The food retailing sector points to a number of initiatives by individual companies working with local groups and partners. But their most successful joint venture has probably been *Provision*,[14] a charitable scheme for food industry support to voluntary sector free food distribution. Day Centres and other food distribution to the 'homeless', marginally housed and vulnerable, has been a huge growth industry throughout the 1990s.[15] *'Spare some change for a bite to eat'* is a common cry on city streets: it highlights a visible part of the widespread poverty today, and that food, a basic daily need, is still a marker for its presence and experience.

Notes

1   'My primary poverty line represented the minimum sum on which physical efficiency could be maintained. It was a standard of bare ***subsistence*** rather than ***living*** [italics in original]. The dietary I selected was more economical and less attractive than was given to paupers in work houses. I purposely selected such a dietary so that no one could possibly accuse me of placing my subsistence level too high.' (B.S. Rowntree, 1941, *Poverty and Progress*, London, Longmans Green, p.102; quoted in Veit-Wilson, 1986).

2   This 'newer knowledge' led to an almost exclusive focus on nutritional explanations during the 1920s and 1930s as causes of, and solutions to, major public health problems (Petty, 1987). However, in contrast to the nineteenth century approach of public responses - housing, sanitation and other social reforms, in the 1920s emphasis shifted to individual, private behaviour: choice of food items, or the ability to manage a household budget appropriately in relation to food. This shift was a reflection of the discovery of and resulting intense research interest in, vitamins, and hence in 'protective' foods. The causes of malnutrition came to be identified as ignorance of dietary 'quality', rather than simple 'quantity' of food which could be purchased, which was more usually represented by counting calories (Rivers, 1979).

3   Boyd Orr in fact used the Stiebling standards from the USA Government Bureau of Home Economics: a level which *'provide[d] a sufficiency, with a safety margin, of all essential dietary constituents'* (Boyd Orr, 1936, p.12). This description suggests the level was probably not the optimum Boyd Orr hoped for, but similar to the present reference nutrient values: mean requirement plus two standard deviations, or sufficient to meet the needs of 97 per cent population.

4   Although Boyd Orr lost this particular battle, his personal intervention in the internal ministerial discussions about wartime food rationing did have a positive effect, in that the system used during the war was based on principles of equity rather than food purchase (James, 1994, p.29; personal communication).

5   In practice there are technical shortcomings in the *National Food Survey* for commenting on low income households: they are poorly represented in the sample and those who take part may be more prone to changes in behaviour while being surveyed than richer households (Leather, 1992).

6   Lipton, writing for the World Bank, took the ideas of variability in requirements a stage further, and characterised the 'ultra-poor': those who by expending 80 per cent of their income could not obtain 80 per cent of their calorie requirements - known as the 'double-80' rule.

7   Measurement of poverty and/or food deficits internationally often concentrate on energy intakes alone, on the assumption that they represent the basic need. There are a number of problems with these approaches. First, measurement of energy intake other than by dietary survey of some kind is unreliable; food balance sheets, often the source of data, do not measure consumption but availability or supply. Secondly, it is difficult to interpret low energy intakes; energy requirements are either based on intake distributions in healthy populations, or from factorial measurement of energy expenditure components. As Payne argues, the latter approach requires the user to specify average body weight and activity level for the population in question. Objectivity is again illusory: the question of whether the levels of weight and activity specified by those setting reference standards should be desired optima or based on present practice in the population concerned is unresolved. Thirdly, of course, people need more than energy; obtaining a suitable diet may cost more than obtaining basic energy needs.

8   By 1994/5, large supermarkets had captured about 70 per cent of average total food expenditure, from about half in 1991: the market has concentrated in all senses (Piachaud and Webb, 1996).

9   'My Lords, we do not believe there is any reason why people on income support should not be able to follow a normal, healthy diet. [...] people tend to eat different diets whatever their income. Some quite well-off people eat inadequate diets. Plenty of food is available at reasonable cost and people can thus maintain a reasonable and sensible diet.' (Minister of State, Department of Social Security (Lord Mackay of Ardbrecknich), during debate on reductions in lone-parent benefit, House of Lords, 14th March, 1996.)

10 In the survey of diet and nutrition in lone parent families, we found that answers to the question 'do you think you can afford to eat/give your children as much fresh food as you want to?' differentiated individuals and households with adequate and high risk nutrient intakes very well. Despite the lack of rigor or quantified definition in the question, respondents understood it perfectly well and gave answers that were verifiable from food and nutrient outcomes (Dowler and Calvert, 1995).

11 Dowler, E., Donkin, A., Stevenson, S. and Turner, S. *Mapping access to healthy food in a deprived area*, London School of Hygiene and Tropical Medicine & Institute of Education, University of London.

12 See Leather, S. (1996) *The making of modern malnutrition: an overview of food poverty in the UK*, London: The Caroline Walker Trust, and *Citizenship and Food Rights: the Policy Options*. Unpublished report for the National Food Alliance Food Poverty Working Party. See also writing from the Glasgow based Poverty Alliance's Foodworks Enquiry,

where the language of rights, entitlement and food security has consistently been used to great effect.
13 In practice, definition of rights as an attribute of citizenship can bring its own problems: the marginalised in a society, or those labeled as refugees or asylum seekers, have needs and rights to food too.
14 Provision Charity Services Ltd, Grange Lane, Letchmore Heath, Herts WD2 8DQ.
15 A National Day Centre Project is now run by CHAR, co-ordinating Day Centre activities and promoting networking through a regular newsletter.

References

Acheson, D. (1998), *Independent Enquiry into Inequalities in Health,* The Stationary Office.
Berhman, J. (1988), *Nutrition and Incomes: Tightly Wedded or Loosely Meshed?*, PEW/Cornell Lecture Series, Cornell Food and Nutrition Policy Program, Ithaca, Cornell.
Boyd Orr, J. (1936), *Food Health and Income: Report on A Survey of Adequacy of Diet in Relation to Income*, Macmillan & Co, London.
Bradshaw, J. (ed.), *Budget Standards for the United Kingdom*, Avebury Press, Aldershot.
Callan, T., Nolan, B. and Whelan, C.T. (1993), 'Resources, Deprivation and the Measurement of Poverty', *Journal of Social Policy*, vol. 22, no. 2, pp.141-72.
Craig, G. and Dowler E. (1997), 'Let Them Eat Cake!' Poverty, Hunger and the UK State', in Riches, G. (ed), *First World Hunger: Food Security and Welfare Politics*, Macmillan Press, Basingstoke, pp.108-33.
Department of Health (1996), *Low Income, Food, Nutrition and Health: Strategies for Improvement*. A Report from the Low Income Project Team to the Nutrition Task Force, Department of Health, London.
Department of Health (1998), *Our Healthier Nation: A Contract for Health*, February 1998, Cm 3854, The Stationery Office, London.
Dallison, J. (1996), *RDAs and DRVs: Scientific Constants or Social Constructs? The Case of Vitamin C*, unpublished PhD Thesis, University of Sussex.
Dandekar, V.M. (1981), 'On Measurement of Poverty', *Economic and Political Weekly*, vol. xvi, no. 30, 1241-50.
Davey Smith, G. and Brunner, E. (1997), 'Socio-economic Differentials in Health: The Role of Nutrition', *Proceedings of the Nutrition Society*, 56, pp.75-90.
Dobson, B., Beardsworth, A., Keil, T. and Walker, R. (1994), *Diet, Choice and Poverty: Social, Cultural and Nutritional Aspects of Food Consumption Among Low Income Families*, Family Policy Studies Centre, London.
Dowler, E. (1996), *Nutrition and Poverty: The Case of Lone Parents in the UK*, unpublished PhD Thesis, Faculty of Medicine, University of London.
Dowler, E. (1998), 'Budgeting for Food on a Low Income: The Case of Lone Parents', *Food Policy*, vol. 22, no. 5, pp.405-17.
Dowler, E. (1998), 'Food Poverty and Food Policy: Poverty and Social Exclusion North and South', *IDS Bulletin*, vol. 29, no. 1, pp.58-65.
Dowler, E. and Calvert, C. (1995), *Nutrition and Diet in Lone-parent Families in London*, Family Policy Studies Centre, London.
Dowler, E. and Calvert, C. (1997), 'Budgeting for Food on State Benefits: Poor Lone Parents in the

United Kingdom', in: Köhler, B. Feichtinger, E., Barlösius, E. and Dowler, E. (eds), *Poverty and Food in Welfare Societies*, Sigma Edition, Berlin, pp.307-15.

Dowler, E.A. and Dobson, B.M. (1997), 'Nutrition and Poverty in Europe: An Overview', *Proceedings of the Nutrition Society*, vol. 56, pp.51-62.

Dowler, E., Draper, A., Thomas, R., Dobson, B. and Nelson, M. (1998), *Scoping Study for a Proposed Survey of Diet and Nutritional Status in Low-income Households*, Report to MAFF, Joint Food Standards and Safety Group.

Dowler, E. and Rushton, C. (1994), *Diet and Poverty in the UK: Contemporary Research Methods and Current Experience: A Review*, Working Paper for Committee on Medical Aspects of Food Policy and the *Nutrition Task Force*, Department of Health, Department of Public Health and Policy, Publication no 11, London School of Hygiene and Tropical Medicine, London.

Dowler *et al.* (1999), *Food Projects and How They Work*, YPS for the Joseph Rowntree Foundation.

James, W.P.T. (1994), 'The Nature of Food: Essential Requirements', in B. Harriss-White and R. Hoffenburg (eds), *Food: Multidisciplinary Perspectives*, Blackwell, Oxford, pp.27-40.

James, W.P.T., Nelson, M., Ralph, A. and Leather, S. (1997), 'The Contribution of Nutrition to Inequalities in Health', *British Medical Journal*, vol. 314, pp.1545-9.

Kempson, E. (1996), *Life on a Low Income*, Joseph Rowntree Foundation, York.

Köhler, B., Feichtinger, E., Barlösius, E. and Dowler, E. (eds) (1997), *Poverty and Food in Welfare Societies*, Sigma Edition, Berlin.

Lang, T. (1997), Dividing up the Cake: Food as Social Exclusion', in Walker, A. and Walker, C. (eds), *Britain Divided: The Growth of Social Exclusion in the 1980s and 1990s*, Child Poverty Action Group, London.

Lasker, G.W. and Mascie-Taylor, C.G.N. (1989), 'Effects of Social Class Differences and Social Mobility on Growth in Height, Weight and Body Mass Index in a British Cohort', *Annals of Human Biology*, vol. 6, no. 1, pp.1-8.

Leather, S. (1992), 'Less Money, Less Choice: Poverty and Diet in the UK Today', in National Consumer Council (ed), *Your Food: Whose Choice?*, HMSO, London, pp.72-94.

Leather, S. (1996), *The Making of Modern Malnutrition: An Overview of Food Poverty in the UK*, The Caroline Walker Trust (6 Aldridge Villas, London, W11 1BP), London.

Lipton, M. (1982), *Poverty, Undernutrition and Hunger*, World Bank Staff Working Paper, World Bank, Washington.

Mack, J. and Lansley, S. (1985), *Poor Britain*, George Allen & Unwin, London.

Mooney, C. (1990), 'Cost and Availability of Healthy Food Choices in a London Health District, *Journal of Human Nutrition and Dietetics*, vol. 3, 111-20.

NCC (ed.) (1995), *Budgeting for Food on Benefits: Budget Studies and their Application in Europe*, National Consumer Council, London.

NCH (1991), *NCH Poverty and Nutrition Survey (1991)*, National Children's Home, London.

Nelson, M. (1997), 'Developments in the UK: The Work of the Low Income Project Team', *Proceedings of the Nutrition Society*, vol. 56, pp.91-100.

Nelson, M., Mayer, A.M. and Manley, P. (1993), 'The Food Budget', in Bradshaw, J. (ed), *Budget Standards for the United Kingdom*, Avebury Press, Aldershot, pp.35-64.

Nelson, M. and Naismith, D. (1979), 'The Nutritional Status of Poor Children in London, *Journal Human Nutrition*, vol. 33, pp.33-45.

Payne, P.R. (1992), 'Assessing Undernutrition: The Need for a Reconceptualisation', in Osmani, S.R. (ed), *Nutrition and Poverty*, Clarendon Press, Oxford, pp.49-96.

Petty, E.C. (1987), *The Impact of the Newer Knowledge of Nutrition: Nutrition Science and Nutrition Policy, 1900-1939*, unpublished PhD Thesis, University of London.

Piachaud, D. and Webb, J. (1996), *The Price of Food: Missing out on Mass Consumption*, Suntory and Toyota International Centre for Economics and Related Disciplines, London School of Economics, London.

Plant, R. (1983), quoted in Leather, S. (1996) *op. cit.*

Plant, R. (1984), *Equality, Markets and The State*, Fabian Society.

Radimer, K.L., Olsen, C.M. and Campbell, C.C. (1990), 'Development of Indicators to Assess Hunger, *Journal of Nutrition*, vol. 120, pp.1544-48.

Reutlinger, S. and Selowsky, M. (1976), *Malnutrition and Poverty: Magnitude and Policy Options*, Johns Hopkins University Press, for the World Bank, Baltimore.

Riches, G. (1997), 'Hunger, Food Security and Welfare Policies; Issues and Debates in First World Societies', *Proceedings of the Nutrition Society*, vol. 56, pp.63-74.

Rivers, J.P.W. (1979), 'The Profession of Nutrition - an Historical Perspective', *Proceedings of the Nutrition Society*, vol. 38, pp.225-31.

Shetty, P.S., Henry, C.J.K., Black, A.E. and Prentice, A.M. (1996), 'Energy Requirement of Adults: An Update on Basal Metabolic Rates (BMRs) and Physical Activity Levels (PALs), *European Journal of Clinical Nutrition*, vol. 50, *Supplement 1*, February, S11-S24.

Smith, D. (1995), 'The Social Construction of Dietary Standards: The British Medical Association - Ministry of Health Advisory Committee on Nutrition Report of 1934', in Maurer, D. and Sobal, J. (eds), *Eating Agendas: Food and Nutrition as Social Problems*, Aldine de Gruyter, New York, pp.279-303.

Townsend, P. (1979), *Poverty in the United Kingdom*, Penguin, Harmondsworth.

Townsend P. *et al.* (1987), *Poverty and Labour in London: Interim Report of a Centenary Survey*, Low Pay Unit, London.

Veit-Wilson, J.H. (1986), '*Paradigms of Poverty: A Rehabilitation of B.S. Rowntree*', Journal of Social Policy, vol. 15, no. 1, pp.69-99.

Veit-Wilson, J. (1994), 'Condemned to Deprivation? Beveridge's Responsibility for the Invisibility of Poverty', in Hills, J., Ditch, J. and Glennester, H. (eds), *Beveridge and Social Security: An International Perspective*, Clarendon Press, Oxford, pp.97-117.

Walker, C.L. and Church, M. (1978), 'Poverty by Administration: A Review of Supplementary Benefits, Nutrition and Scale Rates, *Journal of Human Nutrition*, vol. 32, pp.5-18.

Woolf, B. (1946), 'Poverty Lines and Standards of Living', *Proceedings of the Nutrition Society*, vol. 5, pp.71-81.

12 Eking Out an Income: Low Income Households and Their Use of Supplementary Resources

GILLIAN ELAM, JANE RITCHIE AND ALPER HULUSI

Contemporary research among low income households has shown that a variety of personal and domestic resources are used to support or extend levels of regular income. These include help from family and friends; sale or exchange of goods, possessions or skills; self provision from craft or land; use of stolen goods; and release of capital from savings or equity. This paper will examine how the nature and use of such resources has changed over time and their varying roles in contributing to standards of living. It will also consider the case for more refined measurement of such additional resources in studies of income maintenance.

> The poverty of the members of Class "A" is indeed such that probably the bulk of them would be driven into the workhouse, were it not that their meagre earnings are eked out by charity, either public or private.
> (Rowntree, 1901, p.42).

Introduction

A number of qualitative studies carried out in the last decade have detailed various personal and domestic resources that are used by households to support a low income (see, for example, Kempson, Bryson and Rowlingson, 1994: Morris and Ritchie, 1994; Speak *et al.*, 1995). These are of four broad kinds:

Informal support from family or friends by way of food, clothes (particularly for the children), furniture, bedding or other household items, decorating and cash gifts or loans;

Sale or exchange of goods, possessions or skills through selling personal or household items or produce; or by providing services in exchange for goods or cash from people outside the household;[1]

Release of savings, capital or equity through the sale or maturity of insurance and endowment policies, the acquisition of second or subsequent mortgages, the release of securities or pension premiums and entitlements, and the use of redundancy payments or inheritances or savings;

Theft and other illegal activity, such as shop lifting, receiving or selling stolen goods or sale of illegal drugs.

All of these resources provide a means of supplementing or extending the regular income[2] coming into a household, whether this is from benefits, pensions, earnings or other sources. As such they are commonly mentioned in studies of the living standards or income maintenance of low income families. They are used either to sustain a standard of living that is tolerable; or simply to 'survive' from week to week. Indeed, for many low income families, they form some of the many strategies that are adopted to try to 'make ends meet' (Kempson, 1996).

> I don't know what we would have done really if it wasn't for our mum. Only this week, the little girl's shoes, the bottoms were all falling off, we couldn't afford new shoes. So mum bought her a new pair of shoes. And Dan's (husband's) mum bought Liam his school uniform ... our mum, she's been ever so good, we'll go and see her and she'll say 'oh, take a couple of ponds of sugar or a quarter of tea ...or a couple of 50ps for the cleaners...
> (Ritchie, 1990, p.50)

A sixth category - ***credit and debt*** - might have been added to the list of additional resources identified. This would include the use of catalogues, clubs, credit and store cards, hire purchase, loans, overdrafts and arrears which are often seen as crucial to supporting a low income. We have initially excluded credit and debt from the supplementary resources reviewed since, unlike all the others, they involve money that has to be paid back. But we reflect briefly later on the changing nature of credit and debt over the century and the role they play in trying to sustain or enhance low income living standards.

Identification and Measurement of Supplementary Resources

The key purpose of this paper is to examine how the nature and use of supplementary resources has changed across the century. Before doing so, it is important to note some general features about the identification and measurement of such resources in income maintenance and poverty research.

First, there have been only limited or selective attempts to measure the extent of use of these resources, either in terms of volume or prevalence. This is largely because the nature of the resources makes them difficult to convert to a monetary value on a reliable basis. It is also because, until recently, their *role* in supporting household incomes has only been investigated systematically within in-depth qualitative research. This has prohibited any statistical determination of the scale of their use either amongst low income families or across the population as a whole.

The lack of statistical measurement leaves a crucial question unanswered which is as relevant to an historical as to a contemporary perspective. To what extent are such resources used more by low income families than by those in higher income groups? In other words, is their use a particular feature or 'outcome' of poverty or is it determined by other factors. Similarly, if they *are* more heavily used by lower income groups, are there other factors that affect their level of input into household budgeting (for example, ages of dependent children; whether area of living is urban or rural; level of income replacement ratio in unemployment). Questions such as these cannot be answered categorically but we attempt to glean some insights from the evidence documented.

A third issue concerns the definition of what counts as a 'supplementary' or additional resource. While there is almost universal recognition that households utilise various means to 'eke out' a low income', there are different perspectives on the classification and measurement of the sources used. For example, casual or occasional earnings, children's' earnings, undeclared income from lodgers or tenants, or the use of credit and debt may be differently treated in understanding the composition (and scale) of supplementary resources.

For the purpose of this paper we have confined ourselves to those which have the following characteristics:

- they are additional to the *regular weekly income* received by household members (whether this income is legally declared or not), even if their use occurs regularly on a weekly basis

- they do not require longer term repayment
- they are generated by individual members of the household or from items/produce contained within, or owned by, the household.

The Nature of Supplementary Resources

In discussing the number of families living above and below the poverty line in York, Rowntree briefly poses a question about the undetected resources which may be supplementing incomes:

> The question may arise: Do the family earnings comprise the whole of the family income? Are there not other sources of income which have not been taken into account? In the country, for instance, the money wage of the agricultural labourer by no means always represents his total income; he is often able to augment this considerably by means of the produce from his allotment, or by keeping hens, pigs etc. Does the town dweller augment his income in some corresponding way?
> (Rowntree, 1901, p.112)

He concludes that while there are other such resources available to people in York, 'the extent to which incomes are augmented by such irregular means is very small' (Rowntree, 1901, p.112). He felt, therefore, that it would not materially affect his main thesis about the numbers falling below the poverty line. But he identifies the possible sources of 'additional income' that he had been considering. They were:

1. Money sent home by children who are working and who are not living at home, e.g. domestic servants etc. ...
2. Allotment gardens, keeping hens and pigs etc. ...
3. 'Stray' money[3] ...
4. Payments for occasional service and 'odd jobs', such for instance as payments made to women for an occasional days washing, or for sitting up at night with a sick person, etc., or payments to children for going errands, and so on ...
5. Charitable gifts[4] ...
(Rowntree, 1901, pp.112-15)

It is arguable whether Rowntree was right about whether 'additional resources' were greater in the country than in the town since there had been no systematic investigation, nor indicative measure, of the extent to which this was so. A few years later, a study of poverty in an English village (Davies 1909) identified the use of land as a potentially significant 'additional source of income'. Townsend, for example, attempted to measure the scale of resources generated through home production (the net value of garden and farm produce for personal consumption) and gifts (worth £25 or more) as part of the 'private income in kind' that households receive. He concluded that for these and other non income resources 'The problem lies not merely in identifying such resources but in translating them into equivalent values' Townsend 1979). In emphasising this point, an example is given of what one of the village wives had done with 'an ordinary cottage garden':

> I have a patch of the garden to myself; in this I have a strawberry bed, raspberry bed, gooseberry-trees, currant-trees (black and red), apple-trees and a fowl pen. I have to look after this myself and keep it clean; the fowls enjoy all the weeds which I hoe off and throw into the pen. ... When I am selling my fruit in the summer, I sell off the finest fruit, and boil down into jam all the fruit, which makes quite as good jam, but does not command so good a price at the market. The jam I find very useful in the winter when butter is dear.
> (Davies, 1909, pp.136-7)

The annual income made from these produce was £8 8s 5d in addition to all the fruit, vegetables, eggs and poultry used for home consumption. This was a sizeable sum being over £3 more than the annual rent paid for the family's five roomed cottage and the garden. From these and many other budgetary examples, Davies concludes:

> The produce of the garden furnishes a large proportion of the food of the people. Potatoes, onions, greens and other vegetables figure largely in the menu of the poorest households, especially those with many children. Bacon is almost universally eaten.
> (Davies, 1909, p.193)

The early twentieth century literature also tells us about other sources that were used to 'eke out' a low income, both in town and country. But in the main, they are hard to detect as they were rarely systematically investigated and often tangentially referenced. With some exceptions, this very same pattern continues across the decades with only selective or passing reference to their presence or value. But even from such glimpses it is possible to build a picture of the ways that households have supplemented their incomes, either from sheer necessity or to soften the consequences of low income living. The documented evidence suggests that in nature, if not in precise form, these resources have remained remarkably similar over time. The following analysis considers each of the main categories in turn.

Informal support from family and friends encompasses a range of different kinds of help, both monetary and in kind. These include help with making ends meet, such as food, clothes, small loans; contributions towards, or gifts of, furniture, household items and appliances (either new or second hand); money for school uniforms or educational activities for the children; and, in more severe circumstances, repayment of debt or household arrears. Support of this kind appears to have remained a permanent and central feature of additional support to low income families (Rowntree (1901), Davies (1909), Bowley (1915), Orwell (1937), Shaw (1954), Young and Willmott (1957), Bottomley (1971), Townsend (1979), Hughes (1985), Bradshaw and Holmes (1989), Ritchie (1990), Middleton *et al.* (1994), and Kempson (1996).

There is little doubt that kinship support is present amongst families of all income levels, both as parents help their adult children to establish homes and families of their own and as children then support their parents in their older years (Young and Willmott (1957). However, it is less clear whether the nature of the support given to low income families, which often takes the form of help with food, clothing, or even rent or fuel bills (Clark, 1978; Kempson, 1994) is so universal. Morris and Ritchie, who carried out a comparative qualitative study of living standards among low to median earning families, suggest not. Their research indicates that both the level of dependency on such help and the form it takes differs with income levels:

> ... many of the families on lower income receive material help from their families by way of necessity rather than as natural familial support or engagement. ... There is therefore some dependency for basic week-to-week living as well as for other, more occasional, items. Such references disappear among median earners and in the higher ranges of those on in-work benefits, although clothes, particularly school uniforms for children, and household items remain and were clearly of significance. ...
> (Morris and Ritchie, 1994, p.57)

Similarly, at the start of the century, Rowntree was of the view that there was a high level of dependency on charitable gifts amongst the poorest people in the York. He did not think this applied to higher income groups.

For, broadly speaking, the recipients of charity are the poor i.e. those who from causes 'primary' or 'secondary' are below the poverty line; and the number who are lifted above it by charity must be small. ... Any gain in material comfort would have been dearly purchased at the cost of independence of character, and the consequences of such artificial support would be grave, economically as well as morally.
(Rowntree, 1901, pp.114-5)

The price of charity in the late 1990s is perhaps not as 'grave' as Rowntree perceived. Nevertheless, households which receive such help by way of necessity often speak of their dislike of such dependency and its effects on their 'pride' (Kempson, 1996).

Sale or Exchange of Possessions, Goods or Skills

Various studies of poverty or low income families have identified items that have been sold or exchanged to generate money for the household (see for example Davies (Townsend, 1979; Bottomley, 1971; Kempson *et al.,* 1994). These have included:

- personal or household items such as clothes, jewellery, domestic appliances, bikes, cars and caravans, tools that have either become outdated or obsolete, musical instruments, furniture, or, in the second half of the century, televisions, video recorders and musical systems.
- items made by family members specifically for the purpose of selling or trading, such as food, soft toys, clothes etc.
- the sale of produce from gardens, allotments or land.
- the collection of unwanted personal or household items for selling in house to house or local sales.

Similarly, much documentary and biographical literature identifies goods and possessions that have been sold to raise capital or cash.

To sell my clothes I went down into Lambeth, where the people are poor and there are a lot of rag shops. At the first shop I tried the proprietor who was quite polite but unhelpful; at the second he was rude; at the third he was stone deaf or pretended to be so. The fourth shopman was a large blond young man, very pink all over, like a slice of ham. He looked at the clothes I was wearing

and felt them disparagingly between thumb and finger. 'Poor stuff,' he said, 'very poor stuff, that is.' (It was quite a good suit.) 'What yer want for 'em?' I explained that I wanted some older clothes and as much money as he could spare.
Down and Out in Paris and London
(Orwell, 1933, p.129)

Although the sale of goods and possessions is by no means an exclusive activity of those on lower incomes, the *need* to sell may well be more pressing. There are several accounts, for example, of goods being sold to buy items for the household; to meet basic living expenses such as a large household bill or even food; or to cover the costs of special events like birthdays, Christmas or a school trip (Bottomley, 1971; Forster, 1995; Townsend, 1979; Kempson *et al.*, 1994; Morris and Ritchie, 1994). These, too, span different parts of the century.

The use of time or skills to generate small occasional payments was well illustrated in the early poverty literature cited above. It clearly has continued through the century and appears not to have changed greatly in form. For example, there are many contemporary examples of people being paid in cash or in kind for decorating a friend's or relative's house, repairing a car, doing occasional baby sitting or selling or exchanging produce from gardens or allotments.

Savings, insurance, capital and equity have been documented as important means of releasing money when families face 'hard times'. Although different types of capital may be used for different purposes (e.g. large bills, large household items, 'luxuries', emergencies etc.), savings, inheritances and severance payments (where these exist) are often drawn upon to support regular household expenditure (Marshall, 1972; Clark, 1978; Townsend, 1979; Bradshaw and Holmes, 1989; Kempson *et al.*, 1994, Morris and Ritchie, 1994). However, this is more by necessity than choice and in general there is a deep reluctance to use savings, or to cash in policies or investments just to get by or to make ends meet. Such reluctance is keenly felt by low income pensioner households who have little means of ever restoring their capital through increased income (Finch and Elam, 1995).

The importance of life and medical insurance schemes in the first part of the century is emphasised by the high proportion of families who made weekly payments from very low incomes (see for example Rowntree, 1901; Davies, 1909). The introduction of the national health service and social security provision has inevitably changed the role of such schemes, although arguably, this is reversing again. Nevertheless, it is clear that, more recently, insurance policies are sometimes relinquished in times of low income, either to release capital or to save the weekly or monthly payments (Kempson *et al.*, 1994; Morris and Ritchie, 1994).

The relative value of property has risen steeply in the second half of the century and may therefore account for the increased reference to the use of housing equity or housing equity schemes. Nevertheless throughout the social documentary literature there have been references to the rent or sale of land or property when income is low or reduced. For example, the early poverty research contains regular references to income from 'lodgers' that is needed to extend a low household income (Rowntree, 1901; Davies, 1909; Bowley, 1915). More recently, there is mention of the sale of property to release some of the equity or additional mortgages to release capital (Kempson *et al.*, 1994; Morris and Ritchie, 1994).

Stealing and other illegal activity. We speak here not of 'professional' crime but of theft or other activity which is used to support the every day needs of low income households. Although apparently much more rare[5] than the use of other resources, it has been tangentially noted as a last, or perhaps necessary, resort by some low income families. This, again, appears to be persistent feature over time even though the nature of the 'stolen' goods may well have changed.

> I've gone out of here in the mornings, I've come back with a box of groceries, chicken, bag of coal and that. One way or another I'll find food; you know what I mean. I'll get money one way or another. But I shouldn't have to do that. I shouldn't have to do that, but I do, I mean I think nothing of going into - store - and putting a coat on under mine - not that much (clicks fingers). I'd do it again tomorrow, you know, I'd do it for her. If I haven't got it then I'll nick it. The fact of the matter is - I haven't got the money ... Don't get me wrong, I don't go out nicking every week - I'm talking about when the bills come in or something like that, when I'm really stuck.
> (Ritchie, 1990, p.51)

> ... there is immense and systematic thieving of coal by the unemployed. I call it thieving because technically it is that, though it does no harm to anybody. In the dirt that is sent up from the pits there is a certain amount of broken coal, and unemployed people spend a lot of time picking it out of the slag heaps.
> (Orwell, 1937, pp. 90-910)

'Bad party; no good to anybody'. Poacher by trade , but can't be caught, as he has leave to catch his employer's rabbits. (The 'General Character' of one of the families in primary poverty.)
(Davies, 1909)

As noted earlier, the use of credit and debt has been regularly recorded as a means of supporting a low income. Indeed, there are few studies of low income households that do not make some reference to the use of credit of some kind (such as Christmas clubs or catalogues) or to personal loans or repayment arrears. In all cases they are a means - albeit a temporary one - for households to try to make ends meet.

The use of credit and debt has been statistically measured both amongst the general population as a whole and among low income households. This shows that low income households rely on certain forms of credit or loans such as mail order, HP, tallymen, money lenders and so on. This appears to have been so throughout different decades even though the credit industry has experienced significant expansion, particularly since the 1980s and changed in form (Berthoud and Kempson, 1992; Rowlingson, 1994).

The evidence accumulated suggests that the kind of supplementary resources on which low income households rely have remained fairly constant in character over the century. It also appears that there may be greater reliance on such resources among lower than among higher income households, although this conclusion can only be tentative. However, the evidence that does exist, whether statistical, qualitative or biographical certainly points in this direction.

Measuring Supplementary Resources

As was noted at the outset, many small scale qualitative studies have investigated the use of one or more of the additional resources discussed above. Increasingly, there is recognition that these items can mount up in terms of the supplement they provide to regular income. As a consequence, large scale statistical enquiries now will include items which measure the extent of use of items such as financial help from families or friends or use of savings (see, for example, Marsh and McKay, 1993; Department of Social Security, 1997; Townsend, Corrigan and Kowarzik, 1987). More exceptionally, there have been attempts to measure the monetary value of these additional resources, although not without some acknowledged difficulties (see, for example, Townsend, 1979).

Virtually all of the studies in which some measurement has been attempted have been confined to low income families. More systematic investigation across a broader income range would reveal the extent to which variations in use occur with income levels as well as with other socio-demographic variables. If, as the qualitative evidence suggests, low income households are more dependent on such resources than those in higher income groups, then the scale of this would be known. Such evidence will also help to address other questions. Do households with supplementary resources fare any better in terms of the duration and impact of low income? How important are such resources in transitions between benefits and work? If survival on a low income depends on access to these resources, how do those without such access survive? Are some infrastructures and networks better than others in the provision of additional resources? Answers to such questions will help to inform our understanding of living standards and the nature of income inequalities.

There are inevitably data collection problems. These include identifying resources which are inconsistent by nature, fluctuate over time and may be barely visible to the recipients. There are also difficulties in calculating an equivalent monetary value for help in kind or for items which rely on estimation and may be complicated by reciprocity over time. While difficulties of both identification and conversion undoubtedly exist, it should prove possible to get at least some gauge on scale and prevalence of use. It would seem that the resources concerned have been a sufficiently important and persistent feature of low income living to warrant more systematic statistical measurement.

Notes

1   Income from casual work, undeclared for purposes of tax or benefit receipt, could be viewed as regular income or as an additional resource, depending on its certainty and frequency. For the purpose of this paper, payment for time or skills have been included only where they are occasional or informal (i.e. from relatives or friends).

2   This includes all sources of income coming into the family unit, including undeclared earnings, payment of rents and regular earnings by children.

3   'Stray' money was income received for pasturage on common lands.

4   Charitable gifts included '*money, food etc.*'

5   Investigation of theft or other illegal activity has been undertaken in some qualitative studies (see, for example, Ritchie1990) although is not a common feature of low income research.

References

Berthoud, R and Kempson, E. (1992), *Credit and Debt: The PSI Report*, Policy Studies Institute, London.
Bottomley, V. (Winter 1971), ' Life on the poverty line', *Poverty*, no. 20-21, pp.20-21.
Bottomley, V. (1972), 'Families with low-incomes in London', *Poverty*, no. 22, Spring, pp.11-17.
Bowley, A.L. and Burnett-Hurst, A.R. (1915), *Livelihood and Poverty, A Study in the Economic and Social Conditions of Working Class Households in Northampton, Warrington, Stanley and Reading (and Bolton)*, King, London.
Bradshaw, J. and Holmes, H. (1989), *Living on the Edge - A study of the living standards of families on benefit in Tyne and Wear*, Tyneside Child Poverty Action group.
Burghes, L. (1980), *Living From Hand to Mouth; A study of 65 families living on supplementary benefit*. A joint FSU/CPAG publication.
Clark, M. (1978), 'The unemployed on Supplementary Benefit', in *Journal of Social Policy*, vol. 7, part 4.
Cohen, R. (1991), *Just About Surviving: Life on Income Support Debt and the Social Fund*, Family Service Units.
Consumer Credit (1971), Report of the Crowther Committee Cmnd.4596, HMSO, March 1971.
Davies, M.F. (1909), *Life in an English Village: An Economic and Historical Survey of the Parish of Corsley in Wiltshire*, T. Fisher Unwin.
Department of Social Security (1997), *Household Below Average Income. A Statistical Analysis 1979-1994/95*, The Stationery Office, London.
Finch, H. and Elam, G. (1995), *Managing Money in Later Life*, DSS Research Report.
Ford, J. (1991), *Consuming Credit: Debt and poverty in the UK*, Child Poverty Action Group.
Foster (1995), *Hidden Lives*.
Hughes, J.O (Winter 1985/6), 'Unemployment and Personal Circumstances - an investigation in to the situation of the unemployed on Supplementary Benefit, with particular reference to their clothing requirements', in *Poverty*, no. 62, pp.33-37.
Kempson E., Bryson, A. and Rowlingson, K (1994), *Hard Times - How poor families make ends meet*, Policy Studies Institute, London.
Kempson, E. (1996), *Life on a Low Income*, Joseph Rowntree Foundation.
Marsh, A. and McKay, S. (1993), *Families, Work and Benefits*, Policy Studies Institute, London.
Marshall, R. (1972), *Families Receiving Supplementary Benefit: A study comparing the circumstances of some fatherless families and families of the long-term sick and unemployed*, HMSO, London.
Middleton, S., Ashworth, K. and Walker, R. (1994), *Family Fortunes: pressures on parents and children in the 1990s*, Child Poverty Action Group, Poverty Publication 89.
Morris, L. and Ritchie, J. (1994), *Income Maintenance and Living Standards*, Social and Community Planning Research, London.
Oppenheim, C. and Harker, L. (1993), *Poverty - the facts*, Child Action Poverty Group, London.
Orwell, G. (1933), *Down and Out in Paris and London*, Penguin.
Orwell, G. (1937), *The Road to Wigan Pier*.

Reeves, P.M. (1994), *Round About A Pound A Week*, Virago Press Limited.

Ritchie, J. (1990) *Thirty Families: Their Living Standards in Unemployment*, HMSO, London.

Rowlingson, K. (1994), *Moneylenders and Their Customers*, Policy Studies Institute, London.

Rowntree, B.S. (1901), *Poverty: A Study of Town Life*, Macmillan and Co. Ltd.

Rowntree, G. (1954), 'The finances of founding a family', *Scottish Journal of Political Economy*, vol. 1, no. 3, p.201.

Shaw, L.A (July 1954), 'Impressions of family life in a London suburb', *The Sociological Review*, (New series) vol. 2, no. 1.

Townsend, P. (1979), *Poverty in the United Kingdom: A Survey of Household Resources and Standard of Living*, Penguin Books Ltd.

Townsend, P. (1995), 'The Family Life of Old People: an investigation in East London', *The Sociological Review*, vol.3, no, new series, pp.175-95.

Townsend, P., Corrigan, P. and Kowarzik, U. (1987), *Poverty and Labour in London*, Low Pay Unit, London.

Social Policy Research Unit (1983), *A review of the research on the adequacy of the scale rates of supplementary benefit*, University of York, Department of Social Administration and Social Work, DHSS 3, KC.

Young, M. and Willmott, P. (1957), *Family and kinship in East London*, Penguin Books Ltd.

Young, M. (September 19-20 1975), *For Richer, For Poorer: Some problems of low-income consumers*. Preliminary report prepared as one of the discussion papers for the Congress, Manchester, HMSO.

13 Disabled People, Poverty and Debt: Identity, Strategy and Policy

LINDA GRANT

Living with problem debts transforms people's lives. Materially debt invariably leads to a way of life encased by deprivation; an endless process of juggling scarce resources and doing without. But beyond the material outcomes, more or less imposed on people, the experience of living with debt can engender new personal identities and surprising strategies. For disabled people and their partners or carers the transformative effects of debt are superimposed upon lives partially fashioned by prejudice, discrimination, hardship and exclusion. This paper explores the identities and strategies imposed upon and adopted by a group of disabled people in debt.

The paper is based on qualitative research which explored the experience of living with debt and the circumstances surrounding and leading to debt amongst a broad range of disabled people and people with long-term chronic health problems (Grant, 1995a). The principal aim of the initial research was to identify ways in which independent debt advice services might be developed to be more attractive and appropriate for disabled people. The research involved detailed interviews with 76 disabled people and the carers of disabled people, including people with physical impairments, learning difficulties, mental health problems and sensory impairments. All of the informants had problem debts, that is: they were unable to repay debts at the rate initially agreed with a creditor; they were not repaying debts at all; they had had to borrow money to repay a debt or meet a regular payment; or they were in arrears with general household payments such as rent, mortgage or fuel bills. This chapter draws on evidence from 18 of these interviews.

The transformative effects of problem debt on people's lives and identities take place within a range of circumstances and relationships created by debt. Debt is often the inevitable outcome of long-term poverty, with all its well-documented, negative consequences for people's lives (see, for example, Cohen *et al.*, 1992; Kempson, Bryson and Rowlingson, 1994; Oppenheim and Harker,

1996; Kempson, 1996). Sometimes debt arises unexpectedly as a result of a sudden change of circumstances. Whatever its cause, debt creates and constitutes in itself a critical new set of circumstances and relationships for those affected. For example, relationships with creditors are altered. Once payments to creditors stop or become erratic creditors will seek a response from those in debt and debtors must either negotiate with them or ignore them. In either case, and often people pursue both strategies with different creditors simultaneously, new relationships are created in the financial transactions with a range of organisations. These new relationships can be infused with threats, harassment, legal action, or compromise which can, in turn, engender fear, anxiety, shame, guilt, depression or bravado amongst debtors. But whatever form the relationship with creditors takes it is the fact of a changed relationship with creditors which distinguishes living with debt from living with poverty.

The process of repaying problem debts locates those who experience it amongst the poorest of the poor. What may be a more or less adequate income without problem debts is rendered critically meagre as debt repayments swallow it up. The pattern and content of everyday life is changed; spending priorities have to be reassessed and reorganised. These and other factors distinguish living debt from living with poverty.

For disabled people the emergence of a debt problem often brings with it a personal realisation that debt is overwhelming and inescapable. Whether debt arises in the context of long-term exclusion from the labour market or the sudden onset of disability and loss of employment, a future of long-term dependence on state benefits is often likely, making the heavy weight of a debt problem more substantial. For disabled people debt is often inescapable for a number of reasons. It is well known that poverty can have very significant consequences for physical and mental health amongst the population in general (Oppenheim and Harker, 1996; Cohen *et al.*, 1992). People in debt similarly report that dealing with debt has led to a deterioration in their health. But disabled people often have difficult lives without debt because of the discrimination associated with disability. This discrimination stems from a society which fails to accommodate people with physical and mental impairments and so excludes, marginalises and degrades them. Debt can deepen these difficulties and trap people in a downward spiral where disability has led to debt and debt leads to poor health and illness (Grant, 1995a; Beresford, 1996). This downward spiral renders the possibility of taking up or returning to work more remote. Discriminatory processes and practices can, in any case, obstruct disabled people's access to the labour market and intensify their insecurity within it (Beresford, 1996). Debt becomes inescapable because the key route of debt - paid employment - is often not a feasible option. Thus, it is unlikely that there will be a new level of income to resolve debt.

Debt, Disability and Identity

If debt can be said to turn people's lives upside down, what is its impact on people's identities: on their sense of themselves as a partner, parent, son, daughter or friend; on their sense of themselves as a worker or a citizen; on their sense of themselves as a human being?

Living with debt recasts the nature of relationships with significant others and in this process transforms self-identity. For example, parents can find they can no longer count on receiving respect from their children because they are not fulfilling the role of provider.

> I think my children have realised that if you can't provide them with a decent living you don't deserve their respect. I've noticed, if I've told my 14 year old, 'can you make me a cup of tea I have to take some tablets', some time ago she wouldn't have dreamed of saying 'No'. But now she turns round and says, 'No, you've just had one half an hour ago'. (...) They are beginning to realise now - he's just an old bugger that's sat there, what can he do. They have said, you know, 'what have you done for us'. And I said, 'I used to do this and I used to get you that.' 'Oh, that was a long time ago. What are you doing for us know.' This means a lot, it hurts you a lot.
> (Interview 1)

Specific incidents are often poignant markers of a role stripped of what are regarded as its essential elements. The negative impact on parents of having insufficient money to be able to fulfil a providing or caring role in the way that they would wish can be experienced by unemployed people in general (Sinfield, 1981). But for disabled people, and often their carers also, it is the very inescapability of debt which is so significant in this regard. In these circumstances debt can become the haunting theme of people's sense of themselves in their personal relationships. For many disabled people in debt the key route out of debt - paid employment - is not an option. Even after death, and many of the people interviewed talked of death as a potential 'escape route' from debt, debt it is thought, will continue to define these changed relationships.

> I keep thinking all the time - if anything ever happens to me how are my kids going to pay these debts. Because these people would want them to pay, no matter how they paid. They are not going to turn round and say to them, 'Right, your dad's dead, forget about the money.' They are not going to say that. You don't want to think about it but it still keeps coming to you, especially at night when I am on me own downstairs.
> (Interview 1)

The experience is not simply about doing without material things which were affordable in the past, or not being able to meet the material expectations of children. It is that life has become irreversibly altered by debt.

> Things will never change. For me it is just an on-going, long-term care, can't see any to it. I don't think it will ever end quite honestly.
> (Interview 13)

> You think, quite honestly, you've dug yourself such a big hole and you are at the bottom of this hole and you just can't get out. And it's just never-ending, it's just there for ever.
> (Interview 5)

Debt becomes all-consuming, a constant point reference for self-identity across a range of relationships.

Friendships, similarly, can be changed by the experience of debt. Some people sensed that old friends now regarded them primarily and essentially as 'a person in debt', affirming this all-pervasive impact of debt.

> I have lost all my friends. I don't even go out much now. I used to go and see my friends but as soon as they saw me the first thing that struck them was maybe I was coming to borrow something if I had come to say hello.
> (Interview 1)

Living with debt, of course, leaves people with little money to pursue social pleasures; people in debt become excluded from everyday social activities through lack of money. But this also means an inability to fulfil the role of friend in an established relationship.

> People used to ring up and say, 'are you going fishing', and things like that. Now it doesn't happen. They ring for a bit and then it just tails off. It HAS A bigger impact than what you think.
> (Interview 3)

Friendships can become unequal and uncomfortable. Sometimes friends and families pay for treats and holidays. People struggle with their limited finances in an effort to keep some equality within the friendship and to live out the accepted patterns of friendship.

> I mean my friends, they pay for a lot of stuff for my daughter and they'll say 'we'll go out for the day to Matlock', or some'at. But you need money to go with. (...) I feel so guilty that they do things for us. So we've got to at least feed 'em when they come here and things like that. But I mean that - it's £10 off somewhere else (...) you've got to or you can't face people, you've got to keep some kind of dignity.
> (Interview 4)

However welcome the financial support and generosity of friends and family, financial dependence changes these relationships in ways which highlight the financial situation of the person in debt. Debt becomes a key point of reference in their identity as a friend.

For some of those interviewed an increased dependence on the financial support of significant others had coincided with an increased physical dependency on the care of others. Thus, when reflecting on the consequences of debt, people linked this with disability.

> You've gone from being active to being pushed in a corner and - look, it's time somebody helped you. You don't like it really. Apart from that, which is bad enough, its financial as well. You're having to come to terms with being secure and suddenly all that's gone. It's very difficult to get over.
> (Interview 5)

Two distinct developments can become linked in people's consciousness, sometimes triggering depression or other health problems, sometimes engendering an intensely negative sense of self.

> My wife, she does everything. She does the cooking, she takes the kids to school, brings them back, does the housework and sometimes, when we have an argument, she says to me, 'unfortunately you have just turned into a lump of wood and you are good for nothing'. At that particular time, when she says that, it's drove me crazy and I've blown my top but later on, when I think about it, she is right, she is just being honest because that is what I really am.
> (Interview 1)

The experience of debt becomes enmeshed with the ideas and practices embedded in a society infused with disablism. Debt erects additional barriers in the way of disabled people's insistence on the value of their lives.

> You're ashamed about being mentally ill and you're ashamed about being in debt as well. People say you shouldn't be ashamed but that doesn't comfort you. (Interview 9)

Disabled people in debt are often caught up within sets of complicated, and at times bewildering, relationships with private and statutory agencies and systems, including creditors, the Benefits Agency, the legal system and the health service. Many of these relationships can take on an oppressive nature when a person is in debt which can have implications for people's sense of themselves as members of society, as citizens. Poor communication between creditors and debtors, between claimants and the Benefits Agency, and between legal representatives and debtors was a strong theme emerging from the interviews (Grant, 1995a). People who have dealt adequately and competently with these kinds of agencies before debt find themselves unable to elicit clear and unequivocal answers to their questions, leaving them confused, misunderstood and frustrated. Often creditors fail to apply a constructive or understanding response to a debt problem and are only willing to negotiate with a debtor after the intervention of an independent debt advisor. For debtors there is a sense in which professionals and 'experts' come to dominate the process of dealing with debt. Occasionally creditors harass people in debt by calling frequently at the person's house, constant phone calls and threatening physical behaviour (Grant, 1995a).

Court appearances can have a devastating impact on people's sense of self-worth. People whose debts had resulted in court action invariably felt that they had been treated like 'scum', or like 'criminals'; that they had been stripped of their citizenship.

> In court I was treated with absolute disgust because we were in debt. That is a terrible feeling, no matter how you've got into debt, whether it's your fault or not, it's a terrible feeling.
> (Interview 5)

These negative references also infuse the interviewee's descriptions of poor relationships with creditors. Encounters with creditors' agents and attempts to negotiate over a debt problem often left the person in debt feeling intensely degraded. The experience is one in which a deep contrast is drawn between the status that debt confers on them and their status before debt.

> Because somebody owes money are you going to make them feel like criminals, wield the big axe over their head. Let's not talk to them civilly - they owe money. That's the way you are treated.
> (Interview 2)

> When you are telling the truth and people are treating you as if you are a non-entity, lying toe-rag, well, I just can't explain it, you can#t relate to it. (...) If you're talking to them people from building society, you get that down that if you had a crow bar in your hand satisfaction would be that you've smashed their face in. That's really only way I can explain how low, how bad it makes you feel.
> (Interview 3)

The discrimination associated with disability sometimes informed these encounters with creditors. The message that disabled people and their carers wanted creditors to understand was that disability had played a part in creating their financial circumstances. But creditors often refused to accept this. One woman whose husband had started to come home from hospital for short periods, following a brain haemorrhage which had left him severely mentally impaired, described her encounter with a debt collector.

> He came round here one afternoon and unfortunately (my husband) was home from hospital for the afternoon. (...) He looked at (my husband) and said, 'He looks quite healthy to me, what are you on about?' He said, 'I don't believe your circumstances, I'll just take the telly, the video, the stereo. I'll take you to court and we'll have every item in the house removed.' And my husband started trembling. He can suffer from epileptic fits now, since his operation.
> (Interview 17)

Such responses from creditors had forced some of the informants to consider exploiting disability or a disabled person in order to encourage fair or sympathetic treatment. To contemplate this was distressing. People were aware that they were playing into a perception of disabled people as dependent and needy, a perception at odds with their own views.

> I think if only they could see (my husband's) wheelchair they would believe what I'm trying to tell them. But why should I have to use his disability in that

way.
(Interview 5)

I mean I go out there and I don't expect special treatment just because I have this daughter with difficulties. But I do expect people to understand me. She is a human being and I don't think I should have to exploit her.
(Interview 18)

Living with debt appears to shape new identities within a range of relationships and roles, and leads people to assume a new sense of themselves as 'a person in debt'. Yet outside these relationships and roles, in so far as individual human beings can be de-contextualised, people's experience of debt is, at once, both all-consuming and hidden. Debt becomes both an essential dimension of a new identity and a lonely experience to be shared with as few people as possible. There is a sense in which the potential of debt to transform and contaminate social relationships, identity and status must be contained and controlled by the person in debt. This determination to limit the contaminating effects of debt is revealed by the tendency to hide debt and its consequences from as many people as possible. Despite the severe mental stress and depression which often envelopes the person in debt, attempts are made to conceal aspects of living with debt even from immediate family. For example, one man faced with the repossession of his house had not told his wife about a court appearance, 'she didn't even know I'd been to court. It were an ordeal for me to go' (Interview 3). People choose to bear the burden of debt alone.

You feel degraded. You think other people know that you are in debt. You think you've done something wrong. It's very lonely because you don't tell anyone. I never tell my sons things like that, no, I don't mention it to them.
(Interview 9)

The desire to contain debt as a pollutant of relationships, and in turn identity, is also revealed in the interviews by people's constant references to their lives before debt. 'Life before debt' was invariably portrayed by the interviewees as in stark contrast to 'life with debt'. Life before debt was often described rather glowingly - it was carefree, happy, comfortable, easy.

When I was working my main priority was to pay my bills, my mortgage, the food. (...) We really had a very comfortable life. I had a beautiful car (...) I mean, one minute you are a really happy, carefree family. I used to work 5, 6 days a week and me days off we used to take the kids all over the place and now, even during the holidays they haven't been out, just for a single day. (...)

They want to know why and you can never answer that, you've never got an answer to their questions.
(Interview 1)

Life before debt was recalled as ordered. Payments to creditors were never missed and, indeed, the failure of creditors to acknowledge this was a source of anger and disgust for many of those interviewed. Life before debt was a key reference point for the present; a time not only to be hankered after in terms of its greater material security but at a time when a person's value as a human being was incontrovertible. Life before debt was a time when a person could make a material and emotional contribution to the happiness of their family and friends. These unsolicited reflections on the past within people's description of living with debt are about reaffirming an ability to make a positive difference to other people's lives, an ability to which debt has seemed to strip away. Debt is all-consuming in the present but reflections on the past are not simply an escape from current reality.

Just as looking to the past involves an assertion of an ability to change others and make a difference, so people also look to the future and imagine a life with money.

For us to get up in the morning and have peace of mind. It hits you debt, as soon as you wake up. To wake up knowing there's nothing there, nobody's coming after you for anything, it would be fantastic.
(Interview 6)

But this imagined future life with money is one in which, again, the person in debt could make a difference to the lives of those for whom they care.

I wish I could make a lot of money and send my mum and dad on a fantastic holiday. I wish there was some way I could repay them for what they've done for me. I never will, I never can.
(Interview 13)

Living with debt freezes people within a life defined by debt.

Debt was the most important thing at the time. I couldn't think of anything else. I couldn't sleep for thinking about it. I don't think you went through an hour without thinking - oh you've got this to pay, you've got the other. I don't think you thought anything else existed, only this shame and debt.
(Interview 9)

Relationships, projects, life itself is swallowed up, 'You can never start living with debt' (Interview 14). Thus the possibility of a future with money, where all debts are repaid would signify the re-start of living; the longed-for opportunity to re-establish life.

Strategies Adopted in Response to Debt

There are a range of what might be called 'rational' responses to debt. Such strategies would include: seeking the advice of an independent debt advisor from an organisation like the Citizens Advice Bureau; devising and following a careful household budget of essential expenditure; and cutting back on, or doing without, some material goods and services. Many people do adopt these kinds of strategies. But others resist or reject them.

Those interviewees who had sought independent advice about their problem debts tended to establish a structured pattern of expenditure and debt repayments, a strategy which, when supported by a debt advisor, often relieved the anxiety and financial chaos which can envelop households in debt. Yet many people in debt do not seek advice.

The social stigma attached to debt is a significant barrier to seeking advice. The vast majority of people only approach an advice when their own efforts at managing debt and dealing with creditors have broken down. Indeed, it is usually when people have reached a crisis point that they seek help.

> I went to the CAB because I thought somebody is going to have to try and help me because I was getting to the state where it were affecting your mental state. I could kind of feel it coming on and I thought, well, if I don't shake myself or do something I'm going to be in trouble.
> (Interview 3)
>
> I was suicidal, truly. I couldn't see a way out at all.
> (Interview 2)

Some people are simply unaware that independent debt advice services exist or are unsure about the kind of service a debt advisor can offer and thus cannot identify the potential value of advice. Many advice centres are physically inaccessible to some disabled people and an agency's failure to offer a home visit can exclude some disabled people from access to advice (Grant, 1995b).

But a reluctance to seek help with problem debts often stemmed from a longer-term experience of prejudice. Disabled people's status as citizens is already compromised by a society which fails to accommodate their needs. Seeking help may further damage a person's identity as a citizen, a view typified by the comments of a man who had had schizophrenia for many years.

> I mean, you go into one office and say, 'Hello'. They'd say, 'God, he's here - what do you want?' I say, 'Oh, it's all right, it doesn't matter', and go away. It helps if they're not like - Oh, you've got a psychiatric illness, or they don't feel afraid. They don't think, he's a nutter, he'll do this and that, oh fucking nutter.
> (Interview 7)

The fear that an outsider might make specific and negative judgements about a disabled person in debt held people back from seeking advice and led others to stress their ability to cope, to hide their debt problem, even though advice might have been helpful. As the wife of a man with a visual impairment explained:

> I think it goes down to the fact that in the era I was brought up in disabled people should be looked down on. You couldn't really see a disabled person as a person to love so I was marrying beneath myself (...) and I think a lot of it stemmed from that, my pride. I wouldn't let anybody know we'd reached such a level because it was proving them right (Int.8).

For many disabled people just trying to secure the benefits to which they are entitled has been an invasive process and a struggle. The most intimate and personal aspects and consequences of an impairment have been categorised and scored by state officials. Amongst the interviewees some people's had been subjected to intensive scrutiny and investigation which sometimes led to the loss of benefits.

> You're on the edge all the time. Because even though you're off sick they're checking up on you all the time. You're obviously having to go for them medicals. They're after knocking you off that and putting you on unemployment and then money would obviously drop down again. Then they'll start sending you for hopeless jobs that you haven't got a prayer of living on.
> (Interview 10)

The surveillance experienced by one family reveals why some disabled people are wary of involving a further agency in their financial affairs. Helen is the mother of two boys, both in their early 20s. Helen had split up from her husband 13 years ago, he remarried and she brought up her sons alone. Her youngest son, aged 23 at the time of the interview, has cerebral palsy. Although he is able to do many day to day things for himself, he still needs care and support with aspects of his life which Helen provides. Helen had faced pressure from the Department of Social Security (DSS) to take up paid employment.

> In the past they used to threaten me, when I were on my own, they'd threaten me with income support. They said they were going to stop paying it because there was no reason why I couldn't go out to work (Int. 6)

Four years before the interview Helen was diagnosed as having breast cancer and she was admitted to hospital to have her breast removed. She was forced to arrange alternative care for her son and turned to her ex-husband, who had now divorced his second wife, for help. When Helen came out of hospital her ex-husband stayed on at her house to give her support. The effects of Helen's surgery made it difficult for her to lift her son in and out of his wheelchair and into the bath. Helen continued to claim her benefits as before. However, a neighbour contacted the DSS to report the fact that her ex-husband was staying with her. At the time he was in paid work. Helen was accused of fraudulently claiming benefits and for the past four years had been repaying the alleged overpayment of around £400 Income Support and £400 Housing Benefit.

> The social haven't understood, they couldn't care tuppence. (...) They said 'well, it's not our fault you've had your breast off'. And I thought - it's not ours either. That's a woman at social security. She said, 'it's not our problem, it's not our problem you've had your breast off'.
> (Interview 6)

For some disabled people and their carers the option available to citizens in general to seek out free advice for a debt problem can appear to contain more potential pitfalls than advantages. People are fearful that additional investigation into their personal circumstances and finances, by whatever agency, may lead to a further loss of income. In these kinds of circumstances the suggestion that advice might be helpful is not necessarily accepted.

It's just that we don't want any more hassle regarding our situation, we don't want to go to that trouble. We plod on as we are. (...) I know it would be alright, I appreciate what you are saying but if you'd put up with as much as what we had you just feel like getting in a corner and hiding, that's what you feel like.
(Interview 6)

For people with learning difficulties, anxiety about the possible consequences of seeking advice may be particularly acute. One couple who were interviewed, both of whom had learning difficulties, had been denied access to money for most of their lives. Before they approached an advice centre they were concerned that they would, once again, lose control over their money.

I was nervous at first, very nervous. I thought - now, is she going to take all us money. Even my wife thought they were gonna take us money of us. And I said, 'no, they can't do that', you know, reassuring her. But I was already thinking, you know - Oh God, are they?
(Interview 15)

Disabled people's strategies in relation to debt advice can be informed by social processes and practices embedded within a disablist society. People's awareness of prejudice, their experience of intense surveillance, the long-term denial of their independence shape their response to debt. By not seeking advice disabled people appear to be challenging the discrimination and social exclusion which haunts their lives.

One obvious strategy in response to debt is to devise and follow a careful household budget of essential expenditure, cutting back on, or doing without, a range of material goods and services. Fifty per cent of the people interviewed stated that they had gone without food and/or heat at some time since their financial difficulties had begun, often with very significant consequences for their mental and physical health.

This time last year, February, I was really down. I were going without heating. I had my coat on, I had a thick coat on, cardigans, socks. I daren't have heating on. (...) I tell you, I was in the mood, if I could have smelt gas I should have put gas on. (...) I were ready to do away with myself.
(Interview 16)

Yet the value of using scarce resources to buy only essential goods and services is not always regarded as rational when money is tight. On the contrary, securing tangible outcomes from spending may make more sense.

> You know, people that's short, and there's millions of us these days that's living on insufficient money. (...) They are reluctant to spend money on things that they can't see, like gas. If you wanted to buy your kiddy a toy motor car for Christmas it can see that, but gas, you can't see it. (...) So if there is anything that you're not going to pay it's things like your electricity, your gas and your rent because there's nothing for it.
> (Interview 11)

And the desire to spend money on treats and to seek distractions from the endless grind of making ends meet is an understandable response to living with debt. Most of the interviewees conveyed a powerful sense of lives made difficult by disability without having also to continually employ careful spending patterns.

> At first we were really going crackers, like going to Netto and I was spending £40 a fortnight for three of us, so we were really, I wasn't eating. Let's say it, it got to the point where I wasn't eating. (...) Over the last two years it's been money all the time, literally all the time, we do nothing but think about money, it really gets you mad ... but I mean sometimes we do really stupid things (...) We have a take away meal once in a mad while, that's £10 or £12. We can't afford it, we know we can't but we do it. If you don't you go round the twist.
> (Interview 4)

Similarly, a man bringing up two children with learning difficulties, one of whom had frequent violent episodes, spoke openly about his need to escape periodically to the pub.

> I can keep to a budget for a while then after a while I think - no, I have had enough, 24 hours a day with this crap, I want away. And as I say, I can't go and have 3 pints ... I've got to go and get rat arsed, if you pardon the expression, come back and not know what day it is, kind of thing. It's not a week long thing it's just a day thing but I make a meal of it, I make a pig of myself. I never drank during the week before, but now if I've go money I'll go for a drink and I'm not fussy if it's rent money if I'm in that mood - I'm going out and that's it.
> (Interview 12)

Guilt and a fear of disapproval were evident in these revelations.

Expenditure that people not experiencing debt or poverty might regard as routine had to be justified by those in debt. Yet as George Orwell (1965) observed in *The Road to Wigan Pier*, in a discussion of the wholesome diet recommended for unemployed people in the 1930s

> ... the peculiar evil is this, that the less money you have, the less inclined you feel to spend it on wholesome food. (...) When you are unemployed, which is to say when you are underfed, harassed, bored and miserable, you don't **want** to eat dull, wholesome food. You want something a little bit 'tasty' (p. 96).

In the context of lives constrained by a lack of money and social exclusion, enjoying something 'a little bit tasty' is a strategy which enables people to reassert control over their lives.

People in debt would be advised to identify priority debts, such as mortgage repayments, and to arrange with creditors to make regular, if reduced, repayments on debts. Many interviewees had adopted this strategy, particularly those who had received advice from a debt counsellor. Most of the interviewees were also aware of the potential value to them of prioritising debts, like mortgage and fuel payments, and establishing structured relationships with all creditors. The strategy involved not taking on any further credit. Yet people did not always follow this strategy. Part of the reason for this lies in the very nature of living in debt. Using credit is often the only way to buy non-everyday goods. Thus, retaining access to at least one source of credit is seen as a priority. For those disabled people who are unlikely to enter or re-entre the labour market formal sources of credit through banks and building societies are not accessible. Thus keeping up payments with creditors who arrange credit on the doorstep and who call weekly for repayments is a common strategy even though interest rates from this form of credit may be high. This is a vital and possibly the only potential source of credit for the future.

> He comes every week (...) If I had to miss him he would understand but I try not to, it's not beneficial to us.
> (Interview 11)

In living and dealing with debt people's identity can become distorted and demeaned. For disabled people this outcome of debt is infused with the prejudice, discrimination and social exclusion associated with disability. The evident resistance to 'sensible' responses to debt suggests a rejection of enforced social exclusion and a reassertion of people's sense of their right and desire to control their own lives. The strategies adopted by this group of disabled people in response to debt represent an insistence on their dignity, value and purpose as citizens and human beings.

Disability, Debt and Policy

Disabled people are vulnerable to debt. The tendency to poverty amongst disabled people largely explains this vulnerability to debt. The link between poverty and disability is well-established (see, for example, Thompson *et al.,* 1990; Berthoud *et al.,* 1993; Martin and White, 1998). Despite a popular conception that disabled people are well-protected by a benefits system which meets the extra costs of disability, disabled people's access to 'additional costs' benefits is not universal and the amount of benefit to which many disabled people are entitled is often too low to counteract the tendency towards problem debt apparent among low income households. Taking on credit might be the only way to cover extra costs. But the general problems of living on a low income often make repayments on credit difficult to maintain.

This research, conducted in 1994, revealed very low levels of income. For example, 50 per cent of the single people interviewed had an income of less than £85 a week. Thirty-six per cent of households with children had an income of less than £150 a week. Thirty-six per cent of households were dependent on means tested benefits as their main source of income. Far from being targeted for help, disabled people can face appalling levels of hardship and deprivation (Walker and Walker, 1991).

Debt is above all a problem for the poor (Ford, 1991). Of course, not all people living in poverty experience debt. Some live with severe deprivation in order to avoid debt. But many poor people experience a combination of circumstances which make debt virtually unavoidable. In addition, individual disabled people and their families can face a range of specific financial circumstance and difficulties associated with disability which compound this vulnerability to debt (Grant, 1995a).

Disabled people claiming social security benefits have recently been thrust onto the centre stage in the Labour Government's on-going discussion of welfare reform. The current murky policy agenda, involving suggestions to replace the cash benefits of Disability Living Allowance (DLA) with services in kind and to encourage and support disabled people to enter the labour market, has generated some support amongst disability organisations, fierce opposition from others, and a sense of anxiety amongst many disabled people concerned that their standard of living will be reduced and that they will be forced into a hostile labour market. Given the already strong associations between disability, poverty and debt the anxiety among disabled people about possible changes to current benefit provision is well-founded.

Once disabled people are experiencing problem debts there are a range of potential outcomes. Materially, because debt repayments can consume a significant proportion of a low income, disabled people in debt can find their income reduced to a critically meagre level which leads to deprivation. This can involve not only doing without basic needs, like food and heat, but also doing without additional goods and services which are essential to maintaining a quality of life and independence comparable to that of non-disabled people. These goods and services would include care and cleaning services, and appropriate transport and housing. The anxiety of dealing with debt problems often leads to poor mental health and sometimes poor physical health. Moreover, problem debt can have a distorting and negative impact on disabled people's sense of themselves within a range of important relationships. In combination, these outcomes can push disabled people into a downward spiral where disability has led to debt and debt leads to poor health, an inadequate quality of life and isolation. Given these potential outcomes of debt what impact would the policy changes suggested have on disabled people in debt?

Replacing DLA with services in kind would be detrimental to disabled people in debt. Not all disabled people receive DLA in any case and thus a tendency to debt problems and deprivation amongst disabled people would not be removed for these groups. And being in receipt of DLA is not a protection against debt as this research demonstrated (57 per cent of the total sample qualified for an amount of DLA) (Grant, 1995a, p.17). For those who do receive DLA, and bearing in mind that the amounts of DLA received by individual disabled people can be very small, because the income available from other sources can be insufficient to meet their needs, DLA often has to be used to make debt repayments and to meet general household payments, like fuel and telephone bills (Grant, 1995a, p.51). Those who qualified under a new 'services in kind' policy might receive services which they are currently unable to afford but they might also experience greater difficulties in meeting general household expenses and resolving problem debt. Unless income from other sources is increased for those receiving DLA the vulnerability of debt amongst DLA claimants will be not be removed. The policy would also deny disabled people control over their spending; it would prevent them from exercising the spending options available to the population in general. As has been argued, the circumstances of the lives of some disabled people and their carers can engender strategies which are aimed at rejecting enforced social exclusion. Without a cash benefit these choices would not be available.

Providing additional support to disabled people to enter the labour market is on the face of it a positive policy proposal. Those disabled people who wish to take up paid employment would no doubt welcome further measures to challenge and address the discrimination which excludes them from the labour market. Yet not all disabled people are seeking employment or in a position to take up paid work. In this study 91 per cent of the people interviewed were of working age, yet only 33 per cent felt able to contemplate paid work as a potential aspect of their future lives, and only nine per cent believed they had a realistic chance of overcoming the barriers facing them in the labour market (Grant, 1995a, p.11). Secure well-paid employment does provide a crucial route out of debt, but access for disabled people to such employment is likely to be limited without major changes in the labour market and employers' practice. Research reveals that disabled people in work tend to be concentrated in low paid, low status jobs (Martin and White, 1998; Barnes, 1991; Berthoud, Lakey and McKay, 1993). Low paid employment would not guarantee an escape from a vulnerability to debt, particularly if 'additional costs' benefits, like DLA, were simultaneously withdrawn.

One of the earlier outcomes of this research was a set of good practice guidelines for debt advisors, outlining low cost, practical ideas for improving debt advice services for all disabled people in debt (Grant, 1995b). Good quality advice, based on a clear understanding of the experience of disabled people in debt, is a valuable resource and can ameliorate the experience of debt and improve people's quality of life. But the debt problems experience by disabled people arise in the context of a benefits system which fails to provide an adequate standard of living or an income sufficient to meet the additional costs of disability for all disabled people. Good quality debt advice does provide support and help to disabled people in debt but it cannot replace an acknowledgement by government that the current levels of income available to many disabled people are insufficient to meet their needs. Current policy proposals do not address this issue.

References

Barnes, C. (1991), *Disabled People in Britain and Discrimination: A Case for Anti-Discrimination Legislation*, Hurst, London.

Beresford, P. (1996), 'Poverty and Disabled People: Challenging dominant debates about policies', *Disability and Society*, vol. 11, no. 4, pp. 553-567.

Berthoud, R., Lakey, J. and McKay, S. (1993), *The Economic Problems of Disabled People*, Policy Studies Institute, London.

Cohen, R., Coxall, J., Craig, G. and Sadiq-Sangster, A. (1992), *Hardship Britain: Being poor in the 1990s*, Child Poverty Action Group, London.

Dally, G. (1991), *Disability and Social Policy*, Policy Studies Institute, London.

Ford, J. (1991), *Consuming Credit: Debt and Poverty in the UK*, Child Poverty Action Group, London.

Grant, L. (1995a), *Disability and Debt: The Experience of Disabled People in Debt*, Sheffield Citizens Advice Bureaux Debt Support Unit, Sheffield.

Grant, L. (1995b), *Good Practice Guidelines for Debt Advisors: Practical ideas for improving advice services for disabled people in debt*, Sheffield Citizens Advice Bureaux Debt Support Unit, Sheffield.

Kempson, E., Bryson, A. and Rowlingson, K. (1994), *Hard Times*, Policy Studies Institute, London.

Kempson, E. (1996), *Living on a Low Income*, Joseph Rowntree Foundation, York.

Martin, J. and White, A. (1988), *The Financial Circumstances of Disabled Adults Living in Private Households*, HMSO, London.

Oppenheim, C. and Harker, L. (1996), *Poverty: The Facts*, Child Poverty Action Group, London.

Orwell, G. (1965), *The Road to Wigan Pier*, Heinemann, London (first published 1937).

Sinfield, A. (1981), *What Unemployment Means*, Martin Robertson, Oxford.

Thompson, P., Lavery, M. and Curtice, J. (1990), *Short Changed by Disability*, Disability Income Group, London.

Walker, A. and Walker, L. (1991), 'Disability and financial need: the failure of the social security system' in Dally, G. (ed), *Disability and Social Policy*.

14 Neighbourhood Destabilisation, Youth Crime and the Destabilised School

JOHN M. PITTS

The Rising Rate of Crime

The Home Office criminal statistics for 1981-1991 record a 30 per cent fall in the numbers of children and young people involved in crime. This drop is a product of a 25 per cent reduction in the numbers of 10-17 year olds in the population, a sharp rise in the informal cautioning of 10-14 year olds by the police, an overall decline in the police 'clear-up' rate and a fall in court conviction rates. However, data published in 1992 indicated that the number of recorded offences committed by children and young people had risen by 54 per cent over the same period (Hagell and Newburn, 1994). Thus, it appeared that fewer children and young people were committing a great deal more crime.

An analysis of British Crime Survey data for the period 1981-1991 went some way to explaining this bald statistic. Not only did it reveal a substantial increase in the volume of crime and victimisation in the preceding decade, it also showed marked changes in its nature and geographical distribution (Hope 1994). Taken together, these data suggested both an intensification and a concentration of youth crime in the UK in the 1980s and 1990s.

The British Crime Survey divides neighbourhoods into ten categories on the basis of the intensity of the criminal victimisation. By 1991, the chances of a resident in the lowest crime neighbourhood ever being assaulted had fallen to a point where it was barely measurable. Residents in the highest crime neighbourhoods, by contrast, now risked being assaulted twice a year. This polarisation of risk is made clearer when we recognise that by 1992, residents in the highest crime neighbourhoods experienced twice the rate of property crime and four times the rate of personal crime than those in the next worst category. These findings point to a significant redistribution of victimisation towards the poorest and most vulnerable over the intervening ten years.

251

As we have noted elsewhere:

> In parallel with the regional restructuring of the British economy during the 1980s, the inequality in crime risk grew amongst local communities, especially those in less advantaged 'Northern' regions of England; ... and local studies at the end of the 1980s registered large increases in crime victimisation over a relatively short period (Hope and Foster, 1992).
> Pitts J. and Hope T. (1998) p.38

The Redistribution of Wealth

It is salutary to note that this remarkable redistribution of victimisation was parallelled by an equally remarkable redistribution of wealth. Between 1981 and 1991 the number of workers earning half the national average wage or less, the Council of Europe poverty line, rose from 900,000 to 2,400,000. In the same period those earning over twice the national average rose from 1,800,000 to 3,100,000. During this period, recorded crime in the UK increased by 111 per cent.

Housing the 'Have Nots'

As the 1980s progressed a combination of the government's 'Right to Buy' policy, 'Tenant Incentive Schemes', the curtailment of the right of local authorities to spend housing revenue on house building, and progressive reductions in central government's financial contribution to local government ensured that less and less public housing stock was available for rent. These developments presaged significant demographic changes in which relatively prosperous older and higher income families left housing estates in the inner city or on its periphery, to be replaced by poorer, younger families (page 1993). As a result, whereas at the beginning of the 1980s the average council house tenant's income was 73 per cent of the national average, by the beginning of the 1990s it had fallen to 48 per cent.

By 1995, over 50 per cent of council households had no breadwinner (Rowntree, 1995). The estates which experienced the greatest changes saw increasing concentrations of children, teenagers, young single adults and young single parent families. These neighbourhoods also became a last resort for residents who had previously been homeless, hospitalised or imprisoned, and for refugees from political persecution. A recent study by Rowntree found that

20 per cent of Britain's children and young people now live in such neighbourhoods (Dean, 1997).

Neighbourhood Destabilisation

These rapid demographic changes quickly eroded relationships of kinship and friendship ... transforming these estates into aggregates of strangers, who were often deeply suspicious of one another (Pitts and Hope, 1998). This had a number of consequences.

(a)   These changes meant that those people most vulnerable to criminal victimisation, young single parents, Black and Asian families and the single elderly, and those most likely to victimise them, adolescent boys and young men, were progressively thrown together on the poorest housing estates. In their study of one such neighbourhood in the early 1990s, Tim Hope and Janet Foster (1992) found that a 40 per cent turnover in population over three years was parallelled by a 50 per cent rise in burglaries. However, rapid population change meant that traditional forms of informal social control were also eroded.

(b)   Alongside the disappearance of informal systems of social control we witnessed the erosion of traditional systems of informal social support for parents, young people and children, which often make the difference between whether a child or young person can be sustained in a fragile or volatile home or not. The American criminologist Elliott Currie (1991) notes that:

> Communities suffering from these compounded stresses begin to exhibit the phenomenon some researchers call 'drain': as the ability of families to support themselves and care for their children drops below a certain critical point, they can no longer sustain those informal networks of social support and help that can otherwise be a buffer against the impact of the economic grinding of the market.
> [p.346]

(c)   Because people were disconnected from one another, participation in local political and social life fell away and so they had no basis upon which to join together to exert political pressure, bid for resources and make demands on the local and central government agencies with responsibility for the problems they confronted. Some sense of connectedness and a willingness to co-operate, however slight, is the base upon which a 'virtuous circle' of mutually reinforcing neighbourhood factors which determine both the quality of life and the standard of living in poor neighbourhoods is elaborated. These factors include demographic stability, the availability of appropriate housing, the quality and strength of schools, social services and family support. Since 1990, Robert Sampson *et al.* (1997) has been investigating whether, or to what extent, neighbourhood crime rates are a function of that neighbourhood's social and organisational characteristics, rather than the characteristics of the individuals and families who live there. This research has involved 8,782 residents in 343 Chicago neighbourhoods. Sampson concludes:

> Past research has consistently reported links between neighbourhood social composition and crime. In the current study, the researchers found that in neighbourhoods scoring high on collective efficacy (social cohesion and trust), crime rates were 40 per cent below those in low scoring neighbourhoods. This difference supported the researchers' basic premise - Crime rates are not solely attributable to individuals' aggregate demographic characteristics. Rather, crime is a function of neighbourhood social and organisational characteristics.

(d)   High crime neighbourhoods tend to be highly concentrated and have a distinctive economic structure. Harrison (1972) identifies a dual economy in urban centres in which the labour market is divided into primary and secondary sectors. The primary sector labour market is characterised by steady jobs with reasonable wages and prospects for advancement. Workers in this sector tend to be older, better qualified, more reliable and better motivated, but these are qualities which are strengthened and reinforced by the higher quality and the greater stability of their jobs. The secondary sector labour market, by contrast, is characterised by low wages, sporadic, dead-end jobs which attract younger, less skilled, less well educated and less reliable employees. Like primary sector employment, the characteristics of the secondary sector work force tend to be shaped by, and mirror, their conditions of employment. Residents in poor, high crime, neighbourhoods tend to derive their livelihood from a variety of sources; government transfers, employment and training programmes, crime and illegal hustles which, as McGahey (1986) has suggested, 'constitute important additional sources of income, social organisation and identity for the urban poor'. In low crime neighbourhoods, residents tend to derive their incomes, identity and sense of self-esteem from one, primary sector, employment source. The economic, demographic and policy changes of the 1980s were instrumental in eroding primary sector employment in the poorest neighbourhoods and, by default, promoting the development of secondary sector employment with its inevitable concomitant; the proliferation of illegitimate economic enterprise. Richard McGahey (1986) notes that:

> the relative abilities of different neighbourhood economies and social organisations to cope with urban, regional and national economic transformations may help explain why some neighbourhoods turn into persistently high crime communities and others do not. By viewing urban crime in relation to particular neighbourhood economies and the broader urban labour market, we may be better able to understand crime's generation and persistence and to devise more effective policies for its control and reduction.

The Vera study, undertaken in New York in the 1980s, showed that the key factor determining the level and nature of crime in working class neighbourhoods was adult involvement in primary sector employment (Sullivan, 1989). The study found that the quality and quantity of jobs in a neighbourhood determined the ways people formed households, regulated their own, and the public behaviour of others and used public services. The resulting neighbourhood atmosphere then helped to shape the incentives for residents to engage in legitimate employment or income-oriented crime. A high level of adult involvement in primary sector employment spawned stable households, stable families, stable social relationships and enhanced vocational opportunities for the next generation. A low level of involvement had the opposite effect. This study also revealed that, in the first instance, the factors determining a neighbourhood's crime rate and its capacity to contain crime, were almost all visited upon it from the outside in the form of social and economic policies, economic fluctuations, the drugs trade, demographic destabilisation and benefit levels.

In Britain in the 1980s, neighbourhood destabilisation, by eroding economic links between poor neighbourhoods and their local economies reproduced this structure in growing numbers of poor neighbourhoods. In the process inner city retail, industrial and commercial concerns, which had once been central to the social and demographic stability of working class neighbourhoods, either went out of business or relocated in the industrial and retail parks on the periphery of the city. The impact of this mass evacuation was compounded by a political shift in the mid-1980s which meant that training resources followed employers out of high crime neighbourhoods.

A Concentration of Disadvantage

These are the neighbourhoods in which racist attacks, small-scale riots and drug-related crime and violence proliferated in the 1980s (Pearson 1987, Lea and Young, 1988; Campbell, 1993; Sampson and Phillips, 1995). Pearson observes that:

> ... even within a town or a city with a major problem it will tend to be concentrated in certain neighbourhoods and virtually unknown in others. Moreover, where the problem has tended to gather together in dense pockets within our towns and cities, this will usually be in neighbourhoods which are worst affected by unemployment and wretched housing.
> (pp.190-91)

Not surprisingly, perhaps, these are also the neighbourhoods from which the bulk of the children in the Care, or being 'looked after' by the local authority are drawn and where the preponderance of young people who run away, and stay away, from home originate (Currie, 1991; Pitts, M., 1992; Shriane, 1995; Pitts J., 1996). An analysis of data supplied by the Homelessness charity *Centrepoint* (1995) reveals that, overwhelmingly, young people who run away from, or are thrown out of, home come from regions with the highest levels of unemployment in general, and youth unemployment in particular. Many of them have spent some time in Care. Many reported that they left home as a result of conflict with parents, and that this conflict often concerns money, or its absence. An analysis of the data for London reveals that over 70 per cent of the runaways who reached *Centrepoint* came from the poorest Inner London boroughs. A study undertaken by Hugh Shriane in Luton showed that 46 per cent of the young people who ran away from home came from the poorest public housing estate with the highest crime rate, lowest levels of youth employment and political participation in the borough.

Domestic Violence and Child Abuse

While it is possible to produce evidence to support a link between economic and political change, neighbourhood destabilisation and running away, familial abuse might well be regarded as a problem of a different order altogether. However, recent scholarship (Segal, 1990; Messerschmidt, 1993; Campbell, 1993) suggests that rather than being randomly distributed throughout the social structure, violent and sexual crimes against women and children tend to be concentrated in the poorest neighbourhoods. If as many commentators argue, however, the violent sexual abuse of women and children by men is first and foremost a question of power rather than sexual desire, it is less surprising that it should be most prevalent amongst men who experience the greatest discrepancy between what they have become and what they believe, as men, they are required to be (Segal, 1990). This begins to explain the prevalence of child abuse and domestic violence in destabilised neighbourhoods. In response to these developments Currie has advocated 'a wide range of supports for parents in coping with real world stresses in their communities', however, the political changes of the 80s and 90s have served only to erode these services.

A Youth Crime Implosion

The bulk of the crime and violence in these neighbourhoods is committed by local children and young people and is, more often than not, directed against other local children and young people, in and out of school. Pitts and Smith (1995), in their Home Office study of the violent victimisation of young people, noted that these are the neighbourhoods in which racially-motivated violence and gang fighting is most prevalent. The crime and violence in these neighbourhoods is implosive in that it is committed by, and against, local residents. This intra-neighbourhood crime pattern is a distinguishing characteristic of high crime areas in Britain (Hope, 1994). Their other distinguishing feature is that the young people involved in this crime appear not to grow out of it (Hagan J., 1993; Graham and Bowling, 1995).

Adolescence is a period of transition but how long it lasts and when it ends depends upon whether a young person has the social and economic wherewithal to proceed to the next stage in the life-cycle. In his study, undertaken in the USA during the great depression, W.F. Whyte (1943) 'hung out' with a group of 'corner boys' in an Italian neighbourhood. As the book proceeds, we realise that Doc and the Nortons are not teenagers but men, some of them their mid-to late twenties and that they have been hanging out on the same come for over ten years. They have been doing this because, having no steady jobs, they have no money to pay rent, buy furniture or do all the other things one would need to do to become a 'family man' in Cornerville. They are, as a result, frozen in a state of perpetual adolescence.

In East London in the early 1990s, black youth justice workers observed that the upper age of members of the local 'posse' had risen to over 30 (Pitts, 1997). One of the consequences of this has been that the older members have introduced some of the younger ones to more serious crime. Like Doc and the Nortons, these men could not make the transition from adolescence to higher status adult roles because they simply did not have the means to do so. In a period of economic boom, the young people in these neighbourhoods would have cut their ties with the school and the neighbourhood and got on with adult life. Today, people of eighteen and older are condemned to seek such status as they can from a peer group whose members may be as young as 12.

Thus, they are only semi-detached from the neighbourhood and the school, its social networks and its tensions. Conflicts which begin in the school can spill over into the neighbourhood where they attract older unemployed teenagers and young adults. Conversely, conflicts which begin in the neighbourhood may sometimes be fought out in the school. Pre-eminent among the factors which make for higher levels of crime in these neighbourhoods is that young people who, under other circumstances, would have grown out of crime, leaving it behind with other adolescent enthusiasms, become more deeply and more seriously embedded in a criminal way of life (Hagan, 1993).

Maverick Masculinities

A number of commentators have argued that the phenomena described above are, attributable not to poverty, unemployment or neighbourhood destabilisation *per se*, but to family breakdown, single parenthood with a concomitant deterioration in moral values, which have fostered nihilistic and destructive, modes of masculinity.

From the neo-conservative right, Charles Murray (1994) asserts that:

> Adolescence and testosterone are a destructive combination, and the only antidote is a civilising process which begins in infancy and is completed by

marriage. I am arguing that the civilising process cannot occur in communities where the two-parent family is not the norm.

From the 'post-Marxist left' Beatrix Campbell (1993) argues that:

> Among unemployed men - so the argument goes- poverty produces an identity crisis, their unemployment leaves them without a role. 'Is it any wonder', we sigh, 'that they turn to crime?' However ... these conversations about men and crime tell a different story, one that shows how unemployment reveals a mode of masculinity whereas commonness has been that it causes a crisis of masculinity.

These arguments raise a number of questions. If it is the case that family breakdown and/or expulsion from the labour force have served to neutralise the social bonds which previously held these young men to the conventional order, why is it that, thus freed, only a tiny minority opt for, or are propelled towards, violent and destructive masculinity. In truth, by far the most common reaction of young people to family breakdown and worklessness is resignation, depression or withdrawal. West and Sweeting (1996) in their study of young people, health and unemployment observe that:

> Economic recession, unemployment, low-paid jobs and the sense of having no future are potentially all components of a social malaise that may affect the health of us all but especially the young ... nine per cent of males and seven per cent of females who were unemployed reported attempting suicide, much higher rates than those found for those at work or in education.

On the other hand, if the problems of crime and disorder in destabilised neighbourhoods are a product of single parenthood and the consequent absence of the steadying hand of a father, we have to ask why significant numbers of the young people involved in the crime and disorder in these neighbourhoods come from ostensibly caring two-parent families? It seems more likely that what unites these young people with their singly parented peers is a shared sense of relative deprivation rather than the urgent demands of their unconstrained testosterone (Lea and Young, 1988). The 'masculinity' argument also fails to account satisfactorily for the involvement of girls and young women in the crime and disorder which, as Graham and Bowling (1995) have indicated, is far more prevalent than was previously imagined.

Of course, a disproportionately large number of young people in destabilised neighbourhoods become involved in crime. However, the bulk of this crime is instrumental, concerned with raising the wherewithal to maintain the relatively modest lifestyles to which these young people aspire (Sullivan 1989).

Murray suggests that these young people subscribe to an entirely different set of principles which invert taken-for-granted morality. David Forrester *et al.* (1988) interviewed 76 burglars on a high crime estate in Lancashire. This is one of the very few 'in-depth' studies of offenders and their motivation undertaken in the UK. The interviewers discovered, unsurprisingly, that the burglars did it for pecuniary gain. More surprisingly, they also discovered that most of them 'hated' doing it. They believed that it was wrong, and felt sympathy for their victims. However, they could see no other way to raise to money they needed to subsist. While we may feel little sympathy for these respondents, it is evident that they subscribe to conventional values, even if these values are insufficient to constrain their behaviour.

A consideration of how young, unemployed working class men from single parent, and dual parent, families express their masculinity is an important component of any explanation of the changing distribution of youth crime and victimisation in the 1980s and 1990s. However, it is not at all evident that those engaged in this crime are simply acting in accordance a culturally determined, misogynistic and destructive 'mode of masculinity' (Campbell, 1993), or the alternative values of an anti-social underclass (Murray, 1990). As I have noted elsewhere:

> While proceeding from the notion that crime is a gendered activity, these accounts, by misrepresenting the nature, and overstating the dimensions of the problem, over-predict massively, the amount of crime which will be generated. ... They explain neither why youth crime takes markedly different forms in different neighbourhoods, nor why different people in the same neighbourhood respond in markedly different ways to similar pressures towards criminality. (Pitts J., 1996, p.272)

The Destabilised School

The capacity of the school to resist pressures towards crime and violence coming from these neighbourhoods, and to offer young people the means to transcend their social predicament is severely limited by the knock-on effects of neighbourhood destabilisation. State schools have been under pressure since the 1970s. However, cuts in education budgets, demographic change and the fragmentation of the large urban education authorities, which were sometimes able to 'engineer' the social and economic mix of secondary schools, have meant that many of the relatively successful comprehensive schools in poorer neighbourhoods of the 1970s, have been transformed into the 'failing' schools of the 1990s. A recent study of 15 schools, identified by OFSTED as 'failing', entitled *Learning From Failure*, revealed that they were all serving communities with high levels of social deprivation and unemployment, a high proportion of single parent families and a high uptake of free school meals (Centre for Educational Management, 1997). The report notes that these schools tended to have poor premises and that their intake represented the residuum of children that selective secondary schools had rejected. Many of the schools in the sample had recently amalgamated or reorganised in the face of demographic change and local competition.

The reasons for this 'failure' are complex. In our study of student-student violence in a school in East London (Pitts and Smith, 1995), it was evident that with the introduction of Local Management of Schools and real cuts in school budgets, school governors faced increasing difficulties in maintaining pastoral services for the growing numbers of socially-disadvantaged students entering the school. This increase is attributable, in no small part, to the wholesale decarseration of children and young people in need and in trouble between the late 1970s to the present. As Figure 14.1 indicates, between 1977 and 1996/8 the numbers of children and young people in residential or custodial institutions, or attending off-site educational or day-care units, fell from around 66,000 to 27,000. However welcome these developments may have been on humanitarian grounds, they meant that mainstream education was confronted with a substantially increased number of abused and/or neglected children and young people with serious behavioural problems and few, if any, additional resources with which to fashion a response.

The Dynamics of Destabilisation

Sidney Burnell is a mixed secondary school in London where the present author and his colleagues are currently undertaking a study of student victimisation. The school has 1,043 students, of whom 670 are male. It is estimated that 85 nationalities are represented on the school roll and only 44 per cent of students describe themselves as white British. 'Black' students (Afro-British, Afro-Caribbean, Eritrean, Ethiopian, African) comprise 17.4 per cent and South

Asians 17 per cent of the school roll. The largest non-white 'minority' are Bangladeshis who comprise 11.8 per cent of the school roll. In the past few months some homeless Polish Romany families have been rehoused in hard-to-let accommodation on a neighbouring housing estate, and some of the children are now finding their way into the school.

	1977	1996/8
Children's Homes	25,000	7,000(1)
Approved School/ Community Homes & Children's Homes with Education	6,003 -	750 375(2)
Borstal/Young Offender Insts.	8,625	6,615(3)
Boarders in Special Schools	21,184	9,784(4)
Education Dept. Behav.Units/ Pupil Referral Units	3,962 *(FT)*	3,244(5) *(P/T 5-15 hrs.)*
Intermediate Treatment Centres	1,500(FT)	0(6)
Totals	66,274	27,768

Sources:

(1) Berridge D. (1998) *Children's Homes Revisited*, Jessica Kingsley.
(2) DHSS (1975) *Young Offenders in Care, Preliminary Report* (unpublished), DHSS (1978) *Preliminary Report on Care Order Survey*, (unpublished), DoH (1996) *Annual Return*.
(3) *Prison Statistics* (1977), HMSO, Millham, S. (*et al.*) (1978) *Locking Up Children*, Saxon House' NACRO (1998).
(4) D*f*EE June (1998) *Unpublished Statistics*.
(5) Her Majesty's Inspectors of Schools (1978) *Behavioural Units*, DoE, DfEE (1996) *Survey of LEAs* (101 of 109).
(6) DHSS (1978) *Survey of Local Authority Social Services Departments* (unpublished).

Figure 14.1 Changes in the numbers of children and young people educated/contained outside mainstream provision

The transience on the neighbouring estates is reflected in a 50 per cent turnover in the school roll between years 7 and 11. Because the nature of the changes in the neighbourhood has been to replace more prosperous residents with less prosperous ones, by 1997 over 50 per cent of school students qualified for free school meals, indicating that their parent/s are in receipt of state benefits.

Poverty and transience generate educational disadvantage in children, and erode the capacity of adults to offer consistent parenting. Thus, like the school in East London where an earlier study was undertaken (Pitts and Smith 1995), Sidney Burnell school must absorb a higher proportion of children with special educational and behavioural needs. The school currently has twice the borough average of 'statemented' students (students with officially recognised/diagnosed behavioural and learning difficulties) on its roll. As a result, behaviour in the school playground and the corridors has deteriorated. The impact of the resultant atmosphere can be measured in increased truancy and lateness amongst students who were previously seen to pose no particular problems.

Absorbing Trouble

A further consequence of rapid student turnover is that schools like Sidney Burnell have a large number of vacancies. In the current economic climate, in which local education authorities are striving to reduce surplus capacity, these schools are under constant pressure to absorb students who wish to transfer from into them. At Sidney Burnell, 30 per cent of year 10 (14/15 year olds) and 64 per cent of year 11 (15/16 year olds) have previously attended another secondary school. Beyond the destabilising effect on the established peer groups, and the 'pecking order', of this steady influx of new students, is the fact that many of them bring additional academic and behavioural problems with them. It is, of course, ironic that schools in 'destabilised neighbourhoods', confronting formidable social problems, of crime violence and racism are, nonetheless, required to accept a disproportionate number of older, white adolescents, many of whom are transferring as a result of exclusion or conflict triggered by racist incidents in their previous school. One of the consequences of this is that, when inter-racial conflict arises in school, it is not uncommon for each of the parties to call up 'reinforcements' from other schools on their mobile 'phones.

Student Victimisation

At Sidney Burnell school, between September 1996 and April 1997, 41 per cent of year 11 students were assaulted, with 30 per cent of these assaults occurring in the vicinity of the school or on the way home from school, in the hour or so following the end of the school day. Eighty per cent of the perpetrators were male, and 48 per cent were described as being either strangers or students from another school. Twenty-four per cent of respondents reported being threatened or assaulted with a weapon. David Porteous (1998) notes:

> Many more pupils from ethnic minorities reported that they had experienced racist abuse or violence, 35 per cent of all 'non-white' respondents compared to 16 per cent of whites. Bengali pupils, 46 per cent of whom said they had experienced racism, seem particularly vulnerable. They were more likely than any other ethnic group to have been threatened with violence and to have been hit or kicked or pushed about ....

Taking Flight

As *Learning From Failure* indicates, seeing 'the writing on the wall', some parents transfer their children to other schools, further destabilising the school. This has the effect of reducing the proportion of parents who have effected a positive choice in favour of the school and increasing the proportion who are unwilling, or unable, to effect a choice about their child's education. These are not simply neglectful parents. Some of them, like the refugees from Eritrea, Ethiopia or Bosnia, speak little English and have been traumatised by the experience of violence, change and loss. The parents who seek a transfer tend to be more prosperous and articulate and are often active in fund raising efforts and the PTA. They are also the parents who are most likely to reinforce the school's espoused ethos at home. Their departure is a double blow for the school, diminishing both the material and moral resources crucial to the development of its 'social capital'. *Learning From Failure* also found that whereas most of the failing schools were serving students from areas with a high level of deprivation, 'better off' students were increasingly congregating in other, better-resourced, schools.

Staff Morale

Not surprisingly, these changes undermine staff morale, and so the problems in the student group are mirrored in staff absenteeism and a rapid turnover of teachers. As a result, destabilised schools usually carry a higher proportion of probationary teachers, supply teachers and, as a result of the transfer of teacher education to the schools in the early 1990s, student teachers. This is particularly ironic since all the teachers interviewed in our studies are agreed that their students do not like 'new faces', take time to trust people, and need to gain experience in forming positive relationships with adults.

The changes afflicting these schools have, of course, been parallelled by the introduction of the national curriculum, school performance league tables, the Conservatives 'local management of schools' initiative, real cuts in funding, serious reductions in the education social work service, school counselling, pastoral care, home-school liaison, home tuition, off-site units, Child and Family Guidance Clinics, the Youth Service and those non-governmental welfare and youth serving agencies not undertaking statutory youth justice and child protection work. These changes have eroded the ability of these schools to deal with the problems presented by their students. In parallel, the additional work generated for teachers by problematic students; meetings with students, their parents, social welfare and criminal justice agencies, the production of reports for, and attendance at, case conferences, court hearings and so on, has burgeoned.

Holding the Line

In this situation, many teachers feel that the ethos of the school is being engulfed by the alternative ethos of 'the street', and they no longer feel in control. One of the consequences of this is that they become less willing to deal with hostile and aggressive behaviour from students. This means that senior staff come to assume increasing responsibility for behavioural matters and 'difficult classes'. But this compounds the problem since the more disruptive or aggressive students recognise the effective withdrawal from such confrontations as a capitulation by junior staff. Feeling disempowered to deal with incidents individually, staff become more willing to involve their trades unions. Thus, relatively minor instances of violence or verbal abuse may become a 'union matter', with the result that the offending child may be excluded from the school by senior staff in order to avert industrial action. Ironically, of course, this serves to undermine the authority of both junior and senior staff in the eyes of students even more. As Menzies Lyth (1960) has observed, in situations of great uncertainty and anxiety, professionals will fall back upon structures and protocols to assuage those anxieties. This tendency is evident in the progressive bureaucratisation of interactions between senior staff and junior staff, and staff and students at Sidney Burnell school.

Paradoxically, the current tendency on the part of Local Education Authorities to respond to these problems by sending in a 'behavioural task force' has the potential to make the problems, described above, worse, further destabilising an already destabilised school. Staff and students interviewed are agreed that such task forces send an unequivocal message that '*The staff can't cut it so they've had to send for the "Team".*'

Conclusion

It is at least ironic that the Audit Commission's report, *Misspent Youth* (1996) and *New Labour's* Crime and Disorder Bill (1998) both locate the schools in high crime neighbourhoods as a bulwark against youth crime whereas, in reality, many of them are, at best, fighting a rearguard action against the violence and mayhem which sometimes appears to be about to engulf them.

References

Campbell, B. (1993), *Goliath, Britain's Dangerous Places*, Methuen, London.
Centre for Educational Management (1997), *Learning From Failure*, The Roehampton Institute, London.
Centrepoint (1995), *Statistics: April 1994-March 1995*, Centrepoint, London.
Currie, E. (1991), *International Developments in Crime and Social Policy in NACRO*, Crime and Public Policy, NACRO, London.
Dean, M. (1997), *Tipping the Balance*, Search, Joseph Rowntree Foundation, York.
Forrester, D., Frenz, S., O'Connell, M. and Pease, K. (1988), *The Kirkholt Burglary Prevention Project, Rochdale*, Home Office Crime Prevention Unit, Paper 13, Home Office, London.
Graham, J. and Bowling, B. (1995), *Young People and Crime*, Home Office, London.
Hagell, A. and Newburn, T. (1994), *Persistent Young Offenders*, Policy Studies Institute, London.
Hagan, J. (1993), 'The Social Embededness of Crime and Unemployment', *Criminology*, vol. 31, pp.455-91.

Harrison, B. (1972), *Education, Training and the Urban Ghetto*, Johns Hopkins University Press, Baltimore.

Hope, T. (1994), *Communities Crime and Inequality in England and Wales*. Paper presented to the 1994 Cropwood Round Table Conference *Preventing Crime and Disorder*, September, pp. 14-15, Cambridge.

Hope, T. and Foster, J. (1992), 'Conflicting Forces: Changing the Dynamics of Crime and Community on a Problem Estate', *British Journal of Criminology*, 32/92.

Lea, J. and Young, J. (1988), *What Is To Be Done About Law & Order?*, Penguin, Harmondsworth.

McGahey, R. (1986), 'Economic Conditions, Neighbourhood Organisation and Urban Crime', in J.A. Reiss and M. Tonry (eds), *Communities and Crime*, Chicago University Press, Chicago.

Menzies Lyth, I. (1960), 'A Case Study of the Functioning of Social Systems as a Defence Against Anxiety', *Human Relations*, vol. 13, no. 12.

Messerschmidt, J.W. (1993), *Masculinities and Crime: Critique and Reconceptualisation of Theory*, Rowman & Littlefield, Maryland.

Murray, C. (1994), *Underclass: The Crisis Deepens*, Institute of Economic Affairs, London.

Page, D. (1993), *Building for Communities: A Study of New Housing Association Estates*, York, Joseph Rowntree Foundation.

Pearson, G. (1987), *The New Heroin Users*, Blackwell, Oxford.

Pitts, J. (1996), 'The Politics and Practice of Youth Justice', in E. McLaughlin and J. Muncie (eds), *Controlling Crime*, Sage Publications/Open University Press.

Pitts, J. and Smith, P. (1995), *Preventing School Bullying*, Home Office Crime Detection and Prevention Series, Paper 63, Home Office, London.

Pitts, J. and Hope, T. (1998), 'The Local Politics of Inclusion: The State and Community Safety', *Social Policy and Administration*, vol. 31 no. 5, December 1997.

Pitts, M. (1991), *Somewhere to Run*, unpublished BA Dissertation, University of Exeter.

Sampson, A. and Phillips, C. (1995), *Reducing Repeat Victimisation on an East London Estate*, Home Office Crime Detection and Prevention Series, Paper 67, Home Office, London.

Sampson, R., Rauden Bush, S. and Earls, F. (1997), 'Neighbourhoods and Violent Crime: A Multilevel Study of Collective Efficacy', *Science*, vol. 277, pp.1-7, American Association for the Advancement of Science.

Segal, L. (1990), *Slow Motion: Changing Masculinities, Changing Men*, Virago, London.

Shriane, H. (1995), *Luton Runaways Profile*, Community Links Project, Luton.

Sullivan, M. (1989), *Getting Paid: Youth Crime and Work in the Inner City*, Cornell University Press, London.

West, P. and Sweeting, H. (1996), 'Nae Job, Nae Future: Young People and Health in a Context of Unemployment, *Health and Social Care in the Community*, vol. 4, no. 1, pp.50-62.

Whyte, W.F. (1945), *Street Corner Society*, Chicago University Press, Chicago.

15 'The Invisible Poor':Young People Growing Up in Family Poverty

DEBI ROKER and JOHN COLEMAN

... for me it's about not being part of things, not having the money to live normally like other people. Everything I do or I want to do, even like really small things, is decided by money, or by not having it anyway.
(14 year-old young woman)

Introduction: Young People and Poverty

This chapter describes research which examined young people's experience of growing up in family poverty. The research involved in-depth interviews with 60 young people aged 13-18, from across the UK. Each young person was living in a family which was totally dependent on state benefits, with a number also living in temporary or bed-and-breakfast accommodation. The interviews examined the impact of poverty on key areas of young people's lives, including physical health, education and future prospects, experience of crime, family relationships, and social lives. Before describing the research undertaken, it is necessary to provide some background to the study, and address some of the broader issues around young people and poverty.

Many different definitions of poverty are in use at present, and it is clear that the term itself is contested (see for example Blackburn, 1991; National Youth Agency, 1996; Oppenheim, 1996). However, whilst most early definitions of poverty used absolute terms - such as defining poverty as not having enough food to stay alive - more recent conceptualisations have focussed on the effects of poverty on people's lifestyles and degree of inclusion/exclusion from society. It is this broad definition of poverty which is used in this research. In adopting this view of poverty, the authors agree with Oppenheim (1996) that poverty is about

... being denied the expectation of decent health, shelter, a social life and
a sense of self-esteem which the rest of society takes for granted ...
(Oppenheim, 1996)

There is now clear evidence that the numbers of families living in poverty, and
therefore the number of children and young people in poverty, has increased
over the past few decades (CPAG, 1996; Dennehy *et al.*, 1997). These figures
show that there are now 4.2 million children living in poverty in the UK, which
is one in three of all children aged under 16 [see also Miller, this volume].
There is also clear evidence that living in poverty is associated with risks to the
health, well-being and future prospects of children and young people. Poverty
increases the risk that a young person will experience accidents, respiratory
illnesses, and mental health problems; it also increases the likelihood of a poor
diet, and higher than average use of legal and illegal drugs (see for example
Blackburn, 1991; Dennehy *et al.*, 1997).

There are three important points which arose from the literature review
undertaken in preparation for the research. First, that much of the work on the
effects of poverty has focused on the experiences of **parents** living in poverty,
or on families with young children rather than those with teenagers. Second,
that much of the work that has looked at young people and poverty has focused
on those who are homeless or estranged from their families, rather than those
who are living at home and growing up in family poverty. Much less is known
about the experiences of this group, and the impact of poverty at a key time in
a person's physical and psychological development. Third, there have been few
studies which have focused in-depth on young people's experiences, and their
views of the effects of poverty on different areas of their lives. Rather, much
of the information available has aimed to demonstrate the situation for large
populations [see also Lister *et al.*, this volume].

The research described in this chapter therefore aimed to focus on young
people's views and experiences, using their words wherever possible to describe
the experience of growing up in family poverty. The following section describes
how the information was collected.

Collecting the Information

The information reported here comes from 60 individual interviews which were
undertaken with young people aged 13-18. All of these young people were
living in families dependent on benefits; some of the young people were also

living with their families in temporary or bed-and-breakfast accommodation. The interviews were conducted in three different parts of the country - the south coast, the west of England, and Scotland. Twenty interviews were undertaken in each of these areas, which were conducted by local interviewers. The young people were commissioned to take part in a variety of ways, including via advertisements in youth clubs, word of mouth, and via social workers and youth workers. Each young person was paid £10 as a 'thank-you' for their time. The interviews were held wherever the young person wanted them, and took place in youth clubs, their homes, and in workers' offices.

In order to allow young people to express their views in their own words, individual semi-structured interviews were used to collect the information. The nine areas of the interview schedule are detailed below, with the question areas that were included in each section:

1. Current situation and family income
    Who lives with, whether they have contact with both natural parents, how long since their parents have worked, type of accommodation and housing history, view of accommodation, family income.
2. Personal finances
    Their own income and sources of income, what they spend their money on, whether they have debts or savings, whether they give any of their income to their family, and whether there are things they think they should have but can't afford.
3. Who their friends are, where they meet them, how they spend their time, whether their income affects the leisure activities they engage in.
4. Family relationships
    How they view their relationship with their parent/s, the cause of disagreements in the family, whether their parents are happy with how they are living their lives, and what their parents want for them for their future.
5. Physical health
    Their view of their current health, sources of advice about health, dental health, food and income, use of legal and illegal drugs.
6. School life and current activities
    What they are currently doing, view of school days, whether they had time off school, whether they could not afford anything they needed for their school life.

7.   Crime and the law
      Involvement with the police and in crime, whether family/friends have
      been involved in crime, whether they have been a victim of crime.
8.   Future prospects and aspirations
      What they plan to do in the next few years, view of whether they will be
      able to do this, age at which they plan to leave home, impact of poverty
      on aspirations.
9.   Living with poverty - now and the future
      How feels about life overall, whether they feel positive about the future,
      what they do when they need help and advice, worries and concerns, view
      of life opportunities in comparison to others.

Each interview took between 40 minutes and one-and-a-half hours to complete,
and was tape-recorded with the young person's permission. All the interviews
were then transcribed.

In total 60 interviews were undertaken, 20 in each of the three areas. All
the families were living on benefits. In addition, six young people were living
in temporary or bed-and-breakfast accommodation. Seven individuals were
from Afro-Caribbean, Asian, and middle-eastern families. In terms of gender,
28 of the young people were female, and 32 were male. The age range of the
young people was 13-18.

The results of the interviews are summarised in this paper in terms of
eight main topics (note that areas 6 and 8 above were combined). This is
followed by an outline of a number of themes that were current across the
interviews. Due to necessary restrictions on the length of this chapter, readers
are referred to the book published on the research, details of which are at the
end of the chapter.

Summary of the Main Findings

A considerable amount of information was collected in the research. The main
findings from the eight areas are summarised below, and explored further in the
thematic analyses to follow.

Family accommodation, parents' employment history and income: The
majority of the young people were living in Council owned accommodation and
privately rented accommodation. Whilst a minority of the young people were
positive about their homes, a considerable number lived in damp and cold

accommodation, or in accommodation in need of repair. Many of the young people did not have enough rooms in order to accommodate their family properly, many using a lounge for people to sleep in. Lack of space became more problematic with age. Further, many of the young people's homes were in areas with a poor reputation, which many felt made people react adversely to them [see also Pitts, this volume]. Two-thirds of the young people did not know how much money their parents had coming in to the house, although all knew that their parents were living on benefits. There was also evidence that at least a quarter of the families also had money coming in from other sources, including doing part-time work. There was a considerable amount of fluidity in many families' incomes.

The young people's income: There was a lot of variety in the young people's income, but over half had £10 or less to spend each week. Those who did have an income received it from a variety of sources, but mainly from pocket money or part-time work, with a number also involved in illegal activities. Few young people had any savings. It became clear that many of the young people contributed all or part of their income to help support their family financially, whereas others did not receive any money at all from their parents, by way of a contribution to family finances.

Friends and social lives: The impact of living in poverty particularly affected young people living in bed and breakfast accommodation (who had often been moved away from friends when re-housed, and who did not have anywhere to bring friends back to), and those in rural areas (where the costs of transport to see friends were often prohibitive). Some of those in poor quality accommodation described themselves as too embarrassed to bring anyone back to their homes. The difficulties of maintaining friendships and having a social life when on a low income was clearly acknowledged by many of the young people, who often talked about being bored and stuck in a routine where they didn't do anything. This was linked for some of the young people to drug use and involvement in crime.

Family relationships: Almost half of the sample were living in single-parent households, with the remainder living with their natural parents and in step-families. More than one-third of the sample had no contact at all with a natural parent, generally their father. Relationships with mothers and step-mothers were generally rated as better than relationships with fathers and step-fathers. Very few young people identified their limited income as a factor that affected their relationship with their parents; however, further probing showed that for many young people income was a source of tension and disagreement within their family.

Physical health: It was clear from responses to this part of the interview that the young people had very subjective views about what counted as good or poor health. Two-thirds of the sample described their health as average or OK. Although a majority of young people said that their families' income did not affect the food they ate, many then demonstrated numerous ways in which they often went without food, eat poor quality food, and had an unvarying diet. In terms of substance use, almost half of the sample were regular smokers, most commonly in the Scottish and west of England samples. Most had started to smoke from a young age. Further, a majority of the young people lived in homes where one and sometimes two or more people smoked. In terms of alcohol use, there were a number of heavy drinkers in the study, again mostly in the Scottish and west of England samples. Similarly, these two areas included the majority of the 20 young people who were regular users of illegal drugs.

School life, current status, and future plans: Many of the young people - one-third of the total sample - had, and were having, very poor experiences in education. This included being bullied, falling behind, and having literacy problems; many also described their acute dislike of education and being at school. Several of the young people had been excluded from school, or had been persistent non-attenders. It is of note, however, that a significant minority of this group now regretted leaving school early and/or with no skills or qualifications, and were now trying to get back into education. The young people named a variety of jobs that they would like to have in the future, but most were not optimistic that they would be able to achieve these goals.

Crime and the law: Over half of the sample had been involved in crime, with 16 young people involved in serious offences. Many of this group identified their criminal activity as stemming from boredom, lack of money to do the things that they wanted to do, and also as a result of the illegal activities of friends and family. Further, over half of the sample had family and/or friends who were or who had been involved in crime. Finally, this section demonstrated that more than a third of the young people had been victims of crime.

Living with poverty - now and the future: The young people had very diverse perceptions of their lives, ranging from those who were extremely positive to those who were very negative. Similarly, there was a range of views about the future, although the majority said they were 'very optimistic'; however, many were only optimistic if certain things were to happen, such as if they managed to get a job, or get back into education. Two-thirds of the young people identified a key individual outside of their family who they believed had been helpful and supportive to them as they were growing up. Finally, a majority of the young people felt that their enjoyment of life was the same or better than anyone else; similar results were found for the young people's view of their opportunities for the future. Only a small group of young people, generally in Scotland and the west of England, felt they were worse off on both these questions.

Key Themes in the Research

Four main themes were identified in the study, themes which ran through each of the areas of the young people's lives were summarised above. Each of these themes is described below, using comments from the young people to demonstrate the points made.

Theme 1: Early and Significant Family Responsibilities

There was clear evidence that a considerable number of the young people in the study had significant family responsibilities, which few young people of their age in other settings would have to bear. These responsibilities took a number of different forms, but two were particularly noticeable.

First, it was demonstrated that many of the young people contributed large amounts of their own money to family income, and effectively helped to manage their family's finances. For example:

> I give my mum a bit every week just in case she's a bit short and I buy some stuff for the family.
> (13 year-old male, south coast, in bed and breakfast)

This young man was also opening a bank account with a cash withdrawal card, so that his mother could take money out of his account whenever she needed. Indeed, one reason he gave for getting a part-time job was to be able to contribute to the family income in this way. Many other young people in the study were in the same situation:

> I give some of [my money] to mum to help her with the shopping because sometimes it's a bit difficult for her so me and my brother help out.
> [Interviewer: And your dad, does-]

Oh no he doesn't know. It might upset him, thinking that she can't manage, so we just keep it between mum, me and my brother.
(14 year-old female, south coast)

If I've got enough I give her money and tell her to go out and have a drink or somat or I lends it her.
(14 year-old male, west of England)

I try to give [mum] what I can. If it's been a really bad month then I can't, but whenever she's got really bad bills I pay them for her cos I know if she doesn't pay them we're gonna get cut off or sent to the courts.
(17 year-old male, west of England)

Many of the young people effectively had no money to spend on themselves, as all their income went to support their family.

The early and significant family responsibilities that many young people had, led some young people to plan their futures around the impact of their decisions on their families:

... I'll leave [home] when I think it's all right to. When me and my brother get married I think he might move in here or we might get a flat nearby. I don't really wanna leave until I know it's all right to.
(14 year-old male, west of England)

This young man was planning to stay nearby in order to ensure that his parents were managing financially. Another young woman described how she was often needed to help with her mother's part-time work, affecting her ability to get on with school work and concentrate on her own future:

[mum does child minding for extra money] ... she needs a lot of help with the babies so if I get home from school and go out she gets really annoyed. I'll come home really tired and she'll tell me to look after them or do something to help ... it's really hard work after a day at school, and I've got homework too.
(13 year-old female, south coast)

Many of the young people talked about having to help with their parents' income generation strategies in this way.

Second, it was clear that a significant number of the young people in the study were involved in caring for one or both parents, or in trying to prevent family violence and disagreements. This led to many being distressed, or at risk of physical injury themselves:

> I get problems with my nerves when our mum and dad's having a row, I wake up in the morning and my legs and my arms are shaking and that ... I was gonna leave the house but I can't leave my [alcoholic] dad in case he gets any problems, so I just came back to the house.
> (16 year-old male, west of England)

> When our dad has a go at our mum, that worries me, if our mum gets up and lashes out at our dad. Cos I know if she hits him in the wrong punch he's gonna die. So I don't let our mum hit our dad. I stand in the way, if she hits me she hits me.
> (16 year-old male, west of England)

A 15 year-old young man described the strain of regularly having to move home on his parents, and how he took the responsibility for that:

> ... it is difficult for them, always packing up. And my mum and dad are getting older now so it's quite hard work, I have to do all the moving of the heavy things, and sorting it all out.
> (15 year-old male, south coast, bed and breakfast)

It is clear from the issue discussed in this theme that many of the young people in the study had significant family responsibilities. These included earning money in order to contribute to their families' income, managing and looking after household finances, and looking after parents with health problems or who were strained by bringing up a family on a low income. Further, many of these young people had assumed these responsibilities from a young age, with many of the 13 and 14 year-olds in the study having considerable family responsibilities.

Theme 2: Comparative Satisfaction

As was demonstrated above, many of the young people in this study believed that they were 'average' or in many ways 'better off' than other young people. This was in many respects a surprising outcome, given the difficulties that many of the young people were experiencing in their lives. A number of young people elaborated on this point, and these views - which we have called 'comparative satisfaction' - are given here.

A considerable proportion of the young people explained how their circumstances were not so bad as they might first appear. This was because, first, they had such a good relationship with their friends and/or their family. These comments included:

> I'm better off than most people because most people are spending their money rotting their liver or blowing their brains out and getting high on drugs. I think I'm better off than any of them, I've got a family who love me, I don't need those things.
> (17 year-old female, west of England)

> I think I'm the same as other people but sometimes I think I enjoy it more because I don't get like loads of stuff. I try and enjoy it more, whereas like my friend will get loads and clothes and things all the time.
> (15 year-old female, south coast)

> [needs anything that hasn't got?] ... no I mean I can always see my friends, and sit and have a beer or a cup of tea here or at their house. You don't really need a lot of money just to relax and see friends do you, it's not essential.
> (17 year-old male, south coast)

Second, other young people, in particular those in bed and breakfast, focused on the advantages or good points about living in the circumstances that they were:

> ... [same as others because] ... we can get out and do stuff. We can't have people back to [the hotel] but we can go out and do stuff, like go swimming or down the park. I wouldn't say that we've got the best life but like people go 'I wish I could do that, it's a hotel so you get your breakfast each morning' and things like that.
> (13 year-old male, south coast, bed and breakfast)

A few of the young people seemed to try hard to find something in their lives that they could say was good, a part that other people might be envious of ('everyone needs to feel good about something' as one young woman said).

Third, several of the young people reflected more generally on why some people are on a low income, and concluded that this was simply the way life was, and that they couldn't do anything about it. They should therefore accept what they have. As one young person said:

> ... well that's just how it is. I don't think it's wrong. People are born into

different circumstances, you know some people have a lot of money and some
people don't have very much, and we don't have very much ... that's just how
it is.
(17 year-old male, south coast)

Many of the young people made comments such as these.

This notion - of being better off, or not as badly off, as some other people
- we have described as 'comparative satisfaction'. This is because many of the
young people, whilst being aware that their lives were difficult, often mentioned
that they were not as difficult as some people's lives - the homeless, those
without friends, and those with poor family relationships. Thus, compared to
others, they were fairly satisfied with their lives.

It is interesting to note, in fact, that several of the young people disputed
the use of the word 'poverty' to describe their situation. Reflecting the varying
definitions of poverty given in the introduction, several young people said that
their family were not living in poverty. Poverty, many suggested, referred to
those people who were completely destitute, in particular the homeless. It did
not apply to people like them, people who were 'getting by'. They were, as
several young people said, 'poor', 'hard up', and people who 'don't have much
to live on'. This is an interesting contribution to the debate about the nature of
poverty.

Theme 3: The Impact of a Limited Income on Young People

This research explored, in broad terms, the impact of a limited income on
young people. However, there were a number of particular issues that arose in
this respect, and which are discussed here.

First, many of the young people talked about the way in which, whatever
they did or wanted to do, they always had to think about money first. This was,
for many, one of the most difficult aspects of growing up on a low income. For
example:

> ... for me it's about not being part of things, not having the money to live
> normally like other people. Everything I do or I want to do, even like really
> small things, is decided by money, or by not having it anyway.
> (14 year-old female, west of England)

> [she misses] ... just the freedom to say on the spot you can do things. Because
> if someone says do you want to go out or there's a school trip you have to check

you can afford it ... you can't spontaneously do things. You have to work out if you've got the money and then maybe ask to borrow some ... which is difficult.
(17 year-old female, south coast)

It's also of note that many of the older young people in the sample, the 16-18 year-olds, said that it was more difficult to be on a low income now they were older. As one young person said:

I'd really like to travel you know, go somewhere different. It's worse now cos my friends are starting to go away as a group, to Butlins or to Malta and stuff, and I could never do that ... it's different now because of my age, I want to go out and do things, and I'd like to start getting more up to date clothes and that sort of thing.

[Interviewer: So it was different when you were younger?]

Oh yeah I didn't mind then, I didn't do that much. I was happy watching TV, taking the dogs out. But now I'm older, I'm nearly an adult and the things I want to do cost money which I don't have.
(17 year-old female, south coast)

Others in the 16-18 age range described how having little or no money affects everything that you want to do at that age - going out, seeing friends, buying things - and also your prospects for the future, in terms of experiences of and access to education, training and employment. One young woman described being poor as a 'vicious circle', where everywhere you turn you find 'closed doors'.

Secondly, the young people often talked about the difficulty of maintaining good relationships with family and friends when you have a limited income, and how this was a major aspect of growing up in poverty. This was because, for example, they couldn't afford to travel to see friends and family who lived a distance away, or couldn't afford to join in leisure and social activities with other people. This was particularly noticeable for many of the young people who lived in isolated rural areas in the west of England sample; here lack of money was exacerbated by the lack of transport available. It was also particularly difficult to maintain relationships with friends when the family did not have a 'phone, which was most common amongst those in temporary accommodation and those living in very rural areas. Also, lack of money also affected relationships within the family, often leading to arguments within the home. For example:

> ... my little brother doesn't understand. He wants more money and more
> clothes ... he gets really angry with mum and dad. So I give my brother
> something, if I've got it.
> (14 year-old female, south coast)

> I shouldn't I know, it's not their fault, but I just want things, like things other
> people have got, and I just go on, you know asking if I can them, and they just
> get really fed up with me.
> (13 year-old female, south coast)

Many described how they tried to keep their frustration 'bottled up', but that
at times it just 'burst out'.

The impact of a low income on the young people's relationships with their
families was often therefore revealed in quite subtle ways. Although initially
the majority of the young people said they had good relationships with their
parents tensions and difficulties often arose, many of which were related to
income. As the quotes above demonstrate, many of the young people felt
acutely frustrated about the limitations that a low income imposed, and this
often led to disagreements and arguments. For many young people this was
exacerbated by living in bed and breakfast accommodation or in homes with
insufficient space.

Theme 4: The Importance of Family Relationships

It was demonstrated earlier in this report that many young people felt that,
although living on a limited income was very hard, it was made easier by
having close family and personal relationships. This was a theme that many of
the young people often referred to. The young people described this in a
number of different ways, such as

> ... I don't need anything really. As long as I've got love off my parents and
> support, things like that. I think that's more important than radios and things
> like that. It's more important to have support.
> (14 year-old female, south coast)

Others compared their lives to those of people they knew who, although better
off materially and financially than they were, had poor family relationships:

... my friend up the road ... her mum and dad just give her TV and stuff like that ... but she doesn't actually get any real love off them.
(15 year-old female, south coast)

It is of note that the relatively small group of young people in the study who seemed particularly depressed about their lives, and who were often most pessimistic about the future, also commented on their poor relationship with their families.

Much other work on this topic has identified the important role of good personal relationships as a 'buffer' against living in difficult circumstances, such as poverty. The results of the research described here give added support to this, with the young people clearly articulating how their good family relationships acted to make their lives enjoyable and meaningful, and which made them feel valued and loved. However, one consequence of this is a clear sense of young people 'putting up with' their difficult lives, accepting that it is just 'the way it is' that some families live in poverty. Without the love and support of their families, however, it is clear that many of the young people in this study would find their lives a great deal more difficult.

Conclusions

This chapter has highlighted the effect on young people of growing up in family poverty. It aimed to provide information about a neglected group of young people - those living with their families and growing up in poverty. This final part of the chapter aims to highlight differences by key variables of gender, ethnicity and age. Second, the implications of the study for research in this area is explored, including a discussion of methodological issues and directions for future research that arise from it. Third, a number of policy recommendations are made, addressing the ways in which specific policy changes could help to improve the quality of life, and the prospects, of young people who are growing up in family poverty.

(i)   Influence of key variables in the research

First, in terms of gender, there were relatively few differences found between the young men and young women on any of the areas explored in the interview.

The only area where a gender difference was found was in relation to involvement in crime, where twice as many young men as young women were currently (or had been) involved in crime. This finding is consistent with national figures for the involvement of young people in crime (see Coleman, 1997). Also, more of the young men had been excluded or were absent from school; again this reflects national figures (Coleman, 1997). Apart from these two aspects, however, there were few differences between the young men and young women in this study. The results of this study, therefore, suggest that the experience of poverty is very similar for young men and young women.

Second, it is difficult to make any firm conclusions from this study about ethnicity and its relationship to family poverty. This is because of the small numbers involved - only seven ethnic minority young people were included in the study. This is in itself an important issue, in that the researchers in all three areas found it very difficult to recruit ethnic minority young people to participate, in particular young people from Asian families. A number of youth workers and social workers, and young people, said that there was a greater stigma attached in some ethnic minority communities to being dependent on state benefits, and also greater fears about confidentiality, and the uses of the material collected. Of those ethnic minority young people who did participate in the study (who represented just over ten per cent of the whole sample), there were no clear differences between them and the white/European young people involved. However, it is possible that the questioning was not sufficiently sensitive to the experiences of ethnic minority young people living in poverty, and that differences that do exist were not picked up in the interviews. Also, no ethnic minority interviewers were involved, which may have affected the responses of this group of young people. This is an important area for future research to address.

The main differences identified in the study were in terms of age. It was clear throughout the study that the older groups felt the effects of growing up in poverty most acutely. Thus poverty was found to affect young people's friendships and social lives, leisure activities, and need for privacy and personal space. Before this age, it was clear that the impact of poverty was not as acute, with the exception of the significant family responsibilities identified, which were found across the age range. This is a particularly important finding, because as demonstrated earlier, most research has focussed on the effects of poverty on young children. This research shows that the effects of poverty on young people (particularly older young people) are very acute.

(ii)   Implications for research into young people and poverty

The research has a number of implications for future work in this area. There are both a number of lessons to be learnt from the research described here, as well as questions raised by the research, which need to be addressed in the future. These are briefly described here.

First, there were a number of important groups who were not included in the research, whose experience of growing up in poverty might be very different to that described here. These include young people with disabilities, young people who are pregnant or who have children, and those from ethnic minority groups which were not represented in the research. It is possible that young people in these circumstances have very different experiences of growing up in families living in poverty. These groups need to be targeted in future research.

Second, one of the issues to emerge very clearly in this research was young people's resilience. It was also clear that many young people were accepting what they have, even in the most difficult and frustrating circumstances. Issues around resilience and coping have only very recently become a focus for research. A renewed effort is needed in this area, combined with a focus on understanding young people's subjective experiences [see also Lister *et al.*, this volume]. In making this suggestion, the authors agree with the American researchers Wilson *et al.* (1997), who conclude from their study of low income youth in the United States that:

> ... it is important for professionals who work with low-income youth to become more aware of and sensitive to how a person's 'interpretation' of his/her circumstances function to modify the meaning and experience of life satisfaction ... [this] does not provide the basis for neglecting obvious deficiencies in the objective conditions of [these youth]. Instead, reports of high life satisfaction in the face of adversity may simply reflect the resilience of youth from low-income backgrounds through the development of coping mechanisms and the lowering of expectations in the face of seemingly insurmountable obstacles.
> (Wilson *et al.*, 1997, p.457)

The relationship between life circumstances, resilience, coping, and life expectations is an important area for future research to address.

Third, a key recommendation for future research is for longitudinal studies of the effects of poverty on young people. The research described here is essentially a 'snapshot' of the lives of 60 young people who are growing up in family poverty. This clearly raises questions about what will happen to these young people in the future. Longitudinal research is therefore needed to answer key questions arising from this study, such as:

- What happens to the young people in this study who are involved in crime, or excluded from school? Are there factors that lead them away from crime or back into education?
- What happens to these young people long-term in terms of employment, training, unemployment?
- How do these young people's family relationships change over time?
- When do the young people leave home, and how does this affect their relationship with their families?
- What are the long-term health behaviours and outcomes of these young people?
- How does resilience and coping develop and change over time? To what extent does young people's sense of optimism or pessimism in the teenage years change in early adulthood?

These and other important questions need to be addressed by following young people such as these through into adulthood.

(iii) Implications for youth policy

There are clear issues raised by the research described here, all of which have policy implications. These are detailed, briefly, below. The list is not exhaustive - indeed, a whole book could be written about youth policy. However, it is believed that, if the policy recommendations below were followed, the circumstances and future prospects of some of the most disadvantaged young people in our society could be vastly improved.

1.   A change in the conceptualisation of poverty in the 1990s

First, the results of this study have implications for the way in which policy-makers, politicians and the public view poverty. It was suggested in the Introduction that there is an ongoing debate in this country about what exactly poverty is [see also Miller, this volume]. The young people in this study demonstrate that, whilst many may not be living in complete destitution, they are living in poverty. In this definition, poverty means living life as a struggle, making sacrifices, putting up with less than someone wants to or is entitled to, and the lowering of horizons and expectations. Most of the young people in this study were experiencing 'poverty by exclusion', as described by Smith (1990) and others (Kumar, 1993; Oppenheim, 1993). Using this conceptualisation of poverty, the urgency of tackling this issue is made real. 'Poverty' has re-appeared on the political and public agenda in the late 1990s. It is essential that the new Social Exclusion Unit, set up by the Prime Minister in 1998, will address the important issues described here [see also Lister *et al.*, this volume].

2.   Changes to family income and benefit policies

Second, the present Labour government is currently in the process of reviewing policies relating to social security and benefits. It was clear that many of the families who participated in this research were struggling to survive on the current level of benefits. Even a relatively small increase in benefit levels would make a considerable amount of difference to most of these families. As a recent Rowntrees funded study demonstrated, an additional £15 a week would greatly improve the ability of many of those living on very low incomes to cope (Kempson, 1996). An increase in benefit payments to these families might also mean that young people, particularly the 13 and 14 year-olds, would not have to contribute part or all of their income to their parents, in order to help them survive. Changes in benefit levels for these families should also include the restoration of benefits to those aged 16 and 17 who are not in education or training, a circumstance which left several of this age group in the study with no income at all.

3.   Increased provision of youth and leisure services

Third, it was clear that many of the young people in this study experienced acute boredom, mainly because they were unable to afford to participate in many leisure activities. Many of the young people described the importance of youth clubs and youth workers in their lives, which provided them with leisure facilities, friendship, advice and guidance. There must be a greater expenditure on the youth service and the provision of inexpensive leisure activities for young people. The costs of not doing this are clear from the young people in this research -many described how boredom and lack of leisure activities led them to get involved in crime and substance abuse. The cost-effectiveness of this policy in the long-term has been clearly demonstrated by the Misspent Youth Report (Audit Commission, 1996). A greater commitment to the youth service and inexpensive leisure activities for young people would be a key investment for the future.

4.   The importance of education

Fourth, many of the young people in this study, in particular those who were involved in crime, had very negative experiences of education. It is important that more attention is given to those who 'slip through the net' as many of these young people did, in particular through literacy problems and falling behind at school. Further, the 1990s have witnessed a dramatic increase in school exclusions, a fact that (as has already been demonstrated) is associated with unemployment and involvement in crime (Cullingford and Morrison, 1997). It is also clear from this study that more 'second chances' are needed, providing opportunities for those who have been excluded or who left school early to return to education. There are a number of important and innovative projects currently underway, but these are few in number, and funding for them is scarce. Education is central to improving young people's futures and prospects, a fact very clearly recognised by all the young people in this study.

5.   Improving youth employment prospects

Fifth and finally, a significant number of the young people in this study felt it was difficult to motivate themselves through education and training, because of the high rates of youth unemployment in the UK at present. Many felt that, however hard they worked, the prospects of ever getting a job were poor. This made many feel that there was little point in gaining qualifications or undertaking training. Policies are therefore needed which improve the employment prospects for young people, and to seriously address the issue of youth unemployment. This research was undertaken before the present government's New Deal programme was set up, and it is unclear at present how successful this will be in tackling youth unemployment. However, a clear outcome from this study is a need for the provision of even more training and employment opportunities for young people, in particular those who have had poor experiences of education.

It is appropriate to end the chapter with some of the comments from the young people, which sum up the urgency of the issues discussed:

... for me [being poor is] about not being part of things, not having the money to live normally like other people. Everything I do or I want to do, even like really small things, is decided by money, or by not having it anyway.
(14 year-old female)

I try not to complain, sometimes I feel guilty you know, but it is hard being poor, you're just surviving, not really living. Sometimes the future seems, like, hard you know, it just feels it'll be such a struggle. I just hope it won't be as bad for us in the future as it is now..
(16 year-old female)

Acknowledgements

The research described in this chapter was funded by a consortium of The Children's Society, The Esmee Fairbairn Trust, and the Royal Philanthropic Society (now RPS Rainer). The full results of the study are available as a book, published by The Children's Society and entitled 'Worth More Than This'.

The authors are grateful to Patrick West, Nick Rose, Helen Bush and Helen Sweeting for undertaking many of the interviews with young people.

References

Audit Commission (1996), *Misspent Youth*, Audit Commission, London.
Blackburn, C. (1991), *Poverty and Health*, OUP, Milton Keynes.
Coleman, J.C. (1997), *Key Data on Adolescence*, Trust for the Study of Adolescence, Brighton.
Cullingford, C. and Morrison, J. (1997), 'The Relationship Between Criminality and Home Background, *Children and Society*, vol. 11, pp. 157-72.
Dennehy, A., Smith, L. and Harker, P. (1997), *Not to be Ignored: Young people, poverty, and health*, CPAG, London.
Hertfordshire County Council (1996), *Poverty Action Plan*.
Holman, B. (1994), 'Research Review: Children and poverty', *Children and Society*, vol. 8, pp. 69-72.
Kempson, E. (1996), *Life on a Low Income*, Joseph Rowntree Trust, York.
Kumar, V. (1993), *Poverty and Inequality in the UK: The effects on children*, NCB, London.
Lister et al (1999), *Experiencing Poverty. Volume 3*, Avebury.
National Youth Agency (1996), *Briefing: Poverty - The Facts*, NYA, Leicester.
Oppenheim, C. (1993), *Poverty: The Facts*, CPAG, London.
Oppenheim, C. and Harker, L. (1996), *Poverty: The Facts. Third Edition*, CPAG Ltd.

Oppenheim, D. (1996), *Families and the recession: Living on the breadline*, CPAG, London.

Smith, R. (1990), *Working With Families: Tackling Poverty*, The Children's Society, London.

Wilson, S., Henry, C. and Petersen, G. (1997), 'Life satisfaction among low-income rural youth from Appalachia', *Journal of Adolescence*, vol. 20, pp. 443-60.

16 The Future of Poverty Research: Panel Session

JOHN HILLS, JONATHAN BRADSHAW, RUTH LISTER and
JANET LEWIS

The final session of the conference was devoted to an open discussion about the future of poverty research. Four people formed a panel and each were asked to introduce their ideas very briefly. This final chapter is based on their notes and are thus presented a good deal less formally than is normal in an academic text.

John Hills

Focus of Research

The focus of poverty research will not be just 'poverty' - in two senses:

- it will include the wider dimensions of exclusion and inclusion
- it will cover not only the poor/underclass, and so on - but more a continuum of problems. To what extent are trajectories of the poor a different shape from those of others, *or* are, echoing Hemingway, the poor only different in that they have got less money.

Dynamics

There will be more work on dynamics as longitudinal datasets open up. This is important in the present Rowntree context given his work on life cycle patterns. But also to identify the precursors and sequelae of poverty, or 'protective' factors when later shocks occur. Also the underclass is not unchanging nor random. We need to distinguish persistently/recurrently/ transitorily poor (and temporarily not poor).

Geography

This is a Rowntree conference, not a Booth conference, but from the papers we are clearly going to have a lot more geography including:

- micro/community studies
- increased use of powerful administrative data

Research and Policy

How far can poverty and related research engage users and influence policy? Examples of a direct and immediate effect of research on policy are rare (I prefer the 'Limestone' model of the varying timescales with which research has an effect), but I would also like to stress the importance of what happened on Tuesday (in the Budget):

- Ruth Lister, Claire Callender and Jackie Goode recently carried out research on the way couples use benefits and produced examples of the lack of sharing. Now the Working Families Tax Credit is to have an option to continue payments to women.
- Research on Earned Income Tax Credit in the United States and WIS in Canada have revealed their administrative problems. These have been taken into account in designing Working Families Tax.
- Sue Middleton and others in Loughborough and the work of the Family Budget Unit have revealed that there is a low variation in spending on children by the age of the child. Now the Budget has announced additional help for under 11s in the Income Support rates.
- Maybe also the accumulation of evidence on poverty and lone parent families as well as, of course, political reaction weighed somewhere in decisions to increase Child Benefit and the Family premium in Income Support.

Speed of Statistics

Lastly I hope that we will know better where we are. There have been several references in the conference to growing inequality/relative poverty. There has been very little discussion of **falling** inequality and relative poverty. We know that poverty and inequality increased very rapidly in the period 1977-91. It is now clear that inequality and relative poverty **fell** somewhat between 1993-95. It is frustrating to be publishing *Income and Wealth: The Latest Evidence* later this month, telling people where we were three years ago! A 'Poverty Report' might speed the appearance of data in the way that ONS has achieved in their reports on inflation/unemployment/money supply/etc.

Jonathan Bradshaw

One of the reasons that we organised this conference a year ahead of the year when Seebohm Rowntree did his first study of poverty in York, and three years ahead of when it was published, was that we thought it was important to get in and involve the social science poverty research constituency as soon after the new government was elected as possible.

As Peter Townsend reminded us, for almost two decades poverty research in Britain has been neglected by Government. The notion has been denied by at least two of the Conservative Secretaries of State for Social Security, a Home Secretary, a Secretary of State for Wales and probably many others. At a time when the living standards of those on benefits have been losing touch with those with access to the labour market, it has proven impossible to persuade the Department of Social Security or the Office of National Statistics that they have a responsibility to monitor the adequacy of state benefits and their impact on the well-being of claimants. Poverty, deprivation, adequacy, living standards, or any other euphemism you may use for the same phenomenon have not been on the public research agenda.

Nevertheless many of you here have been beavering away, many with the support of the Joseph Rowntree Foundation - to whom I think we all owe a tremendous debt of gratitude. Rather like Alcuin of York the Foundation can claim to have kept learning and civilized values alive in the dark ages. However, it would be unfair to claim that it was just those of us outside government who have kept the light shining - just to take two examples:

- I think that the careful and collaborative manner in which the Analytical Services Division at the Department of Social Security developed the Households Below Average Income Statistics was exceptionally good and possibly also very brave.
- Also the ONS can be proud to have published their big report on health inequalities.

But in general the record of the British government can be contrasted with, for example, that of the United States government which commissioned a report on the US poverty line from a high powered committee of the American Academy of Sciences and the Australian government who launched a major research based inquiry into the adequacy of benefits called the Adequacy Project.

Nevertheless, often with JRF support, and with many of you sticking to the laste, despite everything, I think we can claim that the output and capacity of poverty research has been sustained. It is impossible to mention all the important developments, you will have your own selection, derived from listening to papers at this conference. But here is a little list of achievements of the last two decades.

- The development of social indicator methods into socially perceived necessities in the Poor Britain project.
- The development of studies of area deprivation, the utilisation of administrative data at a local level and the associated expansion of local anti poverty initiatives - the increasing involvement of local government in poverty might well become of great significance.
- The reestablishment of budget standards in the armoury of poverty research.
- Advances in research on poverty and ... particularly gender, race and disability.
- Advances in the international comparisons of poverty and income distribution.
- And possibly, though I am still a little uncertain about this because of their diversionary value, the new conceptions of social exclusion and inclusion.

So what! I hear you say. Indeed I have been waiting for someone to make the speech which says - all our work is self serving, it does not help the poor, it just provides jobs for us, and what do *we* know about poverty anyway!

It is not true that our work has had no impact in the last two decades. We heard Harriet Harman at this conference say that the Joseph Rowntree Foundation funded project on the costs of a child at Loughborough University was responsible for persuading the Government to increase the level of Income Support for young children. There are other examples where research turned policy in specific ways. But, of course, as ever, the influence of research on policy has mainly been much more subtle - assisting in stopping things happen. I remember a very senior DSS civil servant thanking me for publishing my UNICEF report *Child Poverty and Deprivation in the UK* - because he had been able to wave it at Treasury ministers in an effort to protect Child Benefit! But during difficult times we have also contributed to changing the climate, challenging the precepts and revealing the consequences of the Thatcher project and this played a part, eventually, in the downfall of the New Right.

What about the future? Many of us have been deeply disturbed and disappointed by the first year of New Labour (and I myself resigned from the Party when they became the first Government since the war to cut the real level of social assistance for lone parents). However, the budget is very encouraging and it is such a relief to hear ministers talking about poverty, in the same terms as we do, and as a priority for action.

So what do I identify as the priorities for the research community?

Tony Blair has committed himself to producing an annual report on their anti poverty strategy and said that 'if the Labour Government has not raised the living standards of the poorest by the end of their time in office it will have failed'. When he was shadow Secretary of State for Social Security, Chris Smith said 'let us see in government whether we can achieve a national consensus about what poverty is, how it can be properly measured and how we can count into the assessments all those elements of exclusion from society and from opportunity that form so much what real poverty is about'. The problem with this is that the baseline evidence is so very thin. Although Households Below Average Income provides a measure of income poverty we still lack a poverty standard which has face value, is communicable with the public and which government is prepared to accept as a target against which to evaluate their policies.

My view is that the best prospect for this comes in the development of a democratic poverty standard based on the notions of socially perceived necessities. The Joseph Rowntree Foundation is presently supporting Dave Gordon, Sue Middleton and I to develop such a standard, and we are hoping to launch a major new national study of poverty in the Autumn which is capable, via replication, of being a vehicle for assessing the achievements of the government.

Ruth Lister

End of the Line

About a decade ago, John Moore gave his infamous speech 'the end of the line for poverty'. Perhaps equally controversially and simplistically, I want to propose that we have come to the end of the line for traditional models of poverty research. The message, though, is a positive rather than a negative one, as I believe that new models are emerging.

Old Models

The traditional models of poverty research have generally counted the poor, told us where they live, how they live, i.e. the impact of poverty on their lives and just how poor they are.

In saying we have come to the end of the line with such approaches, I am not wanting to deny the value of the research that had been done. It has been immensely important in mapping out poverty and the devastating impact it can have and as both an anti-poverty campaigner and an academic I have made considerable use of it. And there is still an important role for such research in so far as it feeds into policy making at national and local level and ultimately we research poverty because we want to do something about it.

But it is time to move on, for the model underlying this research is static, treats those in poverty as a homogeneous group and as passive victims and does not engage them as participants in the research process.

I will take each of these charges briefly in turn.

Static

Traditionally poverty research has been of the snapshot variety. One of the most important recent developments has been the construction of new data sources that allow us to look at what happens over time to people who experience poverty. Robert Walker has been one of those instrumental in developing a more dynamic approach to the understanding of poverty which looks at different kinds of poverty trajectories.

Increasingly, I think that poverty research will be about processes and not just outcomes. A process approach is also encouraged by the concepts of social exclusion and polarisation which, if deployed critically, raise questions about the processes and mechanisms that both exclude and polarise, thereby contributing to the development of theory also.

Homogeneous

Related to this dynamic approach is the problematising of the discourses around poverty - it would be interesting to study how these change over time and between societies and also how they vary within societies - building on the work of Ros Edwards and Simon Duncan in relation to lone parenthood.

These discourses will probably also reflect the fact that 'the poor' are not a homogeneous group. It is only relatively recently that poverty research has paid due attention to gender issues; it is still very weak in relation to 'race' and ethnicity, although people like Gary Craig have started to address this dimension. What is still lacking is an attempt to capture the inter-sectionality of different elements of disadvantage, for example, age and disability as well as class, gender and race and how they interact.

For those experiencing poverty, it may be these other dimensions which are more important in the construction of their identities; indeed for many (most?) poverty may not be part of their identity at all, although debt may be according to Linda Grant's paper. Poverty is an identity which we *as researchers ascribe to them*. Evidence suggests it is one which many actively reject. So, as Fran Bennett suggested in discussion, perhaps we need to come at poverty research sideways, rather than through studying 'the poor' as such.

This brings me to my last two points, which are made also in the paper I've written with Peter Beresford.

Passive Victims

The lack of attention to how people in poverty perceive themselves in relation to the wider society is symptomatic of how poverty research has typically constructed poor people as passive victims, lacking agency, without views of their own and able only to testify to the impact of poverty on their lives.

Of course, there has been a reluctance, among most poverty researchers, to ascribe the causes of poverty to poor people themselves. And there is a thin line between acknowledging the agency of people in poverty and blaming them for that poverty. But I think there has been something of a shift in the literature about poverty from what could be interpreted as a structural determinism in which poor people are represented simply as helpless victims. This reflects wider theoretical developments in sociological and social policy theory, as exemplified in Fiona Williams and Jennie Popay's paper which tries to synthesise structure and agency in welfare research. To paraphrase Marx, poor people make themselves, but no in circumstances of their own choosing.

Participation

And if people in poverty are to be recognised as actors in their own lives, making themselves, then the next step is to ask whether they do not have a part to play as more active participants in poverty research - a question which has been asked most critically hitherto by disabled people.

So, to sum up, I see the future of poverty research lying in three 'd's': a more dynamic, differentiated and democratic approach underpinned by a greater attention to theory, including as Peter Townsend argued in his paper, in an international context.

Janet Lewis

The Conference has covered an enormous number of topics and issues which it is not possible for one person to pull together. My comments are therefore based mainly on what I had prepared earlier, flavoured with some things I have heard at the conference.

1. We should focus on relationships between things. Much work has been concerned with cross-sectional analysis and we need to move away from this to understand processes, and perhaps even explore causal relationships. Eighteen years of Conservative rule perhaps provides us with a 'natural experiment' from which to explore some causal connections.

2. We need to focus on assessing 'what works' in terms of effective action to improve people's quality of life. There is now a great deal of discussion in the health field about 'evidence-based practice'. The Joseph Rowntree Foundation is more concerned with promoting 'knowledge-based change'. The difference for us is that knowledge allows a greater range of factors to be seen as legitimate evidence. We need to go beyond information that is available from Random Control Trials to include the evidence of personal experience and common sense knowledge of what

works in particular circumstances. We also need to give greater attention to thinking about actions that are likely to be effective before we try to incorporate them in new policies. Martin Rein talked about 'weak rationality' in relation to poverty policy. We need to see if we can build on more robust rationalities, based on knowledge.

3.   We need to give greater emphasis to the experiences and perspectives of individuals themselves. Whether this is from the post-modernist position - and the multiple, subjective and objective identities and social positions discussed by Fiona Williams and Jenny Popay - or from other analytic traditions. Part of the function of research should be to empower individuals and to give a voice to people whose views are muffled or lost.